PRAISE FOR *KISS IT GOOD-BYE*

"The 1960 Pirates were one of the great underdog stories of the century. John Moody's book brought back memories for me. *Kiss It Good-bye* is as close as you can get to being in the Pirate dugout with Murtaugh, Clemente, Vern Law and the rest of that great team."

—BILL MAZEROSKI,
Pirates' Hall of Famer

"The book awoke my memories of the Pittsburgh of the 1950s—wiping my fingers across the side of a bus, leaving an inch-thick trail of soot. A successful sports team can bring a community together and elevate the feelings of personal pride and achievement. The Pirates did that in 1960. As a lifelong Pirates fan, I found myself between laughter and tears as I read *Kiss It Good-bye*."

—MARTY SCHOTTENHEIMER,
legendary NFL head coach and Pittsburgh native

"*Kiss It Good-Bye* poignantly captures the spirit of baseball and the role Vern Law played in giving a community a true hero. This is what sports heroes *should* look like."

—U.S. SENATOR ORRIN HATCH

"Vern Law taught me it is possible to be successful in this profession and remain true to what you believe, loyal to your family and your fans, and to succeed with integrity and humility. Thank you, Vern, for blazing the trail and for setting a great example. All who read this book, baseball fans or not, will be touched and inspired by its words."

—DALE MURPHY,
two-time National League MVP, Atlanta Braves

Kiss It
GOOD-BYE

Kiss It
GOOD-BYE

The Mystery, the Mormon, and the
Moral of the 1960 Pittsburgh Pirates

JOHN MOODY

SHADOW
MOUNTAIN

Library of Congress Cataloging-in-Publication Data

Moody, John, 1953–
    Kiss it good-bye : the mystery, the Mormon, and the moral of the 1960 Pittsburgh Pirates / John Moody.
       p. cm.
    Includes bibliographical references and index.
    Summary: A nostalgic look at the 1960 World-Series-winning Pittsburgh Pirates and one of their players, Vernon Law.
    ISBN 978-1-60641-149-0 (hardbound : alk. paper)
    1. Law, Vernon, 1930–   2. Pittsburgh Pirates (Baseball team)
3. Mormon athletes—Biography.   4. Sports—Religious aspects—Church of Jesus Christ of Latter-day Saints.   I. Title.
    GV697.A1M5955 2010
    796.357'640974886—dc22   2009041834

Printed in the United States of America
WorldColor, Fairfield, PA

10   9   8   7   6   5   4   3   2   1

For Kate:
This one is all yours. It comes from my heart.

Contents

Warm-up 1

First Inning 15

Second Inning 49

Third Inning 65

Fourth Inning 79

Fifth Inning 99

Sixth Inning..................... 128

Seventh Inning.................. 141

Eighth Inning................... 174

Ninth Inning 228

Extra Innings 304

What the Others Say 343

Sources 361

Index 363

Warm-up

"A mob is a monster with many hands and no brain."
(From Vernon Law's *Words to Live By*)

THEY LOST, THEY WON.
There is a scent to victory, a salt-edged flavor that covers the tongue, invades the vessels, lines the nostrils, and enlarges the heart. Politicians who declare themselves elected exude it. So do spelling-bee champions, who, after hours of meticulous rote, pump their fists with savage satisfaction and scream with a lust that cannot itself be expressed in any alphabet.

For all our attempts to leech competition out of our lives and to delude ourselves that we are all equally able and glad of it, that we are all winners, there are few substitutes for the pleasures of domination.

Nowhere is the scent of victory sharper or more pronounced than in the world of sport. "Swifter, Higher, Stronger" goes the Olympic motto, and in its antiquity it sometimes seems benign in its intent. Yet there are no measures more satisfying than those. Who is better, or, better yet,

1

best? It is a question that remains worth arguing about and answering because it defines us as a species.

On Sunday, September 25, 1960, that visceral distinction was blurred. The National League–leading Pittsburgh Pirates lost 4–2 to the third-place Milwaukee Braves, in ten innings before 38,108 fans at County Stadium. The Pirates blew a one-run lead in the eighth inning on an error. In the tenth, the Braves' Eddie Mathews knocked a two-run home run off ElRoy Face that ended the game. But the Pirates, though expressing disappointment with the loss, had just won the National League pennant. That was because the St. Louis Cardinals, the second-place team and the only one that could have caught the Pirates, also lost that day, 5–0, to the Chicago Cubs at Wrigley Field, assuring the Pirates their first trip to the World Series since 1927.

On the same day, the Pirates' worst fears were confirmed. They would meet the New York Yankees, who, while Pittsburgh was playing Milwaukee, had sewn up the American League pennant by downing the Boston Red Sox 4–3, while Cleveland was blanking the Yankees' closest rival, the Chicago White Sox, 4–0.

The Yankees were not just any team. This 1960 squad included three players and a manager who would one day be elected to the Hall of Fame: Mickey Mantle, Yogi Berra, Whitey Ford, and manager Casey Stengel. This was the seemingly invincible lineup the ragtag Pirates would face. Vegas bookies put the Pirates' odds of winning at 1 in 15.

The 1960 season was the magic that transformed not just a baseball team, but a city, and, in many ways, America itself. It also made me who I am. This story will trace the intertwined paths of Pittsburgh, its baseball team, and the author, who in 1960 was a boy with six years of life experience and a mindful of questions about the place he lived in and who he would become.

◆ ◆ ◆

The Pirates had been a joke for a generation, the perennial cellar rats of baseball. They had only one winning season between the end of World War II and 1958. Indeed, the 1951 movie *Angels in the Outfield,* starring Paul Douglas and Janet Leigh, in which heavenly reinforcements arrive to rescue a hopeless bunch of baseball bunglers, was based openly on the Pirates.

Even their name was derived through derision. In the late nineteenth century, professional baseball associations (as they were then called) simply bore the name of the city, without a mascot or team emblem. Pittsburgh and its cross-river neighbor, Allegheny City (which was later subsumed by Pittsburgh), had one team in the so-called National League and another in a league calling itself the Brotherhood. The Brotherhood folded in 1891, and some of its players crossed over to the National League.

Philadelphia, which had rights to two of the better Brotherhood players, Harry Stover and Louie Bierbauer,

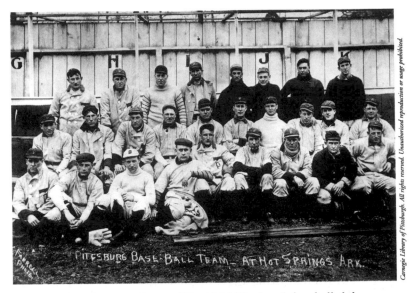

Before they were Pirates. The 1906 Pittsburgh baseball club.

inexplicably failed to file the proper papers claiming them from the Brotherhood. Pittsburgh connived to sign Bierbauer, a second baseman who was married to a popular stage actress. The stealth and questionable ethics by which its club acquired Bierbauer had opposing teams accusing Pittsburgh of an act of piracy. The name stuck. So did the reputation as ne'er-do-wells.

Even Ralph Kiner, a perennial all-star and eventual Hall of Fame inductee, could not save the Pirates from themselves in the early 1950s. The owner of the team, Ohio real-estate millionaire John Wilmer Galbreath, brought in Branch Rickey, the baseball *impresario,* as general manager in 1951. His first season was inauspicious, and in 1952, the Pirates' record was an all-time worst 42–112. They finished 54½ games out of first that year. "In an eight-team league, we should have finished ninth," said the catcher and future TV personality, Joe Garagiola. But things were about to change.

Rickey got rid of Kiner, the highest paid player on the club, to general outrage ("I can finish last just as well without you as with you," Rickey is said to have told the departing Kiner). He brought to the Pirates his invention of a farm system—young prospects playing against others of their own experience level until their skills were honed enough to bring them to the Majors. Rickey's health forced him to retire in 1955, but then another driving force made his appearance in the dugout.

Danny Murtaugh, a pugnacious second baseman from Easton, Pennsylvania, who had had an undistinguished playing career with the Pirates and the Philadelphia Phillies, was named manager 103 games into the 1957 season.

Murtaugh's effect was almost immediate. In his first full season, 1958, the Pirates went 84–70, and finished second to the Milwaukee Braves. Some cynics attributed the upside-down finish of the eight-team National League that year to the move to the West Coast of the San Francisco Giants and the Los Angeles Dodgers, perennial contenders when they had both played in New York City. But Pittsburgh fans credited Murtaugh's management. "He would sit there on the bench in the dugout, chewing tobacco like nobody's business, and never say a word," recalled Bob Oldis, a backup

Courtesy Pittsburgh Pirates

*The smiling Irishman: a rare shot without a chaw
of tobacco in Murtaugh's cheek.*

catcher on the 1960 championship team who later became a
Major League scout. "And if someone made a mistake, like
not running hard from first to third base, someone else from
the team would come up and give that guy hell. And
Murtaugh would just look over and nod and keep chewing."

Murtaugh changed the Pirates into a team some
Pittsburghers could hardly recognize. Even their method of
securing the pennant in 1960 was the stuff of head-shaking
humor. The Bucs (short for Buccaneers to those who loved
them and the nickname behind the team's rallying cry, "Beat

'em, Bucs!") lost all three games in their last series, to Milwaukee, but it didn't matter. On the 25th, the die was cast: The Pirates were going to the World Series.

The game is played on the field, but not all the action in baseball takes place between chalked lines. Locker rooms can be cathedrals of emotional excess. Modern-day players assault the infrastructure of a stadium to vent their frustrations over sub-par days: water coolers, bat racks, and wide-screen TV sets are routinely violated with bats, thrown balls, hurled batting helmets. Kevin Brown of the 2004 New York Yankees famously smashed his fist into a wall after being yanked from a game. The resulting injury cost him most of the rest of the season, and when he returned, he lost the final game of the American League playoffs to Boston in spectacularly dismal fashion.

But in 1960, the locker room was four walls and six splintered benches full of storage space, and, if the visiting team was lucky, a water fountain. County Stadium in Milwaukee was no exception. The Pirates knew they had lost their game. They knew also that the Cardinals' loss had made them league champions. At first, they hardly knew how to react. "We weren't in a celebrating mood, when you lose," explained Bill Mazeroski, the second baseman who would become the iconic figure of Pittsburgh sports history a few weeks later. "But we also knew we'd just won the pennant. So our celebration started real slow." Gino Cimoli, a reserve outfielder and one of the more gregarious members of the team, recalls looking at the other players' expressions and wondering, *is this a morgue?* "They had never been through it before," Cimoli recalled. "They didn't know what the hell was going on." Slowly, as they viewed the bottles of champagne on ice that had been prepared for them, the Pirates realized what they had done, or what the Cubs had done for them. Gradually, the corks popped and the wine and beer gushed, into throats and onto bare heads. "We had a champagne or two," Maz recalled, reddening, still embarrassed fifty years later at his excess.

Here is how Al Abrams, the sports editor of the Pittsburgh *Post-Gazette,* described the celebratory scene: "Within half an hour, the spic-and-span clubhouse was turned into a soggy mess with champagne, beer, water, and anything liquid which could be thrown making a pool at least a foot high. This is not to say anything of the buckets swished on the heads of happy players. It was worth it. Thirty-three years of frustration and disappointment, which in the last three days, dwindled into hours, then minutes and seconds, were finally culminated at 4:43 Pittsburgh time when word was flashed that the lowly Cubs had shut out the second-place St. Louis Cardinals, 5–0."

Joe L. Brown, who had succeeded Rickey as general manager, burst into the clubhouse. Until this moment, Brown had probably been best known as the son of Joe E. Brown, a dog-faced vaudevillian who the year before had been featured

"We've waited a long time for this," said Pirates owner Galbreath.

as millionaire Osgood Fielding III along with Marilyn Monroe in *Some Like It Hot*.

Also there to take in the glorious moment was the owner, John Galbreath. Speaking as only someone whose money is on the line can, he exhaled with reverence: "We've waited a long time for this."

Murtaugh, the manager who had guided the team to its destiny, used the prosaic clichés of the era to describe the roiling emotions within him. "I wish I had words to express how I do feel. I mean it's something you just can't put into words. We've waited so doggone long for this that I think everyone is just tickled pink."

Tickled or pickled? The Pirates were drinking, to be sure, but they were also eating. A whole turkey and platters of spareribs were waiting for them to devour between draughts of booze. They continued the celebration for over half an hour, then staggered into showers and street clothes for the plane ride home to Pittsburgh, where crowds were also erupting in celebration throughout the city.

Two Pirates were not in the clubhouse, amid the mayhem. The Pirates' catcher, Forrest "Smoky" Burgess, and pitcher Vernon Sanders Law, who would start the first game of the Series against the Yankees, disdained the bacchanalia. Neither man drank alcohol, and they found the unrestrained hedonism of their teammates unworthy of newly crowned champions. When Law, shaking hands with team captain Dick Groat, was sprayed inadvertently in the face with a newly uncorked bottle of champagne, he recalled, "It burned my eyes so bad I wondered what it must do to your insides when you swallowed it."

Rather than take on the improbable task of convincing the rest of the team to temper their celebration, Burgess and Law took their showers, dressed quickly, and escaped to the waiting bus that would transport the team to the airport and home.

It was not a long wait, twenty minutes or so, during

which lots of champagne and beer were being consumed inside County Stadium. In wobbly knots, the rest of the Pirates came out and boarded the bus. Law noticed that none of them were wearing ties, which were *de rigueur* for traveling athletes in those days. Then he saw that they actually were wearing ties around their necks; they just didn't reach down their shirts. Giving new meaning to the term *cut-ups,* the Pirates had found the team trainer's scissors and bobbed each player's neckwear. Law told me: "There were two or three on the bus looking to see who hadn't been touched by their mischief. I was the only one so I let them cut my tie in two. But they weren't satisfied with that and pretty soon shirts started getting torn off. The shirts were tied together so there was a long string of them hanging out of the bus window."

Vernon Law was, and is, a devout member of The Church of Jesus Christ of Latter-day Saints—the Mormons. So well advertised was his ardent faith that he was known throughout the league by the nickname The Deacon, bestowed kiddingly on him by teammate Wally Westlake, who first called Law The Preacher, then amended the moniker to be more specific, referring to Law's ordination to the Mormon priesthood, the first office of which is deacon.

Adult Mormons (this book will use the term as it is commonly used and understood and is not intended to be disrespectful to the Saints, as members of the Church refer to each other) who have qualified through their faithfulness are permitted to enter Mormon temples where they make certain

With Wally Westlake, who gave Vern his nickname, The Deacon, 1951.

covenants with the Lord during sacred worship services there. Among other things, those covenants include promises to live faithful, committed, morally pure, and virtuous lives. Each man and woman who makes these promises and enters into the associated covenants wears a white garment under their ordinary clothing as a symbol of their faith. Devout members of the LDS Church (as it is also sometimes called) consider the wearing of a temple garment not just an obligation but a sacred privilege. And given the private nature of the garment, Mormons seldom discuss it with nonbelievers.

And so, when one man on the bus lunged at Vernon Law

to remove not just his shirt, but also what his teammates called his undershirt (but was really his temple garment), Law said, "I wish you wouldn't do that." It was a seemingly mild request, considering how strongly he felt about protecting the garment. The ringleader lunged again, gripping his dress shirt, popping its buttons. Because this ringleader had the status to have stopped the horseplay with a single word if he had chosen to, his conduct was, at best, irresponsible; to most of us, it would be unforgivable. Seeing that this man had no desire to stop the antics, Law fought back. Here is how he recalled it when he talked to me:

"I was picked up out of my seat by four or five fellows. With my sport coat on they couldn't get to my shirt, so one fellow reached in under my coat in the back and started to pull. He popped a couple of buttons but that was all. Now while this was going on, someone had hold of my right foot and was trying to get my shoe off. As he was twisting, I felt something pop. With that, everything stopped and they let me sit back down. At the time, I didn't say anything, but I knew I had strained something in my ankle."

As the others on the bus looked on in suddenly sobered horror, Vernon Law, the ace of the Pirates, the pitcher on whose powerful overhand fastball the Pirates' chances to win the World Series relied, the Mormon who had first asked to be left alone and then had fought off his attackers with all his 6–3, 195 pounds of muscle and determination, rubbed his ankle and forced a smile that fooled no one. By the time the plane reached Pittsburgh, where the team would be hailed as heroes, his ankle was throbbing badly.

Vernon Law has never publicly identified the man he believes caused his ankle to pop, or the leader of the pack, who grabbed his garment, and so bears even greater responsibility. By the time you finish reading this book, you will know who they were.

First Inning

"Noble fathers have noble children."
—Euripides
(From Vernon Law's *Words to Live By*)

TODAY, MERIDIAN, IDAHO, likes to call itself the Star of the New West. Snuggled in the southwest corner of the state that resembles an index finger pointing north, Meridian, ten miles west of the capital city, Boise, is where the webbing between that finger and the thumb would be. Among its 70,000 residents, it is home to a famous NASCAR driver and the first Idaho woman elected to the United States Congress. It is home to the Arnold Machinery Company. It has a Holiday Inn, an Applebee's, car dealerships, pest extermination services, and the other trappings of twenty-first-century life in the United States. In that respect, it is unremarkable, part of the homogenization of America that has undoubtedly improved life for many of its residents but that, in developing Meridian into a copy of every other town and city, has surrendered some of its individuality, its local character.

This is not a criticism. Change is a constant in our world, and nowhere more so than in a country colonized by Europeans looking for something new and different. The Dutch, English, Swedes, French, and Spaniards who came to the side of the ocean that would become known as America wanted to do things their way, to leave behind the past of their customs and competitions. When the colonies they peopled became too much like what they had fled, they and their children and their children's children began moving westward, where it appeared land was not merely available but inexhaustible.

Their westward journeys took most of them *through* Idaho but not *to* Idaho. The region's climatic extremes—suffocating summer heat, bitter cold winter storms—held little appeal for those seeking a, literally, better life. It took—as so often has been the case in this country of enterprise—the rumor of money to be made for Idaho to be worth settling. The Gold Rush of 1849 was a bust for most of those who flocked to California in search of instant wealth. Similar hints of gold in the hills of Idaho swirled around in 1862, and miners streamed into the recently established Idaho Territory. To supply them, towns sprang up, rail lines were extended, and communication links were established. And land was parceled out to those with the commitment to give Idaho a try. To keep track of the land allotments, the territory had to be surveyed and laid out.

In 1863, the founders of Boise, whose sole purpose was

to supply Fort Boise, laid out a city plan of crudely drawn rectangles. The model, though elementary in style, was effective and popular in the emerging towns of the West. The territory, which would not become a state for another quarter century, was established in 1865 and included the county named for Ada Riggs, daughter of the area's legislative representative, H.C. Riggs. With available land came land claimants, with claimants came the need for goods and services, and within a few years, stagecoach service was available throughout much of the territory, including Ada County. As the survey of the entire territory was begun, the surveyor set up at what came to be known as Initial Point, atop a hill from which he (undoubtedly it was a man) could see in all four directions: north, south, east, and west. And when the surveyor's imaginary line was transferred into legal boundaries, the north-south line of intersection ran along what was called Meridian Road, and through a settlement that would be called, not surprisingly, Meridian, Idaho.

"Being as how this is supposed to be a life story, I hadn't better start at the most exciting part of my life, but at my earliest reckonings, which start out in the country, out of the big city of Meridian, Idaho. By the way, Meridian is where I was born on March 12, 1930."

Years after his Major League baseball career ended, when he was living in Japan with his family and coaching a baseball team, Vernon Law laid out his recollections of his early life in a bound volume of typescript he called *As I Remember.*

Intended for his family so its members could know their roots, the hundred or so pages represent an effort at introspection from a man whose entire life was spent thinking of others. Law, as were many of his generation, was taught (and later taught his own children) that he was less important than his family taken together and that his desires were best sublimated to those of others. Those born roughly at the same time, and perhaps a few years before Law, came to be memorialized for their service to their country during and following the Second World War as The Greatest Generation. Because that can-do attitude and that selfless philosophy of life have since so thoroughly been pushed out of American culture, it is useful to study it now, in part to understand what kind of people it turned out in the 1930s and to ask if more such citizens, or fewer, would benefit the country today.

"There is no way I'm going to be able to remember all the events, dates, and important happenings of my life," Law writes at the beginning of *As I Remember*. "But perhaps I can remember a few that might tickle the funny bone here and there." Throughout the typescript, Law's recollections are admittedly selective, but not in a way that casts him in a particularly heroic light. "I don't feel my life's events could be of much interest to anyone other than perhaps my immediate family, and even for some of them, I'm sure it will be boresome [sic]." His relaxed attitude toward English grammar is evident throughout his recollections, but it is not a mark of ignorance. Vernon Law was not a man addicted to what he calls, in Lincolnesque fashion, "book learning." His words do, however, convey the sentiments he feels, and that, by some measures, is the definition of effective communication. Law's wisdom was gleaned largely from sources other than formal schooling: the demands of harsh winter mornings in rural Idaho, the loving but unyielding rules of the house in which he grew up, the smell of spring's buds and new-mown hay, and the luxuriant warmth of a summer's day in the country. And, as much as any of these (but less than the lessons of his faith), the crack of wood against horsehide, the shouted encouragement of teammates, and the satisfying thwack of a fastball cleanly caught, despite a frustrated batter's attempt to do it violence. Vernon Law was shaped by a few important influences; the one he has a right to claim, because of his later accomplishments, is baseball.

For someone who lived his life according to a conservative, even anachronistic set of values, Law's origins were anything but traditional. His father, Jesse Law, already had seven children with his first wife, Audrey Packer Perkins, when she died of what was then called consumption. Within two years, Jesse had remarried, this time to Melva Christina Sanders, who bore him three more children. The first of these was named Evan and would become the closest friend of his little brother, a year younger, named Vernon Sanders Law. With typical self-effacement, Law claims not to know why he got his first name. "I guess because it wasn't taken already."

Courtesy Vernon Law

Brothers and best friends: Evan and Vern, 1936, Meridian.

From the perspective of seventy years of memory, Law said his first recollection was of the temporary shed home, "though one that was plastered," located next to a sandy pit, where he and his brothers played. His summation of his early life is as simple and to the point as it can be. "Life on the farm was hard, but it was good for all of us because it taught us how to work together and get along with what we had."

There. Finished. A complete philosophy of life. No tales

of want and mistreatment. No claims of emotional or physical abuse. Hard but good. This is not a life for Oprah to analyze, Dr. Phil to probe for hidden fetishes, nor a million little pieces of mosaic to be soldered into order by psychoanalysis. Vernon Law was poor as a boy, poor as millions of other boys were, and are, poor in material goods to a degree that most twenty-first-century Americans might now consider scandalous. To him, that life was "hard but good." For all our modern insights into the workings of the human mind, there is a lesson to be learned in the misty memory of growing up in Idaho's mountains.

Because it was hilly and located on the road into Meridian, the Laws' house was often passed in the summer months by slow-moving trucks loaded with baskets of fruit from nearby orchards.

"Those trucks barely crept along the sandy roads," Law recalled, "making it easy for us boys to climb aboard and hand a case of fruit off to one of our brothers. There weren't even mirrors on the trucks in those days, so it was easy to get away with it.

"I'm not sure if Dad and Mom ever found out. I'm sure if they did, they suffered for it, as Dad was an honest and good man, and very strict. To this day, I remember the belt or the switch, whichever was closest and the most convenient."

So there is the picture: The Deacon (as he would later be called), Vernon Law, who was once ejected from a Major

League Baseball game so he would not have to endure the cursing of his teammates, recalling corporal punishment dispensed by a loving but intolerant father. Here is a thought for those who cringe at the thought of disciplining their children: Look at how Vernon Law turned out and consider if an occasional belt strapping is worse than the disintegration of the solid family life that once characterized American society.

There is something else about Law's early life that is worthy of note: the acceptance of death, or at least of its possibility, despite one's best efforts to survive. One day, he recalls, while playing in the sand pit, there was a cave-in. The sand simply gave way to the accumulated weight of a gang of roughneck boys and did what sand will do under pressure: obey the laws of gravity. Atop the pit were large rocks that had been winched out of the ground. With the sand beneath giving way, the boulders began to avalanche their way downward. One struck Vernon head-on and knocked him flat. He felt the sand coming up around his waist, his shoulders, his neck, and then his face and mouth. "I remember trying to rise up, but the weight was too much. The next thing I remember was my brothers above me, digging and pulling me out."

Consciously or not, Law—writing as an adult—was reliving one of the most dramatic moments in the history of his Mormon faith. Though he does not mention it, Law carries the same surname as two of the most vilified Mormons:

William and Wilson Law, who, along with other expelled Mormons, were involved in the circumstances that led to the martyrdom of the Prophet Joseph Smith Jr. on June 27, 1844. A group of Mormon leaders, including Smith and his brother Hyrum, had been locked up in Carthage, Illinois, because Smith had ordered the destruction of a printing press belonging to a group that opposed him. With sentiment against Mormons running high, a mob stormed the jail and shot Hyrum to death. Joseph Smith, according to Mormon lore, hurried to the dying man and shouted, "Oh dear, brother Hyrum!" before he himself was shot and killed.

Vernon Law is in no way related to William and Wilson Law. They simply share a name. The future Pirate pitcher came from a Law family that traces its earliest origins to Isaac Law in Yorkshire, England. Isaac's son, Charles Law, born in 1832, migrated to the New World and began the family tree that would one day include Vernon Sanders Law.

Vernon Law cannot be fully understood without a knowledge of his religion. He is a proud and devoted Mormon, a fact that made him an oddity, indeed a minority of one, in the Major Leagues during part of his career and provided him with the nickname he carried throughout his life: The Deacon. He was not the first of his faith to play in the Big Leagues. That honor, as far as I can determine, was held by Roy Castleton, a left-handed pitcher born in 1885 in Salt Lake City, who spent three years in the Majors: one with the Yankees and two with Cincinnati. During that time, he won three games and lost four. The first Mormon to play for the Pirates was Spencer Adams, a second baseman who spent four seasons, between 1923 and 1927, playing on four different teams, among them, coincidentally, the Pirates and the Yankees. Born in Layton, Utah, in 1898, Adams had an undistinguished run as a player. He never hit .300 and he never hit a home run. He did make one plate appearance in the 1925 World Series for the Washington Senators. He did not reach base. Adams died in 1970 and is buried in his native town. The Majors would have to wait a little longer for a Mormon star to be born.

To understand how Law's faith shaped his character and wrote the code by which he lived as a player and spent the rest of his life, it helps to know what his religion teaches, and why its doctrines and beliefs are a sore point for many Christians who view the Mormon Church with disdain.

The Church of Jesus Christ of Latter-day Saints was once, and could soon again be, the fastest growing religion in the United States, if not the world. This faith—the Mormons, the LDS Church, the Latter-day Saints, whatever one chooses to call it—demands much of its members, including ten percent of their gross income right off the top, for a start. This tithing, like the tithes offered up by the Saints living during Christ's day, is voluntary in most faiths. The expectation with Mormons is more clearly defined, however, with a "full tithe" being ten percent of one's "increase," or annual income. The tithe is paid confidentially, in a sealed envelope, to the local bishop, at regular intervals. At year's end, each member meets with the bishop for a "tithing settlement," to review the annual contributions and to declare whether or not they amount to a full tithing. Faithful Mormons do not regard the payment of tithes as a financial burden or obligation but as an act of obedience and an opportunity to give back to the Lord a portion of what He has given them.

Young male Mormons who are healthy and considered morally worthy are strongly encouraged, even expected, to serve a mission, which means devoting two years of their lives (normally commencing at the age of nineteen) as missionaries for their faith somewhere in the world. Young women who reach the age of twenty-one and are not married are also eligible for missionary service, though there is not the same degree of expectation as for men, nor do their missions last as long—eighteen months.

In the Mormon faith, premarital sex is forbidden. So too are the use of tobacco in any form, the consumption of alcohol, and the use of street drugs. Prohibitions extend to the use of common stimulants such as coffee and tea, which are referred to in early Mormon literature as "hot drinks." Straying from these and other spiritual commitments, depending on the nature of the violation and the exhibition of repentance, humility, and subsequent actions of the person involved, can threaten an individual's membership in the

Church or his or her ability to enter the temple—the most sacred of Mormon places of worship.

The rules of Mormonism are unbending, but they are clear, which separates the Latter-day Saints from many others in these days of moral relativism and may explain an element of the religion's appeal. Former Church President Gordon B. Hinckley, when asked about the Church's steady and significant growth, explained that the gospel of Jesus Christ offers a firm foundation in a world of shifting values. For Mormons, right is obvious and wrong has consequences. This provides a comforting certainty. Mormons regard themselves as followers of Jesus Christ and, having chosen that path, are expected to try to emulate His example in both word and deed. Yet we all make mistakes and fall short from time to time. Mormons who have strayed say they are grateful for the opportunity to repent and try again, with the Savior's help.

There were other Mormons in the rural Idaho hills where the Laws lived, but they were not the majority religion. Today, as then, Mormons make up about 27 percent of Idaho's population. Law doesn't recall the exact proportions when he was a boy, but they were likely about the same. In his world, there were Protestants of various denominations, a sprinkling of Catholics, and a cluster of Latter-day Saints. "What faith were my neighbors?" he asks now in response to the question. "They were farmers!"

In an age when nearly everyone who has achieved celebrity wants to recount a tale of discrimination overcome—racial, religious, gender, or ethnic—Vernon Law chooses to remember the pathology of partnership that characterized his childhood. Sports were his petri dish for friendship. "I think there were three Mormons on the football team," he recalls (that, coincidentally, would be 27 percent of the 11 teammates on the field at any given moment), "but they weren't necessarily the best on the team. I just knew their families and knew they'd be at services." Law's recollections are the stuff of the original American dream of inclusion: putting aside religious and ethnic differences to become Americans, all and one, one and the same. That soup of sameness, as opposed to the various aromas of separation, was what created the conditions where Vernon Law, the once nearly suffocated farm boy from Idaho, would become the heart and soul, the inspiration, for a Major League baseball team whose members believed it was driven by destiny, a phoenix-like phenomenon that would, thirty years after Law's birth, prove itself the best in the world.

Mormons were not always accepted or welcomed in Idaho. In the 1880s, the territorial legislature passed the so-called Test Oath, which required anyone serving on juries, running for political office, or teaching in schools to declare under oath that they did not belong to any group that permitted or encouraged the practice of polygamy. The reason was clear: The Latter-day Saints in those days still practiced plural marriage. It was a custom handed down by the faith's founder and first prophet, Joseph Smith Jr., who said that he had received a direct revelation from God that some men were to have more than one wife at the same time.

Although its theological tenets are indeed ancient, Mormonism is regarded, in many respects, as an American religion. Joseph Smith Jr.—the founder of the Mormon faith and known to its adherents as "the Prophet Joseph"—was born in Sharon, Vermont, in 1805, a son of poor farming parents. His father, Joseph Smith Sr., could barely coax a living out of the rocky soil he owned. One of the few crops, if it could be so called, that grew in abundance was ginseng, a perennial herb renowned in Oriental medicine for its healing powers. Desperate to reverse his family's fortunes, the elder Smith invested in a shipment to China of locally grown ginseng. Like many get-rich-quick schemes, it failed, and Smith never saw his money again. Further, a sequence of unfortunate droughts and other weather-induced disasters led him, nearly destitute, to move his family across the state border to just outside Palmyra, New York, southeast of Rochester.

Palmyra might never have been known for anything but the four churches located on the corners of the intersection of State Routes 21 and 31. It was while living in Palmyra, Smith said, that as a fourteen-year-old boy, he found himself interested in religion and in particular in finding the Lord's true church. On a spring morning in 1820, after reading the promise in the book of James in the Bible, that all who lack wisdom may ask of God and God will respond liberally,

young Joseph retired to a grove of trees to pray and there experienced a theophany—a visit from God the Father and His
Son, the resurrected Jesus Christ. According to Joseph, they
told the boy that none of the religions on earth were pure in
their doctrines or practices and informed him that he should
join none of them.

Most American boys of fourteen are, to put it kindly, not
fully formed. Their waking moments revolve around
thoughts of girls, games, perhaps sports, and whatever other
pastimes they can find to avoid engaging their fertile minds.
In many respects, Joseph was no different, and three years
after his singular experience in the grove—referred to as the
First Vision by Church members—Joseph again approached
the Lord in prayer. Acknowledging that he had "displayed
the weakness of youth, and the foibles of human nature,"
and that he "was guilty of levity and sometimes associated
with jovial company . . . not consistent with that character
which ought to be maintained by one who was called of God
as I had been," he asked the Lord for further wisdom.

It was on that occasion, September 22, 1833, that Joseph
reported being visited by an angel named Moroni, the son of
an ancient prophet named Mormon. This heavenly being
told Joseph of the existence of a set of gold plates upon
which were written the history of God's dealings with His
children on the American continent in ancient days, which
plates he, Moroni, as the last author and keeper of the plates,

had hidden hundreds of years earlier in the nearby Hill Cumorah.

Joseph Smith would have to wait four years for the angel Moroni to deliver him these gold plates. But in 1827, on the same date that he first appeared, September 22, the angel met the now twenty-two-year-old man at the location where the plates rested and directed him to remove them from under a stone where they were hidden. Along with the plates, Smith found a breastplate and attached to it two stones, which he knew to name the Urim and Thummim, transparent stones with which Smith would translate the contents of the plates.

Word of the existence of a new "bible" made entirely of gold did not take long to get around the rural area that was Palmyra, and Joseph later told of repeated attempts by neighbors to relieve him of the sacred pages. To avoid harassment, Joseph and his new bride, Emma Hale, left New York and made their home in Harmony, Pennsylvania. Over the period of a few months, Joseph translated the plates. At first, Emma wrote down what he dictated to her. Later, a well-to-do farmer named Martin Harris helped with the task. When Harris insisted on taking the first 116 pages of manuscript to show his skeptical wife, Joseph was hesitant and at first declined but ultimately relented to Harris's pressure. Joseph's concern proved to be well-founded; Harris somehow lost the translated pages. Ultimately, Joseph resumed translation, with a local schoolteacher, Oliver Cowdery, taking on the scribe's duties. When the Book of Mormon was published in 1830, Harris footed the $3,000 printer's bill.

The book was greeted with everything from suspicion and disdain on the part of naysayers to great faith on the part of believers, who often described receiving a spiritual witness of the truthfulness of Joseph's account of its origin and of the doctrines taught in the book.

The Book of Mormon narrative begins with two families of Israelites who flee the area of Jerusalem around 600 B.C., shortly before the Babylonian conquest of the Kingdom of Judah led to tens of thousands of Jews being taken into captivity. After being directed by God to build a ship, these fleeing families eventually reached their promised land somewhere in the Americas. Conflict eventually separated the immigrants into two rival factions—the Nephites and the Lamanites—each of which over the course of centuries developed its own civilization.

The Book of Mormon is concerned primarily with conveying religious doctrines, principles, and practices and with providing an account of the appearance of the resurrected Jesus Christ on the American continent. The Book of Mormon ends with the story of a great battle between the Nephites and Lamanites at the Hill Cumorah, where, prior to his own death, Moroni stored the gold tablets containing the history that marked the end of the Nephite nation.

In 1829, Smith and Cowdery declared that the resurrected John the Baptist appeared to both of them and conferred upon them an authority known as the Aaronic Priesthood. Thus ordained, they followed John's instruction and baptized each other, in the manner of Christ's baptism at John's hands. Smith and Cowdery further declared that a short while later, they were also visited by Peter, James, and John, the Lord's apostles, who conferred upon them the higher Melchizedek Priesthood. Having obtained that authority, Smith formally organized The Church of Jesus Christ of Latter-day Saints on April 6, 1830, and immediately began seeking converts.

The theology Joseph Smith taught and the claims he made of visits from heavenly messengers were too radical a departure from traditional Christianity to not be met with resistance by some and fury from others. In time, he relocated to Kirtland, Ohio, where he found a willing group of converts led by Sidney Rigdon, and from there the Latter-day Saints moved to Independence, Missouri, which Joseph declared to be "the land of promise and the place for the City of Zion." Continued persecution and violence against Smith and members of the Church made another move necessary, this time to an uninhabited area in Illinois, along the swampy banks of the Mississippi River, where a city known as Nauvoo was built.

The allure of the new faith was obvious. The 1830s were a time of religious ferment and fervor in the prairie lands of the United States. People living on the edge of their subsistence understandably sought a God who knew their situation and who understood their problems and hardships. But beyond temporal explanations, most of those who joined the new church told of a profound feeling that they had been shown the truth, which was the need for a restoration of the Lord's original church.

Members of many established congregations resented the intrusion of the Latter-day Saints, even as the Church's ranks continued to swell with converts. Mormons were again rousted from their towns and sent packing west, where there were vast stretches of unclaimed land as well as new potential converts. In an effort to rid his state of the Church, Missouri Governor Lilburn Boggs declared that Mormons should be exterminated and actually issued an order to that effect. Perhaps as a result of that order, between August and October of 1838—as just one example of the persecution the Saints faced—the so-called Mormon War resulted in houses being burned, mobs attacking one another, and, on October 30, an attack on a Mormon settlement at Haun's Mill, in which seventeen Mormons, some of them teenagers and children, were slaughtered by anti-Mormon forces.

Joseph Smith himself was persecuted many times, including being jailed on several occasions and once being pulled from his home by an angry mob that beat and tarred and feathered him.

Joseph Smith's official revelation on July 12, 1843, that he and other faithful Mormon men had been granted divine authority to have more than one wife at the same time, set the Latter-day Saints even further apart from mainstream American society and made their critics even more deeply resentful of them. Although the Church officially renounced the practice of polygamy in the last decade of the nineteenth century, it remains the stereotype with which the Church is most often associated by outsiders, no matter how unfairly.

Another significant departure from traditional Christian theology was contained in an address Joseph Smith made on April 7, 1844, during a funeral eulogy for his friend, a man named King Follett, who had been killed in an accident. In preaching what became known as the King Follett Discourse, the Prophet Joseph declared that God has a body of flesh and bones, similar in form to mortal men. "God Himself was once as we are now, and is an exalted man, and sits enthroned in yonder heavens!" Smith taught. Additionally, according to Mormon doctrine, followers of Jesus Christ who keep God's commandments, make and keep sacred covenants with Him, and who through the power of the Atonement of Jesus Christ learn, grow, and progress through the eternities, can eventually become exalted, as God is.

The religious and civil conflict between Mormons and their neighbors came to a head in 1844. In that year, Joseph Smith declared himself a candidate for president of the United States. He was also engaged in a constant exchange of charges with two of his formerly loyal followers, William Law and his brother Wilson Law. The brothers brought printing presses into the city of Nauvoo, Illinois, which the

Church had made into its latest bastion. Joseph Smith ordered the presses destroyed, but not before an edition of the newspaper the *Expositor* had publicly accused Joseph Smith of having multiple wives and of having himself secretly crowned a king.

Joseph Smith's private militia, the Nauvoo Legion, destroyed the presses. The Prophet then fled to Iowa but returned to Illinois to face charges relating to the ruined machinery, and it was while awaiting trial that he and his brother Hyrum were killed in a jail cell in Carthage.

Mormons do not worship Joseph Smith, but they do respect and honor him as the Prophet of the Restoration. Everything in Mormonism revolves around their love, respect, reverence, and worship of the Savior Jesus Christ. As Joseph Smith wrote: "The fundamental principles of our religion are the testimony of the Apostles and Prophets, concerning Jesus Christ, that He died, was buried, and rose again the third day, and ascended into heaven; and all other things which pertain to our religion are only appendages to it."

Believe or disbelieve that Joseph Smith saw God the Father and His Son or that he was led by an angelic messenger to gold plates buried a short distance from his home or that he was authorized by heavenly messengers to restore the gospel of Jesus Christ to the earth. What religion is based on logic? Is it any less probable than a Jewish preacher being born of a virgin, walking on water, and rising from the dead?

It is the power of faith that gives religion its hold on us and its influence in our lives. And it is the security imparted by unquestioning faith that gives us strength and hope for the future. If the origins of Mormonism sound outlandish because they occurred in a time not so far removed from our own, that does not make them less meaningful for those who choose to believe in them, literally or otherwise.

After the Prophet's death, his successor, Brigham Young, led the remaining pioneer faithful west, in search of a place where they could practice their religion freely. They found their promised land in what is now Utah. After trekking across the Great Plains, Young looked down from the mountains, spied the Great Salt Lake in the distance, and uttered the immortal phrase: "This is the place."

The Mormons quickly took control of the territory that is now the state of Utah. Their religious beliefs may have been controversial, but their industry and determination were never in doubt. Mormon communities, beginning with Salt Lake City, are notable for their orderliness, tidiness, and clean geographic layouts. In Salt Lake City, streets are named for their distance from Temple Square, a square block that houses both the Tabernacle (home of the world-famous Mormon Tabernacle Choir) and the Salt Lake Temple, which is perhaps the most familiar and iconic symbol of Mormonism. Thus, residents will give their address as 2200 South 1500 East, meaning 22 blocks south and 15 blocks east of Temple Square.

First Inning

They couldn't all fit into Utah, and many didn't want to. The diaspora of Latter-day Saints took the faith to neighboring territories—south to modern-day Arizona, west to Nevada and California, and north to Idaho, especially the southwest corner that now includes Boise and Meridian.

The Mormon Church discontinued the practice of polygamy in 1890. President Wilford Woodruff issued a public declaration, referred to as the Manifesto, declaring that God had revealed to him in a vision that the Church's existence was threatened by plural marriage. It was a theological thunderbolt. The practical effect was to pave the way for Utah's admission to the Union. It also meant that with their strict code of conduct unencumbered by polygamy, practicing Mormons would become some of the best examples of clean-cut, family-oriented citizens in the United States and around the world.

By the time Vernon Law was born in 1930, Mormons had been integrated into the greater American population with a success that other religious minorities could only envy. If Vern was ever discriminated against for his faith, he professes not to remember it. And on the one occasion when he thinks a girl might have broken up with him because he was Mormon, that motive has been disputed by the object of his affection.

Vernon's father was a machinist and a mechanic. He was also the branch president, or highest-ranking Mormon official, in the area where he made his home. Jesse Law's approach to life was that of a technician, exacting, relying on being right instead of being lucky. That trait was passed on to his tall, gangly son, the one who adored his older brothers (especially Evan), protected his sisters, and found his place in a world that does not welcome the average but does embrace the unusual. Vern would demonstrate that he was different, though not by reason of injustices done to him.

He was a boy who made the most of what fortune tossed him and who did not miss what he lacked. "Life on the farm taught us to work together and get along with what we had," he wrote in his memoir. "I remember the long rows of corn we had to weed. It seemed as if I never could get to the other end of the row. I didn't mind too much when the corn got tall as you could lie down in the shade of the furrow and rest without being seen."

Childhood memories of skiving off would eventually be replaced by a philosophy of hard work and no shortcuts. But those first years of his life were the ones Law remembers now with a guiltless abandon, from seven decades of distance, and so they merit attention for their innocence and formative power.

He had a pet named Jack, who Law remembers being part German shepherd and part coyote. "He was a good watchdog but tough on strangers," says Law, meaning who-knows-what befell unwelcome guests to the Law homestead. "I still have a scar on my arm where he bit me accidentally. I was holding him off another dog and he closed his mouth

Jack awaits.

over my arm." Yet Jack would sit for hours on a tree stump at the edge of the Laws' property, waiting for Vernon or Evan to come home from school. When he saw them, he charged full speed, with a welcoming growl that made each homecoming an adventure.

Whether Jack was part coyote or not, it fit a young boy's imagination to think him so. Would such a crossbreed be allowed into a family's house these days? Could it qualify for a license (which of course Law's pet never possessed)? These days, a boy who had been bitten by his beloved pet might be offered counseling or a course on sensitivity to animals and the animal might have been taken away, never to be seen again. But in the 1930s in Idaho you simply patched up your arm and remembered not to do that again.

There is another aspect to Law's boyhood that must be understood and accepted for what it was, and is—a way of seeing things in the times in which he lived. His memoir is not a public record. Its contents were not created to be publicized or scrutinized, and so some of the thoughts it contains are more candid than political correctness might prefer.

He and his brother Evan, to whom he was closer than anyone in the world, used to make the farm equivalent of zip guns, slings, and something called a flipper, which would propel a stone with great force. Law and his brother called them "nigger-flippers," a term that he says now shames him: "We very innocently didn't even know what a nigger was, except that it was our flipper that we used to have a lot of fun with."

Is Vernon Law a racist because he used a term in common coinage in the decade of his birth? Of course not. He has since become a friend, advisor, even spiritual guide to African-American players who recognize in his faith a sincerity lacking in many of the loud mega-churches and megabucks-preachers of Christianity today. The use of the term *nigger* was then so common that any white person who claimed not to use it, or not to have known its meaning, is more to be doubted than admired.

Instead, he was a boy of the West, who experienced all the sharp joys and jolting pain of life on the land. As he was fond of recalling: "Like all farms, we had an outside (two-holer) toilet. It was about twenty yards from the back door and, believe me, when it was zero degrees outside and four in the morning, that was about twenty yards too far. "

He also came to accept the realities of nature. Each Christmas, his father selected a hog from the yard and slaughtered it. Vern recalls a bit of squeamishness at the bloody ritual, a reluctance he overcame when his mother cooked the meat into a smoking, succulent main course. In the dirt-floored basement, the Law family stored potatoes, which had to be sprouted from time to time. "Unless you've had this job, you have no idea what it's like to grab a cold, squashy rotten potato," Vern says. "Spend an hour or two with that job and you'll want nothing but instant potatoes."

Music played its role in the Law household. Though his mother played the saxophone, the instrument was not practiced when Vern and his siblings were at home. Saturday nights often found his mother and father at a church dance where Mrs. Law would play the sax. Says Vern: "I'm sure we were all too busy with chores and school work to spend much time singing or playing instruments."

Nor was he skittish about exterminating pests. Gophers and squirrels that burrowed into the irrigation ditches and drained off precious water were shown little mercy. "With the squirrels, we'd stand by their holes with clubs and as soon as they'd come running out—Bam!" he says. In order to get from the farm into Meridian, where he could spend the 15 cents his father occasionally doled out, Vern and his brothers would hitchhike. One favorite ploy for getting rides was to carry one another, making it appear that one of the boys was unable to walk.

It was, Law happily concedes, a world before PETA, the ACLU, and No Child Left Behind. It was childhood, finally left behind.

When World War II broke out, Vern's father was suddenly in great demand as a mechanic and went to Mare Island, near Santa Rosa, California, to work at a submarine base. When school was out that year, the rest of the family, Vern included, joined him there. The family took to California, the milder climate, the mellower life. Hard work, however, followed the Law boys from Idaho. Vern worked at a veterinary hospital—something he previously scarcely knew existed—where he cleaned the animals' pens. One day, he remembers, a stray dog decided it would not be handled and set the hospital on alert. Despite his efficiency in dispatching squirrels, Vern was an animal lover. He walked up to the dog, extended his hand, befriended the beast, and led the now-docile animal back to his quarters.

Vern and Evan—the brother to whom he was closest in age and disposition—also worked at a bowling alley, despite being too young for employment in an establishment that served alcohol. Automatic pin setters had not yet been installed, so it was up to the boys to reset each alley. Vern remembers being hit more than once with flying pins but adds proudly, "I was able to get out of the way of the balls." Later in Vern's baseball career, hitters could perhaps be grateful that Law knew what it was like to be plunked by a solid object flying at high speed. He had a reputation for never intentionally beaning a batter. Pitching inside, to brush back a hitter and establish respect, was another matter.

He was less agile at dodging skunks. Once, when Evan and he decided to take a shortcut home, they saw the telltale tail and knew what was about to happen. "It was too late, we'd had it," he recalls. "We got out of there fast, and when we got home, Mom knew we were coming. We got about ten feet from the door and were told to take the clothes off, bathe, and then she'd consider letting us in."

There is about Law's childhood recollections a kind of brazen boyishness, as though daring you to make fun of his hickishness. He was nailed by a skunk. He and his brothers bathed in the same dirty water and worked numerous jobs to make a few extra quarters for their family. (Law always makes a point of saying the children turned the money they earned from menial jobs over to their parents.) In a world where children so often are involved in activities unknown to their parents, is Law's mild childhood pitiable? Or should it perhaps be studied by families who hope to regain the

Law Men

Left to right: Evan, Jesse, Dennis, and Vern.

Left to right: Evan, Dennis, Vern, and Jesse.

closeness they seem to have mislaid in the headlong rush into the twenty-first century?

Manners are one thing, cowardice another. Law was no milquetoast, no mama's boy. If he was an obedient son, he was also a fierce, driven competitor on the fields of sports where he played as a youth and later a man. To Vern and his entire family, sports were activities that did no harm and could produce a great deal of good, as long as they were played fairly.

Until he was in high school, Vern had few opportunities to play organized sports. Before that, he and his brothers and neighbors played pickup games (as I would do with considerably less skill, twenty-five years later, in suburban Pittsburgh). But it was in high school that Vern realized something was different about him. "As I look back now and assess the skills of our coaches and what they knew about their sports, I see a huge gap in what they taught then and what's being taught now," he says, from a vantage point of sixty years. "I suppose because we were so few in numbers, they'd take any and all who had the time to practice after school. I weighed 175 pounds as a freshman, and I was 6-foot-3, so I guess they thought I had potential."

That size nearly made a football player of a future World Series champion. Vern was a bona fide football hero. He ran the hundred in ten seconds (an impressive feat without the benefit of the equipment, shoes, and training finesse now available in high schools), could throw a football 50 yards, and kick it 70, which he did once in a game, as a quick kick on third down. In one high school football season, the team went undefeated and allowed opponents only six points all year. Meridian challenged any team in Idaho to play for state supremacy. There were no takers.

But fate—or as Vern would have it, the Lord—had other plans for the tall, lean, farm-grown son of Idaho's Treasure Valley. Because he was a three-sport athlete, Vern was constantly practicing one skill or another, all the while juggling jobs for cash that required him to rise at 5 A.M., work, clean up, and be at school at eight o'clock.

In his third year of high school, he was the team's star pitcher; his brother Evan was the catcher and cleanup hitter. His team was playing Payette, a rival school in western Idaho that would one day produce another Mormon major leaguer, Harmon Killebrew—a home-run hitting machine for the Washington Senators and later the Minnesota Twins. The game was scoreless. Law had allowed only two batters to reach base. In the top of the seventh (scholastic baseball games were seven innings long), Evan led off with a double. Vern singled him home, and Meridian took a 1–0 lead into the bottom of the last inning. Sixty-some years later, Law still remembers what happened, as well he should:

"I couldn't believe my eyes; there was a midget standing there at home plate. He was about 3½ feet tall. They hadn't been getting anyone on base, so he was up there to get a base on balls. He was their secret weapon. Evan came out and said, 'What shall we do?' and I said, 'I don't know, but I guess we're going to have to pitch to him.' Evan went back and held his mitt about 14 inches from the ground. As luck would have it, I threw three straight strikes to him and then managed to get the other two hitters out, so the game ended 1–0."

"As *luck* would have it. . . ." "*they* hadn't been getting anyone on base. . . ." " . . . then *managed* to get the other two hitters." There is nothing in the words to betray ego, yet the pride in his accomplishment is palpable. It was then, as a junior in high school, that Vernon Law, who couldn't avoid a skunk's attack, or flying bowling pins, or the indignities of Saturday night baths in a galvanized washtub, began to think the world might have something to offer him and that his skills might help him realize his full potential.

Someone else thought so too. Sitting in the stands that day in Payette was a local attorney, Herman Welker, who later became a United States senator from Idaho. Welker had spent some years as an entertainment lawyer in Los Angeles and represented the actor Wallace Beery. Through Beery, Welker met a young man named Harry Lillis Crosby, who soon became a pheasant-hunting partner of Welker's in rural Idaho. Because Harry had been infatuated as a boy with a newspaper comic strip called "Bingo from Bingville," he acquired the nickname *Bing*. The odd name and his relaxed, soothing voice made Bing Crosby the country's most popular singer for decades. His recording of "White Christmas" was the bestselling single in American history, making the pop charts nearly every year between 1946 and 1962. *Going My Way* and his "on the road" movies with Bob Hope were wildly popular and made him wildly wealthy. Crosby speculated in California real estate, bred racehorses, and, with some of his spare cash, bought a share in and became a vice president of the country's most woeful professional baseball team, the Pittsburgh Pirates.

Welker watched Law pitch and decided to call his friend with a tip.

Second Inning

"True sportsmanship is usually displayed following defeat."

(From Vernon Law's *Words to Live By*)

"CLASS DISMISSED."

The fifty-three students of Sister Mary Loretta's class at St. Valentine's Roman Catholic school tumbled out of the classroom like earthquake survivors. Was there ever a more jubilant feeling than the end of first grade? It was unlike anything, just as the first day and, indeed, the entire first year had been. First grade is unique—one of those moments designed to live forever in the mind because without those memories, life would hardly be worth enduring.

I was one of those fifty-three (a class size that now would have the teachers' union on the picket line and parents protesting for their innocents' rights), one of the youngest, due to being born in October but having parents who decided not to "hold him back." Thus I was commingled with kids who were ten to fifteen months my chronological superiors. Perhaps that made me more timid. With only five years behind me, and the additional burden of being slightly built and given to self-doubt, fears and tears were only exacerbated by my being younger.

On my first day of school in September of 1959, I arrived with my father, a welterweight reporter for the Associated Press who had spent his entire life instinctively feeling inferior. Having completed a high-school education and that barely, my father approached life with trepidation. But he had determined that his son would never lack confidence. Dad did whatever he could to pump me full of proofs of my capability. For years, upon returning home each night, he had played catch with me in the backyard. No matter that he was tired from work; he wanted to make sure I would know I was good at baseball. And when I tried to pitch, I pretended to be Vernon Law.

Before I went to bed, Dad and I would plunge multicolored pushpins into a Hammond map of the world that hung on the wall of my bedroom, as we tested each other endlessly on countries, their neighbors, and their capitals. He took me to St. Valentine's Roman Catholic Church every Sunday morning, though my mother was not with us. She was Lutheran and did not deign to attend Catholic services. From my earliest days, I was aware of this division within our family. My mother was Protestant, proud and intelligent. My father was Catholic, strong-willed but sometimes angry and unsure of himself. Was that what these religions stood for?

Courtesy Author

Even at the beach, I wore my loyalty to Vern and the Pirates (note cap).

What, then, was I, a hybrid of these faiths and traits, to become?

I knew nothing. My entire life spread before me.

Dad knelt in front of me in the school hallway. "Now, listen, old buddy. I'm going to work and you're going to school in there." He indicated Room 6, the domain of the yet-unseen Sister Loretta. "Don't be afraid. There's nothing to be afraid of. At twelve o'clock, Mommy will be here to get you and you'll go home for lunch with her. Then you'll come back here with Mommy and she'll come and pick you up again at three. Understand?"

I nodded, knowing that if I tried to speak I would

unleash a torrent of tears, snot, and fear. All those things were always just beneath the surface with me then— sometimes still are.

I ventured into the class. There were so many kids, and they all looked bigger, better, and happier than me. I knew a few who lived nearby, but they weren't looking at me. They were busy meeting the new kids, as I should have been. One in particular, a boy named Richard Sebak, seemed already to have befriended the entire room. His chubby-cheeked, dimpled face bore a radiant smile, and he knew just what to say to each of his classmates. How did one learn that?

"John? Take a seat." It was Sister Loretta, looking, already, somewhat perplexed by me. I was just standing there. No one at home called me John. I was Jack. My father was the John of the house. Thirty years later, I would name my own son John, to continue the tradition and confusion.

I could feel it coming. It was—is—a tightening of the throat, an unsteady, fluttering feeling in my stomach. A weakness in my knees. Fear has a feel to it. I have never stopped knowing it.

I started to well up. I didn't want to be here. I didn't belong here. I wanted to be home, with my mother, doing nice, familiar things.

"John? Come with me?" It was not said unkindly, but there was a tiny tinge of derision in Sister's voice. I could hear the others around me sniggering. "He's crying. Crybaby." I didn't care what they thought. I wanted to leave. My mother would have to be called to come for me. That would be all right.

I saw my father standing by a window at the end of the hall. His hat was poised on the sill. He had not, after all, gone to work. He had waited to ensure that I was all right, sensing perhaps that I needed some extra time to accustom myself to my new routine. I ran into his arms. "Okay, old buddy. Don't push the panic button."

It was the advice he always gave me. He even made a wooden box for me, with a brass plaque on top, with those words. "Don't push the panic button." There was a lever that went through the box which, when pushed, cantilevered the brass plaque. Out came a tube with Life Savers in it. I can still remember the soothing taste of Life Savers. My favorites were the chocolate ones. To this day, I think of chocolate Life Savers as the antithesis of panic.

Yes, as you can see, I was a wimp. I had no courage, no manliness that took me to the edge of rage and allowed me to do what manly men do: stupid stuff.

Instead, I placidly did as I was told, and thought that was the same as doing well. I'm not complaining at all; my parents loved me, we always had enough to eat, no great tragedies befell us. There was nothing I would exchange about my upbringing.

Except that I was scared of everything. I lived within a cautious perimeter of activities, friends, family, and experiences. I never challenged those limits, never thought to ask

If it had been a role, fine. Unfortunately, it was real life, too.

why they existed and who had established them. I was the only child of a middle-class family in the suburbs of Pittsburgh.

Pittsburgh.

The Steel City. The Smoky City.

The mills were already beginning to close their doors by the time I was born in 1953. Jones and Laughlin's huge facility upriver on the Monongahela spewed orange vapors all day and night. But U.S. Steel had fallen out of love with

Pittsburgh in favor of less expensive towns that weren't bastions of organized labor as Pittsburgh was, is.

Pittsburgh, eight miles to the north of our ranch-style home, was, to me, the epitome of sophistication, commercial enterprise, medical expertise. My parents took me there, to Dr. Pennington in the Jenkins Arcade, for dental appointments. Because I never had to have any work done, only cleanings with peppermint-flavored cleaning paste on his electric brush, I thought, and declared, for the first ten or twelve years of my life that I wanted to be a dentist. Later, when I realized that it would be helpful to like and excel at science in order to pursue that career, my enthusiasm waned.

We went to Gimbels, and Kaufmann's, and the Joseph Horne Company for shopping expeditions, long before those emporia came to the suburbs and erased any real commercial reason for people to go downtown ("dahn-tahn" is how it's pronounced—"pra-nahnced"—there). At Horne's, if I had been good (I always was), we stopped at the ground-floor candy counter, and I would point to the long bars of white chocolate, and it would be cut with a knife and served up on a wooden palette that I was allowed to lick, before it was dipped in hot water to prepare it for the next customer.

And yet . . .

I watched television, a fair amount (though, my mother made sure, never sitting too close to the black-and-white screen and never so much as to ruin my eyes or imperil my study). Some of the shows I watched were set in suburban

Jenkins Arcade on Liberty Street, where I went to the dentist.

settings similar to the one I called home. *Leave It to Beaver* and *My Three Sons* looked as if they could have been filmed in Bethel Park: leafy streets, kids—always white ones—walking to and from school, mothers in knee-length house-dresses who were cooking dinner when those kids arrived (straight) home from school. Fathers came home and ate dinner still wearing a suit and tie. The demise of the family dinner and the stay-at-home mom is a different topic and not my purpose in recounting these years. The point is, those television portrayals told me I was fine, that other kids lived as

I did, and that some of their lives were exciting enough to make TV shows about them.

But other shows of that day, and particularly movies, were disturbingly unfamiliar. Many were set in New York, a place that seemed so far away from Pittsburgh that I could not understand how its inhabitants existed. How did so many people live in buildings piled on top of each other? How did taxis—nonexistent in my life—know where you were so they could come by when you wanted one? Did all the apartments where people lived have outside terraces with beautiful views of the skyline, as those on the television shows and movies suggested?

And, why did the Yankees always win?

Although I was a wimp, I followed baseball and was pretty good at playing it. And there was ample time and opportunity to play baseball where I grew up. If you could play baseball, and had your own glove, you were accepted, despite other failings such as not being well-behaved, well-spoken, or a good student. At one pickup game, a batter hit a ground ball like a shot in my direction. I cut to my left, bent over, speared it, and threw to first in one seamless motion. "Okay, you can play on my team from now on," allowed Burt, who was several years older than me and a figure of unquestioned worship in our neighborhood.

A year or two later, Burt and Jimmy, a usually gentle giant of Burt's age who lived across the street from me, would borrow a ball that I owned. It was, and is as far as I know, one of a kind. Bigger than a baseball, smaller than a softball, with a durable rubber cover that nonetheless felt like leather, it was a gift from an aunt who at the time lived in Baltimore, which to me was another city full of fascination, mystery, and its own baseball team. My aunt purchased the ball, on sale, at a store that had no branches in any other city. No one had a ball like mine. No matter its frugal origins, the ball was perfect for the hybrid game that had become the mainstay of my life in Bethel Park. We gathered in a field to one side of Benjamin Franklin Elementary School, located just down the street from my house. This would, of course, have been my elementary school, had I been sent to the public school system. But my father's staunch Catholicism overrode geographic convenience (as my own would not, when my children were of similar age), so I went to St. Valentine's, which was a quarter mile away.

Ben Franklin was a spacious garden of instruction. It occupied well over ten acres of land, though the school building itself took up less than a quarter of that. In those days, the land in the suburbs seemed limitless and construction was undertaken not with a thought toward conservation, but more, it seems, to use up the vast tracts of dirt and trees as quickly and inefficiently as possible.

The school itself was one of those modular buildings that had become popular in the immediate postwar period, when Americans were coming to grips with the remarkable fact that theirs was now the most powerful nation on earth. Our military had conquered enemies whose lands contained some of the most renowned architecture of all time. The Champs-Élysées had set out American flags to welcome our liberating troops. The Ginza in Tokyo (what was left of it) had red and blue strips of cloth flying (white being considered the color of death and therefore inappropriate). And the U.S. Army was made up of men like my father, who were now home to take up their lives again.

The question then, was, having seen and mastered the sites of such cultural wealth, what would we make of our own country?

The answer would have dispirited Albert Speer and Baron Haussmann.

Reflecting perhaps the simplistic mind of our president at the time, who had presided over the taming of Europe and its monuments, the Eisenhower era saw a massive expansion of construction in a style reminiscent of Lego. Flat, modular blocks of housing, offices and, yes, schools went up across the rolling American landscape, not because they were beautiful or represented anything, but because they were functional and quickly constructed.

Ben Franklin was a series of yellow brick squares tied together by doorways. The roof was flat, about 18 feet from the ground, and propped up by hollow columns of steel that had been fashioned only eight or so miles away in the blast furnaces of Pittsburgh. In 1950s America, you lived amid the materials that your neighbors produced. The flat roof and the steel pillars are the key to this story.

Burt was thin and wiry and, as I have said, several years older than me. Jimmy was an out-and-out behemoth. Jimmy's physical strength was the marvel of all the mothers along our street, who, for pennies and with his mother's permission, would rent him to move heavy objects, finish arduous tasks that their own good-for-nothing husbands had abandoned, or even, on one memorable occasion, push a stalled car *uphill,* until it reached the top of our street and could be clutch-popped back to life.

"Let us borrow your ball," Burt said without prefix. The request was not unusual. Because my discounted ball had the feel of a real baseball, it was preferable to others with their various plastic coatings. Because it was slightly bigger than a baseball, but not as large as a softball, it could be pitched overhand with greater velocity, and therefore impart a more manly feel.

"Can I play, too?" At my age, the epitome of cool was to be allowed to play ball with the older boys. Burt knew I could field, so the request was not too cheeky to be considered.

"We're gonna hit homers," said Jimmy with the charm of an elevator door.

Because the ball had the solidity of a baseball—hardball, in local parlance—it could be hit longer distances, to more macho satisfaction.

For me, this invitation was as good as an offer to try a cigarette or to play mumblety-peg with an older boy's penknife or snap a girl's bra strap. Fielding the towering shots that Jimmy could launch was for me as mindless a pleasure as a black Lab must feel gamboling after a stick. I grabbed the precious ball that had won me admission to this ecstasy and followed the older boys down the street to the field.

The game was played against the 20-foot-high wall of Ben Franklin, so that missed pitches or balls that did not cross the plate would strike the wall and bounce back to the pitcher. The scuffs the wall inflicted meant nothing. The ball actually became more solid and therefore more hittable, the more scratches and cuts it bore.

Jimmy was a monster of a boy, as I've already mentioned. When he made contact with the ball, it probably soared 150 feet, no small thing for a preadolescent. When he undercut the ball it went straight up in the air, or in the case of the very first pitch he tried to turn on, up in the air and back, onto the roof of the school.

The roof was flat and stretched the entire length of the school. If the ball rolled to one side, it would probably drop off. If its path took it straight back, there was no telling where it would be. But it would be on the roof.

All my life, when I have felt tears coming, my throat would stiffen and I would have a difficult time swallowing. Whether, as a doctor once explained to me, it is bile, or rather, as I romantically think of it, the pure pain of humanity escaping its trap way inside, I know what will happen when I feel that throat tightening. When that ball disappeared onto the roof, I waited, one, two, three seconds for it to roll off on one side of the school. Then I ran around the wall to see if it might fall, or had fallen, on the other side. I ran like a frantic hare, looking for the orb of white in the vast fields of uncut grass.

It was useless. I knew where the ball was, just as Jimmy and Burt knew. It had come to rest on the unreachable roof, 20 feet above, and was lost forever.

I couldn't help the tears—couldn't have stopped them if someone had told me my mother's life depended on dry eyes. Just as at school on that first day when my father sent me into the classroom, my throat went stiff and my knees buckled. I simply began crying—for the ball, which I was sure missed me and wanted to come back home with me from the inaccessible roof. I wanted it back, so it would be safe with me, in my house, and I would never let it out of my sight again.

"You little baby," said Burt, with a vicious accuracy that only made me cry harder.

"Go home, Jack. We'll get you another ball."

"Don't want another one. Want mine," I wailed.

"You baby," said Jimmy, who already topped six-two and was anything but.

It was not rational. It was not manly. It was simply my insides revealing themselves on the outside. I was not a baby,

Wet behind the ears, and destined to remain that way.

not a wimp. I was a little boy who believed that the ball he owned had feelings and would be lonely up on that roof, without him.

Could there have been two boys more different than Vern Law in the hills of Idaho and me in the suburbs of Pittsburgh? He killed small animals, worked menial jobs for extra money, mucked out stalls, hijacked fruit from trucks, feared his father, and feasted on fried food. I was raised wisely, grew healthily, learned prodigiously, and couldn't any more control my male emotions in front of two obviously more type-A superiors than if a needle were being driven under my fingernail.

I ran. It was instinct. Somewhere, up that steep hill, which as I look at it fifty years later is more like a mild incline, was my home, my house, my shelter, my life, and, more to the point, my parents, who were my refuge. I had two people—a mother and a father—who loved me and to whom my interests were the most important in the universe. Vernon Law had a mother and father who had clearly provided him with a sound and enduring moral foundation for life. But his lessons were learned through experience, through mucking out barns and chicken coops, being rescued by his brother from near death, through the unforgiving precision of the baseball diamond and football hash marks, where there was no substitute for winning, no possible excuse for failure that was recognized as valid.

Was I raised to temporize, to worry about the feelings of inanimate objects, and to explain away my failure to hit and pitch like a future major leaguer? Perhaps. It is a question I have been asking myself for decades, often through the prism of Vernon Law's example.

Third Inning

"Have more than thou showest; speak less than thou knowest."
—Shakespeare
(From Vernon Law's *Words to Live By*)

VERNON LAW'S DESTINY was shaped in part by cigars and roses.

Of the first, he knew nothing; of the second, next to naught. Yet the weed and the petals were enough to bring him to the Pittsburgh Pirates, a choice, not his, but a choice nonetheless, that would alter and shape his life.

Herman Welker represented everything that liberals think was wrong with the country after World War II and much of what conservatives wish could be restored. Welker's father moved from North Carolina to Idaho to fulfill a life-long dream of starting a potato farm. In the 1930s there were few places more closely associated with potatoes than Idaho. Herman was born in Cambridge, Idaho, the youngest of seven children. But the farming life was not for Herman. He attended the University of Idaho in Moscow, graduated from its law school, and, after a spell on his home turf, departed for Hollywood, where he represented several clients and be-friended some of the biggest names in entertainment. The wispy young man from Tacoma, Washington, Harry Crosby, whom he had met through Wallace Beery, was a frequent guest at Welker's Idaho home, where they enjoyed pheasant hunting and fishing in the state's trout-rich streams and rivers.

Welker, a Republican, would go on to become the U.S. senator from Idaho from 1950 to 1956. In an age before campaign contributions were too closely examined, he bene-fited from a lavish dinner thrown for his supporters by his friend Bing, who said he hoped to defray the cost by "de-ducting it from my taxes and making the Democrats pay for it." Welker waltzed into the Senate in 1950, defeating former Senator D. Worth Clark. Clark, in the primary election, had ousted Democrat incumbent Glen Taylor, who had made the poor political choice for an Idahoan of running for vice pres-ident in 1948 with Henry Wallace's Progressive Party.

Welker arrived in Washington during the period in which Senator Joseph McCarthy of Wisconsin was conducting ex-tensive hearings on supposed communist infiltration of the government and armed services. Welker was reviled by Democrats for his support of and allegiance to McCarthy. He was derided as "Little Joe from Idaho," to which he retorted, somewhat lamely, "I wear no man's yoke." Six years later, he was defeated after just one term by Democrat Frank Church, who would go on to play a major role in investigating the

Courtesy Vernon Law

Herman Welker (right) with Vern Law in 1950.

Watergate scandal. As a senator, Welker would exert some influence over Vernon Law's career. His first contact with the lanky kid from Meridian, however, was the most important, and it involved no conversation.

Watching the rawboned, unsophisticated right-hander strike out the midget and 17 other batters that day in 1947, Welker had a suspicion about the battery whose name was Law. Major League scouts could not approach a high school player—a code of conduct that explains in part why kids were allowed to be kids in those days, instead of being rushed to stardom for which some are unprepared. But he let his friend Harry, the bobby-soxers' singing god who was also a vice president of the Pittsburgh Pirates, know that there was a kid in Meridian who could toss the pill.

Just as he became my hero, Vern Law had boyhood idols of his own. Not surprisingly for a boy with baseball talent, he had heard the legend of Babe Ruth and was suitably in awe. Ruth had played for the Boston Red Sox, and, famously, had his contract purchased by the rival Yankees in 1919. Ruth's on-field heroics were genuine. Home runs were a rarity in baseball prior to his era. Most runs were scratched out from singles, daring leads on the base paths, hard running, bunts—what today is called "small ball." Ruth's violent swing made homers fashionable, and him a celebrity—the revered "Sultan of Swat."

There was also an off-the-field Ruth, of course. When most athletes take off their uniforms, they also strip themselves of their public perfection. Ruth was perhaps the prototype for this split personality. The product of a Baltimore school for troubled boys, George Herman Ruth—unlike Vernon Law—had had little as a young man to steer him toward living a good life. Because he was talented, he assumed he was also blessed. When he broke his own record of 59 home runs by lofting Number 60 off Tom Zachary on September 30, 1927, it was national front-page news. So well known was the date of the exploit that during World War II, American troops in Europe would ask newcomers to their units, who they suspected might be German infiltrators:

"What year did the Babe hit 60?" Under such circumstances, sports trivia became a life-and-death business.

Vern Law was playing American Legion summer baseball in 1947, a year in which his life changed in several ways. In his last year of high school, he had distinguished himself in three sports and had scholarship offers to play football from three colleges. His baseball coach told him not to play football because he might be injured on the gridiron. Vern tried to listen to this sensible advice but then made the mistake of wandering by the practice field in the fall. The sensation of seeing his classmates having so much fun while he kicked his heels was too much to resist. As he recalled, "The following week, I was in uniform and right in the middle of things. This was the year that our team walked over everybody." The team walked over everyone. Not Vernon Law. The perfect season was a team effort.

Which does not mean that Law was unaware of his prowess. His American Legion baseball team won the district, regional, and state championships. He pitched every game. "I about pitched my arm out during that series as I was striking out 20 or 21 almost every game," he says in his memoir. Twenty or 21 strikeouts per game? Was it any wonder he attracted Welker's attention?

To reward their championship effort, the team was invited to a national sectional American Legion baseball tournament in Billings, Montana. It was there, at a sports banquet, that 17-year-old Vern Law got his first, up-close look at Babe Ruth—his hero. The impression he took away from the encounter was not what he had anticipated. "We all got autographed baseballs from him, which I still have, but I was shocked by his behavior. He was just getting over a throat cancer operation and there he was lighting up a big cigar and holding a bottle of beer. From that point on, he was no longer such an idol."

That comment is worth dissecting. Nothing could take away from Ruth's accomplishments at the plate. And that was bound to attract attention, fans, and adulation. Humans—not just Americans—respect athletic accomplishments. We like and admire winners. But when Vern Law was a boy, and because of the kind of boy he was, his admiration for Ruth was tarnished by his hero's behavior.

In his senior year of high school, Law was at a disadvantage. His brother Evan, a year older, had graduated following the previous season and could not be Vernon's catcher in baseball, nor his favorite target in football. "I really missed him when baseball season rolled around," Law recalls, "because the catcher we had couldn't hold onto my pitches. So we just had a so-so year. I could pitch a no-hitter, which I did, and I would still lose through errors. We did win our share, but I really had to strike out a lot of people to keep them off base in order to win. For the first time in my life, I was without my best buddy."

A different kind of kinship was brewing, however. Nearly perfect in his deliveries from the mound, Vern found it far more difficult to throw a strike in matters *du coeur*. Here's how he explains it: "I dated a couple of girls and thought I was in love with one of them. After a while, she told me she wasn't good enough for me. I guess that was a polite way of getting rid of me without hurting me. But I thought she was OK."

He thought considerably more of VaNita McGuire, one of the most popular girls in his class. She and Vern were in the orchestra together, but he kept his distance, from a probably well-deserved sense of inadequacy. "There were all those boy friends to wade through, and besides, I knew she wouldn't be interested in someone who had holes in his pants and socks most of the time."

Then, one day, Vern and a friend, Darrell Tilley, were driving around in Tilley's car. "We came up behind this car that was parked in the middle of the road. A couple of boys were talking to this girl. When she spotted us, she started waving her hands kind of frantically at us, so we stopped. She came up to us and explained she had waved down this car with these two boys and they weren't who she thought they were. Matter of fact, she didn't even know them, so she was in a bit of a spot. She said, 'What shall I do?' I said, 'Hop in,' and we took off. The other car chased us around for a bit but finally gave up."

It was the high point of his fairly unformed love life, and also a prelude to its nadir. VaNita and Vern got along fine, but after a few months, she broke it off, Vern thought, because he was a member of the Mormon Church. VaNita was a Methodist whose parents were not kindly disposed to any other faith. Before any readers condemn such an attitude as intolerant, remember that this was the 1940s, when what religion you were mattered. It was a part of you, of who you were, and how you were perceived. It was, to draw an uncomfortable but apt comparison, as much a part of your persona as race and sexual orientation are today.

Vern eventually got revenge. VaNita began seeing another boy and Vern another girl. VaNita's new romance went sour first. "He made a mistake and tried to get fresh with her and that was the end of that," Vern writes. "So I guess she decided that she wanted me back, but I avoided her even though we worked at the same place, the Ada County Dairy. Then one day when I was working in the butter room, she opened the door and I was on my way out and I about fell over her. My knees went weak and I got all those same feelings back, so I knew I still cared for her."

Religion was important in Idaho in the 1940s. Important enough to break off a burgeoning romance, especially if it was your parents' wishes. But morals were just as important. And for the impertinence of "getting fresh with her," VaNita's interim boyfriend was quickly shown the door. Vern knew he still wanted to be with her because his knees went weak. And things got better.

"A short time later the school was having a dance so I asked this other girl to go. I suspected it would make VaNita jealous and she'd make the first move to reconcile [in his memoir, Law uses the non-word *reconciliate*], and she did. She told one of her friends to tell me she wanted to dance with me. I played Joe Cool and waited for the right song, and, when it came, she [instead] danced with her brother. She later said she could have killed him because she was sure I was going to ask her. The next song was 'To Each His Own,' so we got together on that one." Though Law said nothing about it in his memoir, it is difficult to imagine he does not recognize the irony of the song's title, given the circumstances.

"To Each His Own" was a song released by the Ink Spots that hit the top of *Billboard*'s charts in August 1946. Here are the lyrics of the song to which Vern Law and his future wife danced that night:

> What good is a song
> If the words just don't belong
> And a dream must be a dream for two
> No good alone
> To each his own
> For me there's you.

After the dance, Vern and VaNita got together at her house—only after Vernon had nobly escorted his disappointed date home—and, in his words, "We talked and made tentative arrangements to get back together."

They would never again be apart.

◆ ◆ ◆

If you're happy and you know it . . . Easter 1947.

Graduation is a big day for most high-school kids. For Vernon Law, it was one day in a week of milestones. On May 20, 1948, Vernon and the rest of his high school class received their diplomas. Vern had already graduated in another respect, earlier in the day.

That morning, he had given VaNita an engagement ring and asked her to marry him. She accepted his proposal, and ring, and scurried around town, showing her classmates the gold and diamond band that would seal her future. "I was so naïve about things back then," Vern told me, "I didn't know there was such a thing as a jewelry store. So my folks suggested that we go to one of those pawnshops. My father thought you can probably get a diamond ring there cheaper than you can anywhere else. So we went to the pawnshop, and I got what I thought was a normal engagement ring, I think I paid $85."

VaNita wore the pawnshop ring for 29 years—though her husband later provided her with a larger diamond, which he purchased with the accumulated $12 daily meal allowance Major League players received—until it literally fell off, having dissolved into pieces.

On the day after Vern's graduation and betrothal, there was a knock at the Laws' door. Outside, the front porch was packed with nine stout men in suits, eight of them smoking cigars and asking to come in. Each was a scout or agent from a professional baseball team, come to convince the family that Vernon should play for them. Vern took no part in the conversations. He stayed in his room, content to let his parents make for him the biggest decision of his life. "My dad would politely tell them to leave their cigars on the porch, then they could come in and we'd talk."

One by one, they told Vernon's parents about his bright future in baseball and what their teams would do for him. None of them mentioned his personal welfare, which was the one thing his parents wanted to hear about. Money was just money. Vernon was their son.

The last team's representative to come in was immediately recognizable. Babe Herman had played for the Brooklyn Robins, later the Dodgers, who would, ten years after Herman stepped into the Laws' sitting room, move to Los Angeles. Herman had a dual reputation as a player—one offensive and one defensive. During his career, he amassed impressive stats at the plate, where he compiled a lifetime batting average of .324, a .532 slugging average, 181 homers, and 997 runs batted in. But in the field, he personified the Brooklyn team's nickname among its fans—"Dem Bums." Herman was such a lousy fielder that one teammate quipped he wore a baseball glove solely "because it was league custom." He took the ribbing in good spirit. In fact, when the police told him that someone was impersonating him and passing bad checks, Herman advised the cops: "Hit him a few fly balls. If he catches any of them, it ain't me."

Herman was not smoking a cigar when he came into the Laws' living room. Nor was he representing the Dodgers. He was working as a scout for the Pittsburgh Pirates. And instead of a cigar, he was holding a bouquet of flowers and a box of chocolates for Mrs. Law. After about 15 minutes of talking with the family, the phone rang. The Laws were surprised, for they received few calls. Herman was not. With a knowing grin, he advised Vern's mother to answer the phone.

On the other end was Bing Crosby. "My mother about

fell over in a faint," wrote Law. "She couldn't believe she was talking to the great singer, Bing. That was about the frosting on the cake and I'm sure a determining factor in my signing with them. They made promises to the folks, that if I made the big leagues and pitched in a World Series, they'd have an expenses paid trip." (The Pirates would live up to Bing's promise thirteen years later.)

Almost as an afterthought, the Pirates signed Evan to a minor league contract as well. They knew that he was Vern's personal catcher. They also knew he was Vern's best friend. Each boy received a $2,000 signing bonus.

The story of Law's recruitment by the Pirates, and the other agents' stupidity in bringing cigars into a Mormon home, is well known in Pirate lore. But the story would not be complete without a footnote. Ten years later, Vern Law, by then an accomplished Pirate pitcher, was on the mound at Dodger Stadium in Los Angeles. After the game, Bing Crosby walked into the clubhouse. Throughout Law's first few years in professional baseball, Crosby kept up a correspondence of letters and telegrams with Vern, sometimes critiquing Law's performance, sometimes just offering good wishes. On this day in Los Angeles, they reminisced about Law's signing, the role Crosby's phone call had played in the decision, and the revulsion his father felt when he saw the cigars at his front door.

"I thought that might work," Crosby said offhandedly.

"What do you mean?" asked Law.

Bing Crosby was proud that he had brought Law to the Pirates. He occasionally imparted personal and professional advice, as in this 1951 letter.

"Well," said Crosby, "I told Herman to go get a big box of cigars and pass them out to the other boys while they were waiting on your porch."

Vernon Law was a Pirate, a member of the club about which the Hollywood spoof *Angels in the Outfield* had been made. Now, another kind of being, not quite celestial, but far from ordinary, was about to take his position on another part of the field.

Fourth Inning

"Master yourself and you can master anything."

(From Vernon Law's *Words to Live By*)

P ITTSBURGH WAS A TRIBUTE when it was named. By the time I was born there, in 1953, it had been turned into a punch line.

The French built Fort Duquesne at the point where the Allegheny and Monongahela (from the Delaware Indian word *Mehmannauwinggelan*, or "river of falling banks") Rivers meet in western Pennsylvania and flow together to form the Ohio River, which in turn finds its way into the Mississippi. Such prime real estate gave whoever controlled it a lock-hold on water traffic going west with the ever-increasing flood of pioneers looking for a few acres of their own. In 1758, the British wrested control of the fort from the French, and General John Forbes (whose name would also be memorialized in later years with a baseball park) named the city in honor of England's prime minister, Sir William Pitt.

The settlement's location, at the convergence of two

*The "Point," where the Monongahela and Allegheny Rivers
meet to form the Ohio. February 1953.*

waterways, ordained that Pittsburgh would be of strategic
importance. It also made nearly inevitable its growth as an
industrial center. Bituminous coal from West Virginia,
Maryland, and western Pennsylvania arrived by river barge.
So did iron ore and lime from Minnesota and Ohio. Those
ingredients, when cooked together, made steel.

And that made Pittsburgh the Steel City.

Jones and Laughlin, Andrew Carnegie's mighty U.S.
Steel, Alcoa, Wheeling-Pittsburgh, Pittsburgh Plate and
Glass—these businesses usurped more and more of the city's

lovely riverside and covered it with belching smokestacks. Lest this be misinterpreted as condemnation, they also created thousands of jobs and put food on families' tables, gave them a life of economic security if not of plenty, and, by the time I was born, allowed them to visit Forbes Field, where the Pirates struggled to become more than the punching bag of the National League.

Draped over Pittsburgh and the vicinity around it, the blanket of smoke created by the accumulated discharge was the stuff of toxic legend. "Hell with the lid off" was how author James Parton described the city as early as 1868. A 1912 issue of *Life* magazine portrayed the globe belching smoke from the approximate location of Pittsburgh, while the moon and other planets curled their noses in distaste.

Things did not get better as smelting methods improved and the demand for steel multiplied. Cars had to have their headlights on 24 hours a day, no matter how sunny the weather. Men who went to their office jobs in white shirts routinely carried a spare in their briefcases, to change at midday because their morning shirt had darkened into gray from the particulate cloud around them. I remember walking with my parents through the downtown ("dahn-tahn") one winter day and actually seeing gray snow fall and accumulate.

Pollution meant production and production meant employment, and Pittsburghers of that era did not complain about air quality. It was things such as losing a job or a Steelers loss to the hated Cleveland Browns or the molar-jarring

"Hell with the lid off." Downtown Pittsburgh as seen from Mt. Washington, 1945.

potholes that the city blamed on the county, the county on the state, and so on that upset my neighbors. Or a failure of the local road works department to clear the roads when occasionally ferocious winter storms snowed us into our houses for a day or more. There were no hysterical news updates on the radio about killer windchill factors (a still-to-be-invented phenomenon). It was winter, so it was likely to get cold. Duh. Bundle up. When a six-foot snowdrift accumulated outside the first house my parents inhabited in suburban Pittsburgh, they dug out of it. It was that simple.

When I was young and the snows came, we would hunker down and wait for the plows to arrive and eat canned

When people expected it to snow in winter: There were no dire warnings on the radio. Pittsburgh 1950.

vegetables, such as squash and pickles, and canned peaches, apples, and apricots that my mother had cooked and carefully ladled into dozens of mason jars we stored in our cellar. Snowbound and half-crazed, I can remember digging a path through two or more feet of snow to my best friend's house. I only had to dig halfway. He was, without consultation, doing the same thing from his house to mine. We met in the middle and hugged like stranded explorers who had rescued one another, as indeed we had—from boredom.

At night, if I was not listening to the Pirates game on the radio, I would tune to AM1020, KDKA—the nation's first radio station, Pittsburghers liked to brag—and listen to *Party Line,* a one-way talk show featuring Ed King and his wife, Wendy. The best part about *Party Line* was that you didn't have to listen to the callers' voices—just Ed's pleasant tenor and Wendy's housewifely hum.

The Kings did not put their callers' voices on the air; it was a way to keep the callers from showing off or becoming argumentative, offending the ears of listeners who were hoping to doze off to the pleasant patter of the party.

You could call in about anything—the state of the trolley lines that connected the city to its suburbs, the humorous condition that Ed referred to as the Sidewalk Shuffle, when two pedestrians approaching each other would bob and weave, first left, then right, only to find the other pedestrian doing the same thing and remaining squarely in each other's path. You did not call to spout politics or complain about your personal problems. At eleven o'clock each night, Ed would serve what he called the Party Pretzel—a question that would win the first caller to answer correctly nothing more than the announcement of his or her name on the air.

"What was the best-selling book of the 1930s besides the Bible?" Ed would ask, then take calls and console listeners who guessed wrong. These were the days before the Internet, and Ed had made sure that the answer to the Pretzel could not be found in the encyclopedia or in that week's *Time* magazine. Sometimes, in order to hear the answer to the Pretzel, which Ed gave at midnight, along with congratulations to the winner, if any, I would intentionally tune the superheterodyne tube radio I kept in my bed-stand just slightly off 1020—the frequency at which KDKA broadcast with 50,000 watts of power behind it. In those days, the airwaves were not so crowded with competing radio stations. And Ed would get calls from as far away as Thailand.

Even better than *Party Line* were the nights when Pirates games were being broadcast. Only away games were ever televised, and not all of those. No home games could be seen on television. I would lie secretly awake, the radio again mistuned to 1010 so that my mother would not hear its whine and rustle, would not come in to tell me to turn it off, so I could listen to the voice of the Pirates, Bob Prince, as he narrated in dramatic detail the nine innings of battle my heroes would wage that night.

Prince was The Gunner; his sidekick, Jim Woods, was The Possum. Every Pirate who Prince described on the field had a nickname. Don Hoak, the third baseman who had once been a prizefighter, was The Tiger. Harvey Haddix, the diminutive left-handed starting pitcher, was The Kitten. Bill Virdon, the speedy, smooth, sweet-swinging center fielder with wire-rim glasses, was The Quail. Bob Skinner, the left fielder who looked like a basset hound wearing a ball cap, was The Dog. ElRoy Face, the short, ruggedly handsome relief ace, was The Little Baron of the Bullpen. Roberto Clemente, the Puerto Rican right fielder and one of the best hitters in the history of the game, was simply The Great One. And, of course, Vern Law had already been christened The Deacon.

Prince never fully explained how he came up with the nicknames. "If someone reminded me of an animal, I started using it," was all the enlightenment he offered. Prince also reveled in his own nickname, The Gunner, bestowed on him by his sidekick Woods, though it was not because Prince bore the slightest resemblance to any sharpshooter. Instead, it was said that Prince was being entertained in Florida one evening by a lady of flexible virtue, when the woman's husband entered the house, deduced the situation, and pulled out a handgun. How Prince escaped being shot remained an intriguing mystery, but the moniker stuck.

Prince was as heedless of safety as he was of impartiality in calling a game. Once, in a hotel, while on the road with the Pirates, he accepted a dare and leapt from a third-floor window into the swimming pool below.

If Prince's unpredictable personal behavior was not advertised to straitlaced listeners, his enthusiasm for the Pirates was. His gravelly voice was at its best when the Bucs were winning, especially when a Pirate hit a home run. "And you can kiss it good-bye!" Prince would shout, and taverns across Pittsburgh would erupt in cheers. And when the Pirates won, as often as

Calling them as he sees them. Prince couldn't hide his partisanship when it came to the Pirates.

not by seemingly divine intervention (remember which team *Angels in the Outfield* was about), he would drag out his victory whoop: "We had 'em aaaaaaalllllll the way!"

A native of Los Angeles who had attended, but did not graduate from, Harvard, Prince became part of the Pirates' radio broadcast team in 1947, joining the estimable Rosey Rosewell, who had his own pet expressions as he called the game ("Oh, my aching back," Rosey would moan when a Pirate error let in a run). When Rosewell died in 1955, Bob Prince was anointed the new voice of the Pirates.

Since I was too young to remember Rosewell, it was Prince's taut-string smoker's rasp that I always associated with my Bucs. He was funny without being silly, dramatic without overdoing it. And his stock phrases created a new lexicon for a sport, and a team, that needed some jazzing up.

"What we need is a bloop and a blast," Prince would observe, meaning a base hit and a home run. And when we got what he had prescribed and the lead changed hands, I would mouth the words coming from Prince's lips: "We had 'em aaaaaalllllll the way!" When the Pirates wound up a road trip, Prince would move closer to the microphone and send a special message to his wife, Betty: "Honey, leave the lights on. Papa's comin' home." Such was his influence that, years later, when I was returning from long reporting trips, I would whisper the same thing to my wife through my hotel phone.

With his grandiose style of broadcasting and the excitement he brought to Pirates games, Prince gave Pittsburgh a thrill. But after I turned the radio off, and awoke the next morning, I had to confront the dull reality around me: Nothing extraordinary ever happened where I lived.

Granted, our three-bedroom ranch home was in the southern suburbs, about eight miles from the city limits. In the 1950s, Pittsburghers were fleeing their smoky city for the greener outlying areas—places where their children could run and play unaffected by the soot wafting through the city air. Even in the safety of our suburban refuge, we were never

The J&L Steel Plant at full tilt.

unaware of what city lay nearby and the effect its principal employer was having on the environment. On clear summer nights, we could stand on a hill near our home and see hot, glowing slag—the waste that was left after steel was made—being poured from the pans of huge dump trucks over the cliffs of South Hills, near Route 51. But the smoke and the slag generated by steel production were tolerated because steel meant jobs, and Pittsburghers were happy to have them.

Few stopped to wonder if this discharge was creating toxic consequences. It was viewed instead as a spectacle—an awe-inspiring industrial fireworks display. Joel A. Tarr, the

Richard S. Caliguiri Professor of Urban and Evironmental History and Policy at Carnegie Mellon University, points out in his book *Devastation and Renewal: An Environmental History of Pittsburgh and Its Region* that "cultural attitudes helped shape the industrial workforce's position on smoke and water purity. Industry's position was also not always uniform: some were heedless in their willingness to use air, water, and land as sinks for their wastes, while others found that degraded air and water quality raised their costs and damaged their products." But pollution aside, the steel mills provided paychecks.

The relative prosperity of the place in my childhood did not relieve the boredom. I can remember hearing one summer morning that the temperature would reach 100 degrees, an event remarkable enough to give people something to discuss. I went outside and sat down on a little hill in our front yard to see what 100 degrees felt like. It was hot. I waited for something to happen: for an escaped convict to run down the street where we lived so that I could cut his legs from under him and hand him over to the cops. Or for a pretty girl to walk up and ask directions (hey, a fellow can dream).

It stayed hot.

There was no air conditioning in those days, at least not in our house. To get cool, you went swimming. To have fun, you played outside. And baseball was the favorite activity.

Burt and Jimmy, Naoto Kato (a Japanese kid who could move faster than anyone else on the diamond), his best friend, Ron Thulin, the Palmer kids, who (like Vern's V-centric family) all had names starting with the same letter—B—would all show up at about the same morning hour, ten o'clock or so, at Ben Franklin, down the street from my house. The school was surrounded by (long-since developed) pastures and fields. Each became a different baseball diamond with its own peculiarities: hidden dips in the grassy mounds around third base, or a sharp rock that lay in wait beneath overlong grass, or a foul line that consisted of a row of wild raspberry plants, a ground-level wasps' hive that it was best to avoid when sliding.

We played until we were called home by our parents. Each kid had a different signal to summon him. One responded to his father's bronze army whistle. Another to a dog whistle (no kidding). A third kid had to keep his ears open for the sound of a cowbell that his mother shook from her back door. Then the game ended, but it didn't matter. We'd be back there the next day and the battle would carry on.

Ben Franklin was also the site of a summer school, more like a summer recreation program that featured such then-exotic activities as box hockey (a rubber puck that you fought with sticks to get through the opponent's goal at the end of a wood framework). There was another game called caroms, which was a variation on pool, played with cue sticks of half-inch doweling, in which checkers took the place of balls. You used the doweling like a cue stick and tried to knock the checker into a hole in the center of the board.

There was some sort of dispute one day over who would play next. I squared off against a black kid named ElBoy. Not ElRoy. ElBoy. It wasn't hard to outwit him or outtalk him. But then he got in my face and sneered, "White patty cake, white patty cake, you don't shine. Call me a nigger, and I'll beat your behind."

I didn't know what to do. Fight? Back down? A girl I liked hissed at me: "Hit him!"

Instead I ran.

In America, in the late '50s, there was no such thing as too much baseball, at least not in Pittsburgh. The Pirates were atrocious, true, but kids played the pastime with a gusto reserved today for video games and fantasy leagues. Our leagues were a few doubles short of fantasy, but they were *real.* For reasons best known to my Creator, I actually had some talent. I was fast, I was adroit in the field, and I had the ability—not necessarily as simple as it sounds—to know where the ball was going to go when I released it.

In addition to our pickup, sandlot games there was organized kids' baseball. It was our church, St. Valentine's, that sponsored the team I played on. This wasn't exactly Little League, in the technical sense of the term. It was called instead "pee-wee," a designation that nowadays would probably provoke a lawsuit on the grounds it was damaging to the egos of the players. Of course, we were five and six years old, so it's not clear that we even knew we had egos. But that's just another example of how things have changed.

Notices for tryouts were published in the church bulletin, which you picked up on Sunday at Mass. Ours was the kind of parish where it could reasonably be expected that you'd know when tryouts were being held because you'd picked up a bulletin when you attended church on Sunday. It wasn't a rigorous or enforced routine, just a social assumption. And because it was assumed you'd do it, you did it. My father read the bulletin, saw the tryout notice, and we went over to try out.

Tryouts were held on a Saturday. My father drove me to the site, the field behind Bethel Park Junior High School. It was less than half a mile from our home, but in the days of 39-cent-a-gallon gas, we drove everywhere. The parking lot was on a hill above the field. You had to goat-step down a packed-dirt incline to get to the diamond—not an arrangement that provided equal access for the handicapped, but there was no such thing as the Americans with Disabilities Act in those days. So you either scuttled down the hill, or you didn't play.

It wasn't that easy, of course. Other kids' parents had read the notice as well but hadn't waited until tryout day to respond. Other parents found out the name of the coach and had already been in touch to put in a good word for their sons.

I, on the other hand, went in innocently ignorant of how it all worked. When finally we figured out the deck was stacked, I felt like a batter caught by a third-strike curve. I figured—and I think my father did too—that tryouts meant tryouts. You showed them what you could do, and if you were good enough, you played.

The reality was different.

The coach—who has since departed—had a few ideas about his team before he'd even met us. He knew, for instance, that his son was going to be the pitcher. He also knew that the son of his wife's best friend was going to play shortstop. And he knew that if either of these things went awry, he'd be sleeping on the couch for the foreseeable future.

So, though I didn't know it at the time, I went to my first-ever pee-wee tryout with only seven possible positions open to me. It was just as well; I was nervous enough. It was one thing to play pickup ball at Ben Franklin, but the team I was trotting toward had a *real,* diamond-shaped home plate. And lots of bats in a canvas bag. And batting helmets. Things I knew the Pirates had. We didn't originally have uniforms, but those would come, eventually.

For the first practice, the coach gave us each a square of yellow material, with a number written on it in Magic Marker and a pin at the top. We were supposed to pin the numbers on the back of our T-shirts. I got number 6. Or was it number 9? To resolve the debate, Coach drew a line under the circular part of the number. The other kid who had the same kind of problem got a line drawn under the tail of his. Any questions?

I won't recount my entire (and entirely forgettable) baseball career. I got to know the other kids, realized I was better than most of them, and discovered that the mound and shortstop were positions where the fix was in. Practice was on Tuesdays at 6 P.M. We played our games on Saturdays.

The first Tuesday, I came home from school, did my homework (that always had to come first), and my mother took me to practice. She parked the car in the parking lot on the hill above the field. I kissed her and hopped out of the car and scrabbled down the hill.

The other kids had seen me.

"You still kiss your mommy good-bye? You baby."

I began to cry. That was not the reaction most likely to make the insults stop. I loved my mother. Why couldn't I kiss her good-bye?

It took me a while to understand that boys of a certain age were expected to leap out of their mothers' cars and run off without a backward look. One life ended, another had begun.

Kiss it good-bye.

I needed more practice than Tuesdays with a 6 pinned to my back. My father knew it. So he began to come home, change his clothes, and immediately spend half an hour playing catch with me. Not just catch, of course. He would roll ground balls toward me and coach me how to field them. He would toss the ball high in the air, making me run right and left. And sometimes he would take the bat and clip the ball so it came searing across the carpet of our lawn, the more realistically to imitate the kind of shots I'd likely see on the playing field. My father was no athlete. And sometimes the ground balls he tried to hit to me would go awry.

And into our next-door neighbor's yard.

This was not as simple as a case of misdirected horsehide. This had the potential to become a neighborhood crisis.

Because our neighbor did not give back baseballs that landed in her yard.

Her name was Mrs. Russell, and she planted flowers in her quarter-acre lot. And when baseballs come in contact with flowers, the baseball comes out of the encounter less damaged. Mrs. Russell—"Russ" as my parents called her, though I had less similar-sounding appellations that I used in my head—watched over her domain from a double window in her dining room. And when she caught sight of an errant baseball ravaging her flowers or saw us sneaking across the borderline of her empire to try to retrieve it, she would say, from behind the dark screens that kept flies out, "Just leave it there, please."

If I am ever brought to trial on a capital crime, that is the voice I imagine the sentencing judge will use.

In 1958, a regulation Major League baseball, made either in the U.S. or Haiti, sold for $2.99. Wilson and Spaulding made most of the ones that were sold to the public. In Bethel Park, the place to buy a baseball was Fizer's Sporting Goods. Losing one, or more, to Mrs. Russell's "Just leave it there, please" dictum was not to my liking, or my budget. We used balls until all the horsehide was off, when they were revealed to have under the leather cover a layer of tightly wound string. There was no ball dirty enough for us to discard. And there were at least three of mine sitting in the yard next door.

My father thought he had the answer. He went out and bought six 20-foot lengths of two-by-two lumber. He also bought about ten yards of chicken wire and a healthy supply of flathead nails. We began work on a Saturday morning, before my pee-wee game that afternoon. We dug holes in our yard and planted the lengths. We were going to build a backstop as big and imposing as the one at Forbes Field, where my Pirates played. It was set about two feet from the border between our property and the Russells'. There would be no more errant baseballs for Russ to capture. I thought our backstop was wonderful. It was going to be the neatest thing in any of the backyards where I played.

We paused in our work, and I went off to my game. My mother picked me up from the game, got no kiss as I climbed into the car, and as soon as we got home, I rushed into the backyard to see what progress had been made.

My father was ripping chicken wire off the two-by-two frame with a viciousness I seldom saw in him.

"What's going on?"

"Ah, dammit, you can't have anything."

Russ's husband had come shuffling over while I was away, tugging on a Chesterfield, and informing my father that his wife didn't think a tall backstop would look good from *their* side of the border. My father said all the right things: We were building it precisely because of their concerns about stray balls, etc. etc. It didn't matter. In those days, when neighbors expressed concern about something that might be happening in your yard, you listened to what they had to say. Neighbors didn't take neighbors to court. It was another era.

I remember asking my angry father what Russ's objections could be? Who wouldn't want to live next door to Forbes Field?

Fifth Inning

"A champion is not always a consistent winner."
(From Vernon Law's *Words to Live By*)

VERN LAW WOULD LIVE next to Forbes Field one day, but not for a while. First it was time to leave home, in order to go home again.

Three days after his high school graduation, Vernon and his brother and catcher Evan were assigned to the Class D team in Santa Rosa, California, where the family had lived during Jesse Law's two years of patriotic service during World War II and where Vern had set up bowling pins for extra cash. His financial situation as a minor league player wasn't much better than as a pin boy, he found. And the working conditions were just about as hazardous. The fields were uneven, the clubhouses drafty and damp. "The lights, if you were lucky enough to have them on your field, were so inadequate you had to light a match to see if they were on," Law recalled years later. Class D was the lowest rung in the Pirates' organization. So regardless of the promise Law showed as a pitcher, the big club had decided he would have to earn his chance to play Big League ball the hard way.

The lessons involved more than baseball. Both Evan and Vern had insisted—and the Pirates had agreed—that their contracts specify they would not have to play on Sundays. It was a choice, not a moral position. Both young men used the Sabbath for praise, not to carouse. The other players on the team knew about the no-Sundays clause and, Vern remembers, were polite about it and demonstrated the proper respect for the Law boys' religious beliefs.

But there was a certain tension in the clubhouse. Many of the other players were members of faiths that also worshipped the Lord on Sundays. Why were these two Mormons any different or better? Vern, though younger, was more perceptive than Evan and recalled, "I could see problems developing." By the end of the first year, he had decided his commitment to do his best for the team outweighed his moral obligation. A contract was a bond. If the normal rotation had him pitching on a Sunday, he would pitch.

This was not the first nor the only time Vernon's faith and his abilities on the baseball diamond would set him apart. For one thing, Vernon Law never went on a mission, a clear expectation for young Mormon men that is now nearly universal. But in the 1950s, and in a place as remote as Meridian, Idaho, the Church did not always call upon a young man to complete this service. "There was not a lot of emphasis put on going on a mission," Law recalled. "I knew quite a few guys who didn't." Later on, when he was enjoying the fame of a Major Leaguer, various General Authorities—the senior spiritual leaders who guide the Church's day-to-day affairs—told Law that his visibility and celebrity had done the Church more good than any mission he might have undertaken. "They said they couldn't buy the positive attention I'd brought to the Church by being a Pirate and winning the World Series," he says now. All that would take years of pitching to develop, however.

In spite of his natural ability, for Vern, the first challenge, surprisingly, was to learn *how* to pitch. He could rear back and throw the ball like a BB—92 miles an hour at the height of his career, by his reckoning. But as every pitching coach, manager, and decent baseball analyst can attest, throwing is not the same as pitching. The first is a show of strength. The second is more a craft that entails varying speeds, placing the ball, and probing a batter's weaknesses.

Vern came to understand this. He later wrote: "It was important that you not only played well, but that you had managers, coaches, and other personnel who could teach, instruct, and help each player develop his skill and make him a prospect for the Big Leagues." He admitted, "I had no coaching growing up, so I had need of a good pitching coach to help me develop a decent windup and learn how to set up a hitter. Another important thing I needed to learn was to throw a changeup and use off-speed pitches.

"In Santa Rosa, my manager was Danny Reagan, a

former catcher, and he helped somewhat but didn't know the ins and outs of helping me in that process, but was helpful in helping me understand the game and how it should be played."

But Manager Reagan had more than that to do. He drove the team bus and fixed it when it broke down—as it often did. He also had to make sure that the twenty or so kids— most were teenagers or in their early twenties and away from home for the first time—didn't get into trouble. It was common for the team to play one day in Santa Rosa, then board the team bus and drive through the night to Klamath Falls, Oregon, 265 miles away, to play the next day.

"Sleeping on the bus was the only rest we got," Law said. "And that was not that easy. Guys would climb up in the luggage rack above and stretch out or lay in the aisles; anywhere that you could get in a prone position was just fine. Today's players in the minor leagues don't have it that tough. Position players back then had to hit .300 in every league before they got a chance to see if they could make it on the Big League level. If you hit .230 in the Big Leagues back then, you were usually shipped back to Triple A to get more seasoning. Today you hit .230, and you get a million and a half and think you're underpaid."

Sixty-some years later, Law—like many retirees from many professions—fixates on the tough road he had to success and begrudges the ease that he believes accompanies the lives of younger generations. There is nothing new or noteworthy in this attitude. Who doesn't think they've had a tough time of life and resent it when younger people seem to skate through the same problems? What parent doesn't tell the kids that they have it easy compared to the old days? Law's complaint is not merely (though it certainly includes) the vast difference in salaries that his generation missed out on. It is also the pluck and added grit he and his peers required just to survive and succeed.

The Santa Rosa team, perhaps invigorated by the arrival of the talented Law battery, played some of its best baseball that season and advanced to the division playoffs. For that, each player got $200 in bonus money, "which of course always helps," Law writes in his memoir. It was during this time that Vernon Law began writing down what he called *Words to Live By,* a collection of witticisms, aphorisms, and rules that he kept in a series of red notebooks. Each inning in this book begins with one of them.

He also wrote down for himself six rules that he tried to follow as a player:

I will never criticize my superiors.

I will never insist I am right to the extent of angering others.

I will never raise my voice or engage in heated argument.

I will never forget that I am one of God's marked men.

I will always remember I am made of the same stuff as the worst sinner.

I will always have a smile for everyone, especially those who like me least.

Of course, Law strayed from these rules occasionally; as he himself pointed out, he was no better than the worst sinner. But he tried harder to be better than just about any baseball player of his or any other era. Word began to get around: this kid is good, *and* he's a good kid.

The next season, 1949, brought changes in Law's career. He moved to Davenport, Iowa, and Class B ball, learned how to pitch instead of just throw, and lost his battery and double-date mate. Evan was a proficient catcher, but even he recognized he was not Big League material. His biggest supporter was Vern, who urged him to test his talent to the limit. Though Vern's support had its source in fraternal love, it was also convenient to have Evan on the same team, to throw to, to be with, and to trust. Evan, however, had decided to wed his longtime girlfriend Joyce Coryell, with whom he had gone on many double dates with Vern and VaNita. Evan and Joyce got married at the Laws' home and started planning a formal temple wedding—which the Mormon Church strongly encourages but does not demand. As it turned out, Evan and Joyce would get their temple wedding, but it would take another year. And it would not be *their* wedding exclusively.

The Davenport Pirates' manager that year was a former Major League pitcher named Bill Burwell. A native of Jarbalo, Kansas, Burwell pitched two seasons for the old

Bill Burwell taught Law the difference between throwing and pitching.

St. Louis Browns and one for the Pirates before embarking on a lengthy career as a minor league manager. A right-hander like Law, Burwell taught the boy from Idaho some of the subtleties of which his still undeveloped arm was capable. "From him I learned how to throw a changeup and also the importance of changing speeds," Law said. "He told me, when you throw batting practice, take a little off your fastball and see what happens. I did as I was instructed and found out I really messed up the hitters' timing and from that point on I became a winning pitcher, instead of just a .500 pitcher. He also taught me a very important lesson: hitters will swing at bad pitches."

The league was known informally as the 3-I—covering towns in Iowa, Indiana, and Illinois. Having graduated to Class B ball, Law found himself pleasantly surprised by the higher level of play and increased talent of the players. "Life in general was a lot more pleasant," Law said. "It wasn't as far between the cities where we played. I also found we had better players and better people to work with. My teammates had better habits and were anxious to make it to the Big Leagues."

It was at this point that Law began to believe he, too, might make it to The Show someday. Effort was never the barrier. "I began to feel my worth as well and felt it was just a matter of time before I'd get my chance. So I really worked hard—did a lot of extra running and throwing and working on those little things that made me a complete pitcher instead of a thrower." The team, though it made the playoffs, didn't offer Law much in the way of run production. The Pirates noticed. Law went only 9–18, but earned another promotion—this time to Double-A ball in New Orleans.

But before he went to the Big Easy, Law made a tough decision. While in Davenport, he was the target of what today might be called a groupie. The woman, whom Law has not named, started showing up wherever he went. For a shy young man with a fiancée far away, it was a tempting situation. "I wasn't one to be rude and would talk to her and her girlfriend," Law recalled years later. "She did get me confused though and unsure and made me wonder if I was doing the right thing." Being the kind of person he was, Law is unlikely to have let the confusion lead him into serious misconduct. It is fair to ask, however, how a twenty-first-century minor leaguer on the road would respond to the attentions of an attractive young woman while far from the eyes of his family and fiancée.

The matter was settled as soon as the season was over. Law married VaNita McGuire on March 3, 1950, in the LDS temple in Logan, Utah. Knowing that Vern would not marry someone not of his faith, VaNita, a Methodist, asked her parents' permission to convert and had been baptized into the Mormon faith shortly after graduating from high school. Years later, she described her mother's response with a mixture of pride and—even after 60 years—some embarrassment. "My mother heard me out, and she asked, 'Are you doing this for Vernon or is it something you believe in? You may do this, we won't stop you, but don't try ever to push your religion on us.'"

VaNita Law is as gentle as a creek flowing over a bed of smooth rock—and just as immutable. Her diction is precise, her meaning clear. Unlike her husband, who is somewhat challenged by the rules of English grammar in both his written and spoken communication, VaNita knows precisely

When VaNita said yes: March 3, 1950.

what she wants to say and how she wants her words to be interpreted. Her family is the center of her life, and she has been a devout member of the Mormon Church for six decades. But she is not a sheltered person. And, despite her love for and devotion to her husband, she is not afraid to contradict him.

Whereas Law recalls that he took the first step in asking VaNita out, his wife of 60 years told me another story when I talked with her by phone one morning while her husband was out playing golf.

VaNita McGuire knew what she was doing. "Our

orchestra conductor was my violin teacher, and she had me pass out the music to the rest of the orchestra. Vern played the trombone. So I'd pass by Vern and I'd always say good morning to him and say his name so he had to look at me. And he was so shy. Girls are more advanced at that age. Boys aren't really a problem for us."

Nor does she concur with Law's recollection that their breakup after a few months of dating was due to Vern's religion. She laughed in her delicate way when I read to her passages of her husband's memoir, *As I Remember,* especially the part dealing with the temporary rupture of the couple's relationship. This, according to Vern, occurred because VaNita was getting pressure from her family not to date a Mormon. VaNita's memory is different: "My mother said to me once, if you're going to go steady with someone, then do it. Don't push your luck and go out with more than one boy. Steady is steady. And I guess I wasn't ready to do that right then. I don't think religion had much to do with it. When we got back together we didn't talk about religion. We talked about us."

VaNita Law could have gone to college. She was smart enough. She was also smart enough to know that a career in professional sports is risky, at best. Thousands of standout high school players are brushed aside when they try to ascend to the ranks of the professionals. Her own brother was an athlete in school, and she knew from observing his victories and reverses how undependable the human body can be as an engine of accomplishment. Injuries could end promising beginnings in an instant. Her boyfriend, by his own admission, was not "one for book learning" (though Law possesses the worldly wisdom of a man who has seen and done a lot of things and has learned from most of his experiences).

VaNita McGuire seems (and professes) never to have doubted that her destiny was linked to Law's, but this decision could not have been reached because she was swept off her feet by her beau's sophistication.

"What did a date consist of?" she asked years later, in response to a question. "Not much. We double dated with Evan all the time. His future wife, Joyce, was the daughter of a Nazarene evangelist, who traveled the land preaching about Christ's life. We'd go to a school dance once in a while. Vern didn't like to dance, and he was terrible at it. Or we'd go to athletic events. We went to a lot of games. Plus, I started going with him to activities sponsored by the LDS Mutual Improvement Association [a church youth group now known as the Young Men and Young Women associations]."

In doing so, in attending Mormon social events with Vernon Law, VaNita was acceding to the inevitable. There was no chance, given his traditional upbringing and his family's devotion to the Church, that Vernon would marry a non-Mormon.

So on March 2, 1950, two weeks before he would report to his third spring training, Vernon Law, VaNita McGuire, Evan and Joyce Law (already wed in a civil ceremony), and the Law boys' parents all piled into VaNita's parents' borrowed car and drove from Meridian to Logan, Utah, just across the border from Idaho, and within the geographic realm of the Latter-day Saints. Arriving just after midnight, the half dozen tired Idahoans were tempted to find a motel. But the elder Laws, determined to school their sons and their daughters-in-law in the value of a dollar, insisted that everyone could sleep in the car.

When the cramped carful awoke, stiff and unrested, Vern and VaNita headed to the Logan Town Hall to obtain a marriage license. Later that morning, Tuesday, March 3, 1950, Vernon Sanders Law and VaNita McGuire Law were sealed to each other "for time and all eternity," and Evan Law and Joyce Coryell confirmed their vows, before ElRay L. Christiansen, president of the Logan Temple, who officiated in the two ceremonies. After the wedding, Vern bought dinner for all six of them at the bus depot restaurant ("big spender" Law recalls). Once again, the newlyweds looked forward to a night at a motel. Once again, they were outvoted.

"Our first night together," Law ruefully remarked six decades later, "wasn't exactly what either of us had in mind. We said we planned to go to a hotel, and my mother said, 'That's not necessary. You can stay at Grandpa's.' We were glad to at least have a door, but felt really conspicuous then and again the next morning."

Imagine a newly hitched couple today being bullied by

their elders to spend the night before their wedding in a car and their first night together in the borrowed bed of a grandparent. Yet Vern and VaNita submitted to the elder Laws' wishes. The couple's motive was not frugality; it was respect for their parents. It was putting others before themselves. It was family.

Back home in Meridian, friends and family hazed the newlyweds with a shivaree, a rural American version of the French charivari, in which neighbors attach cowbells to the couple's bed, and, from outside the couple's room, speculate loudly about what might be going on within the bridal chamber. VaNita did not even have time to open her wedding presents. Her husband's line of work required him to be elsewhere, and for the first—but far from the last—time, she would be going with him.

How many brides honeymoon with 25 men? VaNita McGuire, the new Mrs. Vernon Law, had not just her husband's company, but that of the Pirates' entire spring training organization in San Bernardino, California. "Everyone knew we were just married, and so we had to put up with a lot of comments," Law writes. "VaNita was afraid to even turn over in bed, for fear of rousing suspicion. It was fun though, and the Pirates picked up her bill. After a month of training, I was assigned to Double A ball, in New Orleans." The New Orleans Pelicans would be the only team Law ever played for professionally not to be called the Pirates.

So began the couple's peregrinations. They spent their

On their way: VaNita and Vern at Boise Airport, 1950.

first night at the Jung Hotel and the next day found a studio apartment on Esplanade. Law recalls: "We had to buy a few things to set up housekeeping, and I remember some heavy packages and a long walk with them, but then we were settled and I was glad of it." Imagine the reaction today if a hot pitching prospect for a Major League team injured himself lugging appliances to a new house. There would be lawyers and agents and contract talks, and the media would never let it go. But for the Laws, baseball was just a part of their real life. And the New Orleans Pelicans of the Southern Association had no one to help the Laws carry their belongings down the street.

The Idaho country boy was taken aback by the ethnic and cultural stewpot that he found in New Orleans. And if his baseball skills were not yet fully developed, his sense of justice was, and so his reaction to some of the city's grimmer realities surprised him, as well as his teammates.

Segregation was in full force in the Deep South in 1950, and the price of admission to a ballpark did not include checking prejudice at the gate.

"It was hard for us to see how the blacks were treated by others as this was not how we were brought up," Law told me. "There were separate drinking fountains and black restrooms and white restrooms. Black folks sat in the back of the buses. If there was no room for you to sit down, you moved the little sign back a seat so you sat in front of those in the back. All of this was disturbing to us. Even at the ballpark you found that separation. It was like they had leprosy or something. Even on our own ball club, our one black player couldn't stay in the same hotel or eat in the same restaurant as we did. You'd have to order a meal for him and take it out to the bus so he'd have something to eat. I remember one time on a trip we stopped at a small town to eat after the game and the restaurant refused to serve our black player. When that happened, I got up and left the restaurant and everyone else followed. I know the owners could have made two or three hundred dollars but ended up with nothing. At least we made a statement, which I was proud of."

Remember that passage from Vernon Law before judging him too harshly for—as a boy—having a toy he called a "nigger-flipper." The words an individual uses may have more to do with his surroundings than his soul. His behavior reveals more accurately what is at work within his heart.

The Pelicans and their new pitcher got off to a good start in the Southern Association pennant race. Law was learning the art of the changeup and had a rudimentary curveball that would take years to perfect. Meanwhile, the parent Big League club was headed into an early, though permanent, tailspin, and rumors began to circulate that the Pirates would reach into their farm system to get much-needed pitching help.

Law was hitting his stride, having already won seven games by the first week of June. On Sunday, June 6, the team was on the road, playing in Nashville. Law was scheduled to pitch the next night and was in his hotel room when Joe O'Toole, the team's traveling secretary, called him and asked to meet with him right away. "I didn't dream what was coming," Law recalls. "Usually when you talk to management, it's either a pink slip or being sent down. I was comfortable with the club, and I really wanted to stay to see how many games I could win at New Orleans."

He would never find out. O'Toole told him he would

not be pitching for the Pelicans the next day but instead for the Pittsburgh Pirates. Starting pitcher Bob Chesnes had a sore arm. The club needed help. The club needed him.

Chesnes was a promising six-foot-tall right-hander from Oakland for whom the Pirates had paid $100,000 in 1947. He wowed the anemic team with a 14–6 record in his first year with Pittsburgh. His fastball was his signature, though *Pacific Coast Baseball News* in 1947 had noted that he looked lazy on the mound. Chesnes's debut year with the Bucs was his only winning one. He never recovered from that sore arm in 1950, his last year in the Majors.

For Law, the glory was just beginning. O'Toole told the nervous 20-year-old to get packed and to head for the airport. He was wanted in Pittsburgh as soon as he could get there. First he had to go back to New Orleans to collect VaNita, who was staying with a friend for a few days. Law remembers worrying that he did not have a car to drive to Pittsburgh, and, even if he had, didn't know if he could fit their belongings into one. O'Toole had all the answers, as well as a sense of humor.

VaNita recalls the moment clearly. "It was a Sunday morning. I had stayed with another player's wife, and I was getting ready to go to church when a phone call came for me. I couldn't understand why Mr. O'Toole would be calling me. After identifying himself, he asked if I knew where Vernon was. I answered that he had probably gone to church, and he replied, 'No, I don't think so. We couldn't find him last night when we left Chattanooga, so we just assumed that he had gone back home to you.' I replied, 'Oh, no, he would never leave the team.' I was about in tears with worry, when he said, 'It's all right, he's right here and has something to tell you.' When Vernon got on the phone, he told me that I needed to go back to our apartment and get everything packed as we were going to Pittsburgh and he would be home that night and we would leave the next morning. I was very relieved, but I was so new to the baseball life that I really didn't understand what this move meant. I even went to church to tell our friends good-bye before I went home to pack. The team flew us to Pittsburgh."

Those tickets for two would prove to be one of the best investments the Pirates ever made.

"Since I was born and raised out in the West, I wasn't exposed to any real large cities, like Pittsburgh, New York, or Los Angeles," Law told me. "So it was quite overwhelming to see such large buildings for the first time. I thought the ballpark would be in the city itself, but we kept going along the Boulevard of the Allies next to the river for about three miles and then took a left up Forbes Avenue to Forbes Field."

At the Schenley Park Hotel, where the couple would spend their first few days, Law was greeted by a gaggle of sportswriters from the city's three newspapers, the *Press,* the *Post-Gazette,* and the *Sun-Telegraph,* as well as wire service and radio scribes. He was asked if it was true, as rumored, that he was a Mormon and if so, what did that mean? So

117

A jewel with girders: Forbes Field, in the heart of Pittsburgh.

began Pittsburgh's education into the ways of the Latter-day Saints. Law accepted speaking engagements from nearly everyone who asked. He was not paid; in fact his travel expenses came out of his own pocket. But he believed that the best way to gain acceptance for his church in a part of the country where it was little-known was to answer every question, straightforwardly, and let people decide the merit of the message for themselves.

One of the hardest-to-explain tenets of his faith in the 1950s was the Church's provision that men of color not be ordained to the priesthood. In one of his earliest speaking engagements, Law recalls, an African-American minister stood up and politely asked him to explain why blacks were inferior. "I was looking for a hole to crawl in but found none," Law says. "Half the people in the audience were black, so needless to say, I was a bit taken aback." Law explained as best he could without apologizing for his church's rules. "And suddenly, I was moved, inspired, to say that I was sure that someday conditions would be right for blacks to be ordained to the priesthood. I could see the black people in the audience nodding their heads and smiling. Whether they agreed or not I do not know." After his talk, Law recalls, both blacks and whites from the audience came up to shake his hand.

Given the reality of the day, Law's response was indeed inspired. While some, both inside and outside the Church, regarded the ban against ordaining blacks to the priesthood as racist, LDS Church leaders in that era regarded all men and women as brothers and sisters, as children of God. A quarter century later, the then-President of the Church, Spencer W. Kimball, announced that God had revealed to him that all worthy males, irrespective of color, could be ordained to the priesthood. The revelation went a long way toward bringing Latter-day Saints into the American mainstream. And it made Law's speaking engagements after his years in the Big Leagues less stressful.

Law's initial impressions form a valuable historic record of Pittsburgh in the 1950s. Lifelong residents simply did not notice the dirty air, the hiss of smoke as it belched from

*The new Pirate signs autographs, 1951. Law also answered questions
about his faith, but didn't try to convert Pittsburghers.*

chimneys, the slow-motion ripping noise of barges plying the
Monongahela, loaded with coal to power the mills. "I
couldn't believe all the smoke coming down from the sky,"
said the young man accustomed to Idaho's snowy peaks and
crystalline air. He corroborates what has already been noted:
"It was a well-known fact that, if you wore a white shirt to
work, by the end of the day it would be gray.

"The ballpark was in an area called Oakland. This is where
the University of Pittsburgh is located, along with Schenley
Park. So there were many, many people and businesses to

take care of students and the different ethnic groups of people who resided in that area. The three predominant groups were Italian, Jewish, and people of color. The blacks lived on what was called the Hill, the Jewish lived in Squirrel Hill, and the Italians lived in Oakland, about a block from the ballpark."

That bare-bones assessment of Pittsburgh demographics was not far off. The division of the city according to ethnicity was, in fact, famous even then. The biggest single ethnic group, however, was Slavs—Croatians, Serbs, Lithuanians, Slovaks, Czechs—who had experience with industrial production in their European homelands and who came to Pittsburgh to lend their skills to the art of steelmaking.

Among this stew of humanity, Vern and VaNita had to find a place to live. Major League baseball players in 1950 were no different from anyone else—they were on their own when it came to house-hunting. The Pirates did not provide a real-estate agent. They paid you a salary—in Law's case, $5,000 a year—and expected you to make do. With no car, the Laws looked for a place near the breadwinner's place of employment, Forbes Field.

Their first foray was to Homestead, best known as the site of a bloody encounter between unionized steelworkers and Pinkerton detectives in 1892. The history of the labor movement is as deeply ingrained in Pittsburgh as its legacy as a steel town. The Laws knew nothing of this. A police officer on duty at Law's initial press conference had asked if they needed a place to live and guided them the next day to Homestead. They immediately knew that the two-room apartment above a tavern with a view of steel sheds lining the river was unsuitable. So was Ma Daniels's boardinghouse, where one Pirate wife had reported waking up one night to find a drunken trucker standing over her bed.

After several disappointments, they found a two-room flat three blocks from the ballpark. The rent was $50 a month. Amenities included an upholstered chair in the bedroom and a bathroom that had to be shared with the owner, his wife, and their three boys. The young couple got the flavor of Pittsburgh almost immediately. "If we left the window open for what was supposed to be fresh air, the next morning the silt had to be wiped off the windowsill and most everything else in the apartment."

Law's first start in the Majors came on June 11, 1950, at Forbes Field against the Philadelphia Phillies. Their ace pitcher, Robin Roberts, was on the mound, and the 20-year-old Law, wearing number 20 on his uniform, engaged the future Hall of Famer in a classic pitching duel. With the score tied 2–2 in the ninth, and men on second and third and two outs, the Phils' batter popped up. Either shortstop Stan Rojek or the exalted left fielder Ralph Kiner could have made the play easily. But neither man called for the ball, and it fell between them. Both runners, who had taken off as soon as the ball left the bat, scored, and Vernon Law's Major League record was 0–1. Four days later, this time in Philadelphia's

Raw as an Idaho potato: The rookie, 1950.

Connie Mack Stadium, Law again hooked up with Roberts. With the game tied going into the bottom of the ninth, the same two Pirates failed to communicate on an almost identical popup with men on base. Record: 0–2.

It was a frustrating year for the rookie. He went 7–9 and walked 47 batters. The next year was worse: 6–9 with 50 walks. "Our club was so bad that at times we couldn't play catch without dropping the ball," Law lamented. But forces beyond his

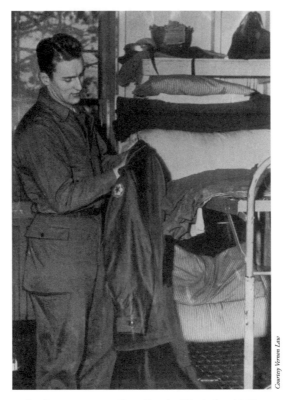

In the army now: Fort Eustis, Virginia, 1952.

control were about to remove him from Pittsburgh. Not a trade to another team, but a war that was never declared.

As an exceptionally healthy 21-year-old male, Law knew he was going to be drafted into the military as the Korean conflict escalated. So he decided to beat Uncle Sam to the punch by enlisting. He and VaNita drove to Fort Eustis, Virginia, where pitcher Vern Law became PFC Vern Law. The choice of locale was not random.

Courtesy Vernon Law

Law wasn't good enough to pitch for the U.S. Army at Fort Eustis in 1952. He ended up playing first base.

Special Services at that time was a branch of the army where inductees with unique skills might contribute their talents in more efficient than usual army fashion. And Ft. Eustis had a baseball program. Law was assigned to the 502nd Transportation Company, where his job consisted of handling paperwork at Special Services HQ, and playing ball. In a hilarious example of army misuse of resources, Law could not make the team as a pitcher. He played first base.

The Laws bought a 26-foot house trailer and lived off base, as did many married GIs serving domestically. Law recalls that though they could live comfortably in it, "the bathroom was just about big enough for me to turn around in. You could shower and brush your teeth at the same time and there were many times it was booby-trapped with VaNita's hose, bras, and what have you. You could get hung up in there and never get out if you weren't careful."

Law was not above gaming the system that makes the U.S. Army such a shuffleboard of fate. He acquired a pass that allowed him to park a car on the base but not one that permitted him to leave with a vehicle. So while he passed through the checkpoint each morning according to regulation, he had to pretend to reach into his wallet in search of his nonexistent exit pass every afternoon. Observing the motion, bored MPs at the gate would wave him through.

When, in early 1952, VaNita announced that she was pregnant, the couple was delighted but also conflicted. Vern had worked his way up to sergeant and been assigned a Military Occupational Specialty, in his case MOS1816, for the movement and transport of trains and supplies. That specialty earned him more money, but it also put him in line for transfer. With VaNita 19 days overdue, the law of unintended consequences kicked in, and Vernon was told he was being sent to Germany. Determined not to miss the birth of his first child, Law went to Colonel Flamm, the officer in charge of the MOS program—who, conveniently, was a

Latter-day Saint. Law's transfer was canceled, and that same day, December 12, Veldon Law was born at the base hospital. Total cost to the Law family: $7.50.

Law's military career was forgettable. He was mustered out a year after Veldon's birth, in December 1953, and after spending the rest of the winter with his family in Idaho, reported to the Pirates' spring training camp at Fort Pierce, Florida. He had given up two full seasons to the service of his country. He had also developed a balky pitching arm, perhaps the result of playing ball for the army. He exchanged one uniform for another, this one with the number 32, which would be his for the rest of his baseball career.

The Pirates finished last in 1954, last in 1955, next to last in 1956, last again in 1957. Pittsburgh stank.

Sixth Inning

"The wheels of progress aren't turned by cranks."

(From Vernon Law's *Words to Live By*)

PITTSBURGH STANK.

Its reputation as the Smoky City, where a pall of filth hung over its streets and citizens, was well deserved. The smell of sulfur was everywhere. The steel mills spat out an enormous quantity of product—a fifth of the national total in 1955—and created jobs for a quarter million workers. More than 5,000 products were manufactured in Pittsburgh in the mid '50s, and though that ensured employment for the enclaves of Poles, Ukrainians, Serbs, Slovaks, Croats, Irish, Greeks, Russians, and blacks who had settled there, it also meant their, and their children's, lives would be lived in the soot and grime of industrial fulfillment.

The truth is, most Pittsburghers did not make a fuss about their living conditions. The Pittsburgh of that era did not rate water purity or warn of UV rays from the sun or calculate air quality or warn that it was going to be hot in July or that snow would cover the streets in winter. You were expected to know these things. If you had a job, you counted yourself lucky, thanked God, and moved along lest something really bad befell you.

In the late 1940s, a Hungarian-born photographer and author named Stefan Lorant was vacationing in the New York resort of Saratoga Springs when he made the acquaintance of one of the few Pittsburghers wealthy enough to visit that luxurious spa. Edgar Kaufmann had built a fortune from the department store that bore his family's name. Kaufmann's was the elite place to shop in Pittsburgh, a tick in quality above its main competitors, Horne's and Gimbel's. Edgar Kaufmann knew who Lorant was, because he had read Lorant's diary of his year in a Nazi internment camp, *I Was Hitler's Prisoner.* Eventually freed from German confinement, Lorant went on to edit a number of illustrated newspapers in Europe. He also tried his hand as a screenwriter and director of motion pictures.

He was right to stick to stills. In 1921, he was approached in Berlin by a woman with a husky voice and sad eyes who asked him to screen-test her. Lorant did so and sadly informed her that she had no talent. Marlene Dietrich proved Lorant wrong but, perhaps even more surprisingly, remained his friend.

When Lorant's latest friend, Edgar Kaufmann, invited him to Pittsburgh, Lorant was not enamored of the idea. In his later life, Lorant recalled: "I was there only once, on my second visit to America in 1940, and I found it terrible! The

High noon, Pittsburgh.

sky was dark, the electric lamps were burning in the morning, the air was thick with grime. I could not breathe, my eyes watered. I went back to the station and got on the next train to Chicago. I never wanted to see Pittsburgh again."

Geniuses are often dopes. Edison didn't like to study. Gene Kelly, a native Pittsburgher, railed at having to take dance lessons. And Stefan Lorant, who would edit the best history of Pittsburgh in existence, never wanted to see the place again. By 1954, Lorant gave in, and was engaged by Kaufmann to write the definitive account of the city named in honor of British Prime Minister William Pitt. *Pittsburgh, the Story of an American City* is one of those books that is printed in ink but authored with love. Lorant later published two updated editions that took the city's story as far as 1980. But the heart of his massive undertaking is the period that he saw for himself when he first arrived—the Pittsburgh of the 1950s and '60s was in its renaissance, when the skies were reclaimed and the buildings scraped clean, the rivers made sustainable, and its citizens bequeathed the respect of twentieth-century beings, instead of Dickensian wastrels and waifs.

I proudly acknowledge that much of the information about Pittsburgh in this inning comes from Lorant's work. For that he has my gratitude, though he is no longer alive to accept it in person.

Nothing in his book is more striking than the pictures of downtown ("dahn-tahn," remember) Pittsburgh in the 1930s and 1940s. It was dark all day. Electric lights were needed to illuminate the streets, so choking was the smoke from the mills. Some pedestrians covered their mouths and noses with handkerchiefs, as though linen would filter out the contaminants all around them.

"Everything was filthy all the time," recalls Sophie Masloff, who was born in 1917 and raised in the Hill District. Masloff in 1988 would become the city's first woman mayor. Contentedly unfamiliar with pop culture, Sophie famously referred to the E-Street Band's lead singer

Why bother with cigarettes? Just take a deep breath. 1941.

as "Bruce Bedspring." When the Grateful Dead played
Pittsburgh, she introduced the group as "The Dreadful
Dead." Yet she remembers acutely the Pittsburgh of her
youth. "You'd go outside and five minutes later you'd look at
your hands and they were black or at least gray. We all knew
where the soot was coming from. It was the mills."

Not surprisingly, in such circumstances, the city gained
a national reputation—not the good kind. One anonymous
magazine editor quoted by Lorant referred to the city as "an

esthetic abortion, a municipal hovel." The short story writer O. Henry called Pittsburgh the "low-downdest" hole he had ever seen and its inhabitants "the most ignorant, ill-bred, contemptible, boorish, degraded, insulting, sordid, vile, foul-mouth, indecent, profane, drunken, dirty, mean, depraved" people he knew. And that was when the pollution wasn't so bad. President Theodore Roosevelt meant to compliment the city when he said, with all too much accuracy, "Pittsburgh has not been built up by talking about it." Its rabbit warren of crisscrossing streets and its neighborhoods built into the hills alongside the rivers baffled outsiders such as correspondent Ernie Pyle, who wrote, "Pittsburgh is undoubtedly the cockeyedest city in the United States. It must have been laid out by a mountain goat."

It was said that Pittsburgh's 500 bars and saloons were the most in any city its size in the country in those days. Until Prohibition became the law of the land in 1920, they were well patronized, and many continued to operate covertly during the so-called dry years. The men who spent long hours in mills, on coal barges, on the filthy railroads that transported raw products in and finished steel out—these men were tired when they left their jobs and often sought to drown their dreary lives in bottles of amber amnesia.

The stew of nationalities seemed to get along, if some-times warily. "We called each other hunkies and dagos and micks and kikes and whatever," says Masloff, whose family is of Jewish-Rumanian origin. "But it wasn't said in a hateful way and it wasn't taken that way. They were just names we used. It was different then, me calling an Italian a dago, because my family was no better off than his was. We were all immigrant families and we all had the same problems. We didn't have pets, we didn't play sports. We didn't have time to do anything except struggle to survive. People can't imagine what it was like. Today, people think it's a catastrophe if the color on their televisions isn't right. Nowadays, there's so much sensitivity, especially between blacks and whites, and you can't say anything. But I think that's because there's an economic gap and lots of people are bitter about that. And so they're sensitive to any perceived slight, even if no slight is intended."

There were constant labor disputes. The Homestead strike of 1892 was one of the more famous confrontations between workers and employers, but it was not the last. Steelworkers went on strike in 1919, and there was daily violence. When the Depression swept the country, Pittsburgh's core industries were devastated. You don't need steel to build things when nothing is being built. And you don't need much coal to make steel when the mills are operating at 6 percent of capacity. Tens of thousands of workers lost their jobs; others accepted ruinous salary cuts.

The New Deal was slow to improve conditions, and then, on St. Patrick's Day 1936, the city was flooded. Streets disappeared. Trolley cars that ran on rails set into the streets

*The 1936 flood, when Bob Prince toured the stricken
city by flatboat with his father.*

were lifted up and carried away. The eternal flames that shot
from the mills were snuffed out. Houses floated down the
Allegheny River like rafts containing lifetimes of memories.
The army officer in charge of keeping order during this time
was Colonel Frederick Seaton Prince, who would take his
son, Robert, for excursions through the flooded streets in an
army barge, on the lookout for looters. Twenty-four years
later, the boy who had sat beside his father and seen
Pittsburgh swallowed by water, buried beneath its floating
filth, would describe it in his trademark style as it reached its
zenith as the home of baseball's champions.

The seemingly endless streak of misfortune left Pittsburghers feeling inferior, as how could it not? New York was the great metropolis, Los Angeles a new and sun-kissed coastal anchor, Miami impossibly exotic and far away. Even Philadelphia, Pittsburgh's cross-state rival, was bigger, more historic, and cleaner. Pennsylvania was the Keystone State and Pittsburgh the Gateway to the West, but those left behind to open the gates and turn the keys could be made to feel pretty miserable. Steel tycoon Andrew Carnegie, whose vast fortune he built on the backs of Pittsburgh laborers, tried to contribute culture to a city that his own mills choked with smoke. He built a library, an art museum, a natural history museum, and, with characteristic humility, named them all after himself.

World War II reignited the need for steel and returned Pittsburgh to its former vigor, if not its extant prosperity. The mills were fired up again and the manufacturers started rehiring to meet the requirement of government contracts. To satisfy wartime demand for steel, the city actually abolished its office of smoke control, which was the only arm of government remotely concerned with controlling pollution. Lorant estimates that Pittsburgh produced 95 million tons of steel during the war. It was a Stakhanovian display of patriotism. When the fighting ended, steel was still needed for the postwar boom that America had entered. And a new mayor, David T. Lawrence, was in office, with a mandate to make Pittsburgh, if not lovely, at least livable.

But Pittsburgh still stank.

A little dirt never hurt anybody, people would say, and, as long as they had jobs, could convince themselves of that local truism. Mayor Masloff remembers: "Men would come straight from the mills to meetings about the various plans to clean up the city and hold their dirty arms up and shake their fists and say, 'I'd rather have my kids suffocate from smoke than starve to death. Don't close the mills.'" But people *were* being hurt. Doctors reported the incidence of lung cancer, emphysema, and bronchial disease around Pittsburgh was significantly higher than the national average. Of course, this was also when doctors were paid to pose in advertisements for filter cigarettes, which they promised were easier on the throat, so it is impossible to blame industrial pollution for every wracking cough. City health director I. Hope Alexander, familiarly known as Ike, began warning of the long-term effects of air pollution and caught the ear, and pen, of the editor of the Pittsburgh *Press,* Edward Leech. Leech ordered crusading (if not always objective) coverage of the issue in the paper and eventually enlisted the support of the city council. The council ordered a significant reduction in industrial pollution, and it looked for a while as if the permanent darkness of the skies might be lifted.

Mayor Lawrence harnessed the influence, wealth, and, most importantly, enthusiasm of Pittsburgh's richest man: Richard King Mellon. It is probably easier to list Pittsburgh-based companies that Mellon did *not* control than the reverse. At one time or another, the Mellon empire had influence with Gulf Oil, Koppers, Alcoa, U.S. Steel, Westinghouse, Pittsburgh Plate Glass, and Consolidation Coal. Between Lawrence's political drive and Mellon's financial clout, the city created the Allegheny Conference, which began planning not just smoke reduction but a wholesale redevelopment of the city and its surroundings. Once committed to clean Pittsburgh up and chart a cleaner future for the city, Mellon worked with other local industrialists such as H.J. Heinz, whose family controlled the food company best known for its 57 varieties of food products, most famously ketchup; Edgar Kaufmann, the department store owner (and Lorant's patron); and Benjamin Fairless, the president of U.S. Steel.

The key to controlling Pittsburgh's pollution—and Lawrence's political genius deserves much of the credit—was cooperation, not coercion. The smoke emission targets were set only after consultation with, and approval from, the companies that created the pollution and the labor unions that represented the interests of their employees. Consol Coal agreed to make Pittsburgh more livable, as did the United Mine Workers. U.S. Steel signed on. So did the steelworkers union. The railroads, which carried coal from the surrounding area to the mills along the rivers, wavered for a while, since their locomotives would have the hardest time controlling their emissions. But they too, eventually, got on board, so to speak.

The broader challenge, to change Pittsburgh's drab profile into something befitting a Gateway to the West, was complicated by conflict over what to tear down to make room for the new. Just as the flood in 1936 created the civic will to look hard at the city's problems, another natural catastrophe offered a starting point for the program that came to be called The Renaissance. On March 22, 1946, the Wabash Terminal, an 11-story beaux arts structure at Liberty and Ferry (now Stanwix) streets, caught fire and burned to the ground. That created the space and the conditions to start rebuilding the city. Gateway Center, as it was called, would be the ground zero of Pittsburgh's rise from, literally, the ashes.

Once the rebuilding—rebirth or renaissance, really—began, it seemed to claim the imagination of every city block. The Alcoa Building, a shimmering aluminum sheath of commerce, rose in 1951; so did the Mellon Building, a 41-story stainless steel block. Mellon Square Park, an oasis of fountains and trees in the midst of concrete silos, opened to the public in 1955. The State Office Building and Bell Telephone headquarters were completed in 1957. The Hilton Hotel at the Point was receiving guests in 1959, and 4 Gateway Center went up the next year. The Golden Triangle, as the downtown business district became known, was suddenly a source of civic pride. Mike Hayden, who grew up on the city's North Side, drove a cab part-time around Pittsburgh and enjoyed surprising passengers on their way in from the airport. "I'd ask them if they'd ever been to Pittsburgh before. If they hadn't I made a point of going through the Fort Pitt Tunnel." Hayden remembers the expressions of startled surprise when, emerging from the dark tunnel, his fares saw the Golden Triangle in its new splendor suddenly appear before them.

These accomplishments took effort and cooperation and the will to overcome seemingly insuperable obstacles. What better city, then, to provide a home for the hopeless Pirates, those perennial losers who couldn't, in Vern Law's words, catch the ball in practice, much less during a game? Pittsburgh was rebuilding itself into a winner. So was its hapless baseball team.

Seventh Inning

"Always run them out. You can never tell."

(From Vernon Law's *Words to Live By*)

J UST AS PITTSBURGH WAS changing the way it looked to the outside world, so were the Pirates. Trade by trade, the bunglers were becoming a solid-hitting, effective-pitching, cohesive bunch that could hold leads, recover from mistakes, and win games. They were a long way from challenging the perennially potent Milwaukee Braves, New York Giants, or Brooklyn Dodgers. But fate would play a hand in all those teams' futures and create conditions under which the Pirates would find themselves playing, for the first time in decades, into October.

After returning from military service, Law had become a mainstay of the Pirates' rotation, as well as a quiet, dignified presence on a team known for having some loudmouths.

Two of the most curious games in his career occurred on days he was not supposed to be on the field.

On July 20, 1955, Law was not the scheduled starter and

was, as per his habit on days when he was not pitching, running in the outfield. (In the 1950s, few players taxed themselves physically beyond what was necessary. Law was an innovator in that he kept himself in shape both during the season and throughout the winter. That, along with his abstemious ways, probably prolonged his career.) Then the scheduled starter, Mel Queen, a journeyman right-hander who spent ten years in the Majors without notable success, came down with a stomach bug. Law volunteered to pitch on short notice against the Milwaukee Braves' redoubtable Lou Burdette. It all happened so suddenly he could not even call VaNita to come to the park, as she normally did when her husband was pitching.

Watching Law and Burdette was like watching twins who were dressed differently. With their clean, angular faces, the two men bore a striking likeness to each other. Each was a few inches over six feet and weighed about 185. Each threw right-handed and relied on heat and deception. They hooked up in an old-fashioned pitchers' duel, and at the end of nine innings, the score was tied 2–2. The Braves pinch-hit for Burdette, and Pirates manager Fred Haney wanted to do the same for Law. The problem, as Law himself proudly argued, was that he could hit as well as some of the position players on the Pirates during that year of misery. So the starter stayed in, until the 12th inning, when Haney again said he wanted to pinch-hit for him.

"I told him I felt fine," Law says. "I was getting them out

Watch out! Proud of his prowess at the plate, Vern escapes an inside pitch.

one-two-three and having an easy game. So he let me stay in. Again in the 15th, he wanted to take me out, but I told him that after pitching this long, I'd like to stay in to win or lose it. When the 18th inning came, he said, 'I've got to take you out. If you hurt your arm, they'll run me out of town.' I could see there was no changing his mind this time, so gave way even though I felt okay."

In 18 innings of work, Law gave up two runs, nine hits, walked two—and struck out 12.

At home, VaNita was startled to hear on the radio that her husband was taking the mound. With Veldon fast asleep, and their second child, Veryl, mewling beside her, she had been on her knees on the living room floor, producing a scrapbook of Vern's growing number of newspaper write-ups. As the game went beyond the normal nine innings, VaNita suspected her hardheaded husband would object to coming out. Admittedly superstitious, she worried that if she got up from her knees, calamity might befall her husband at Forbes Field. And so she ground her knees into the rug until the 19th.

Today, the prospect of a starting pitcher—moreover, the ace of the staff—pitching 18 innings is ludicrous. Coaches keep careful track of pitch counts so that even the hardiest hurlers seldom throw more than 100 times during a game. Vern estimates he threw 220 pitches that night, with no apparent ill effect. His body was tuned to perform and, most of all, he wanted that win.

The conclusion of the game was worthy of an O. Henry short story. Bob Friend, who would be Law's teammate on the 1960 World Series team, relieved his stable mate in the 19th and immediately gave up a home run. In the bottom of the 19th, the Pirates scored twice. And who got the win? Bob Friend. Having made baseball history, but not figuring in the final statistics, Law drove home to his sleeping family, spooned himself an ice-cream sundae, and went to bed.

Law probably got more publicity for *not* getting the win that night than if he had triumphed. The crazy finish to the game underscored the illogic of some of baseball's rules. The

Pittsburgh *Post-Gazette* railed against the outcome and the unbending requirement that Friend, not Law, be credited with the win. "In the end, logic must be the official scorer," the paper chided.

Four days later, in his next start, Law pitched a 13-inning complete game and won 2–1.

His iron-man reputation was secure.

A professional sports career has different effects on different people. For many, the pressure to perform, day in and day out, the unyielding scrutiny from the media that chronicle their public appearances and private lives, and the long stretches spent away from the anchoring effect of families, prove to be too much. Today's sports pages are replete with accounts of misbehavior by superstars, which causes fans, especially the youngest fans, to wonder: If such behavior by their heroes is acceptable, why not for them?

For Law, the temptations were there. He recalls one time in Philadelphia when he was awakened from slumber in his room at the Warwick Hotel to find a giggling young woman standing next to his bed. Law quietly asked her to leave, then watched, stunned, as she disappeared sullenly through the door connecting his room to the one occupied by a fellow player who had bet the woman $50 she could not convince Law to let her share his bed.

Law's sense of morality had been instilled in him by his parents and by the teachings of his church. He was also fortunate to be married to VaNita, the kind of dignified life-partner

Vern and VaNita never forgot what was most important in their lives.

that no man would want to disappoint with his own inadequacies. And he had benefitted from his lifelong habit of surrounding himself with members of his church, on whom he could rely for encouragement, support, and advice.

At the end of the 1955 season, the Laws were back in Meridian, when it came time for their tithing settlement, an annual meeting with the Mormon bishop in which the member has a chance to declare his or her status as a tithe payer. As a Mormon in good standing, Law faithfully observed the Church's custom of donating 10 percent of his gross income to his local bishop, for the Church to use as it saw fit.

He recalls, "We usually kept good track of our finances, but somehow we slipped up, and the amount we had left was just enough to pay our rent, so we had to make a choice: to be full tithe payers, or pay our rent that was due in a couple weeks." Reflecting on the decision he and VaNita made, he said, "I think we had more faith than sense. We used the money to pay the tithe and trusted in the Lord to help us with our other obligations. Before two weeks were up, in the mail came a bonus check for $5,000 from the Pirates. An answer to our prayer? We thought so. I always felt that if I took care of those important obligations to the Church, the Lord would bless me in my career."

In 1956, the new Pirates manager, Bobby Bragan, brought with him a track record of being an umpire baiter, a trait guaranteed to make games interesting. With the club playing Philadelphia at Connie Mack Stadium, Law, not scheduled to pitch until the next day, was just sitting on the Pirates' bench along with relief pitcher Nellie King, who would one day become part of the Pirates' broadcast team. During his playing days, King could be counted on to clown around, keeping the team loose but also annoying the opposing team (and the umpires, if their calls did not suit him).

Even before the game began, while Bragan and the Phillies manager were at home plate, exchanging lineups, someone (Law insists it was not he nor King) from the Pirates' dugout shouted: "Pull down the shades, Stan!" Another inquired, "What kind of call was that last night?"

*Bobby Bragan (seen here in 1931) brought with him
a reputation for baiting umpires.*

Some of the Pirates chuckled, but home-plate umpire Stanley
Landes did not. Several Pirates had reported seeing Landes
the night before, in the same hotel they were occupying, accompanied to his room by a lady who was not Mrs. Landes.

Things got worse. Law recalls: "It seemed like every pitch
was either just in or out of the strike zone, and every play at
first base was bang-bang! and could have gone either way. As

a result, there was a lot of hollering from both benches and some swearing was being done."

By that, Law means a few off-color words, something slightly stronger than "son of a gun," but not the bile-filled screeds that routinely come from aggrieved athletes today. But the code of conduct for players was different then.

The scoreboard in Connie Mack Park was in right field. When Law checked the out-of-town scores and noticed that the Cardinals had scored several runs, he tapped King on the shoulder and gestured to the numbers. "When I looked back to home plate, I saw the umpire was looking straight at me. He said, 'Law, you do that one more time and you're out of the game.' So I kind of tapped the bill of my cap with one finger and gave a halfhearted smile. And he said, 'That's it. Go take a shower.' I ran up to him and said, 'Stan, why are you throwing me out? I haven't been swearing at you.' And he said, 'Maybe not, but you were impersonating me.'"

That was a first. The Deacon had never been ejected from a sports contest of any kind in his life. Still mystified at his punishment, Law slunk into the clubhouse and listened to the rest of the game on radio. His biggest concern, he recalls, was the possibility of being fined by the National League, which often accompanied ejection. "I couldn't afford to pay the League on what I was making," he fretted.

Two days later, a copy of Stan Landes's report to the league president about the Pirates-Phillies game was released. The umpire said: "I threw Law out of the game because I

*Joe E. Brown's grin made him a Hollywood star. His son, Joe L.,
caught flack for bringing Murtaugh in as manager.*

knew he's a minister of some kind and there was a lot of abusive language on the bench, and I didn't want him to hear it. So I threw him out."

It was not that Law had no temper. Rather, he flashed it so rarely that, coming from him, even moderate terms of displeasure sounded like eruptions. Proud of his prowess with the bat, Law also thought himself a good judge of the strike zone. When he was called out on a pitch that he still contends was low, he whirled on the umpire and snarled, "Judas Priest!" Law cringes at the story today. "I suppose I did use that expression when I was really angry. Judas was a pretty bad fellow, wasn't he? So, yes, I'm guilty."

Law played baseball with honor, but he also played to win. And that became possible when a fresh manager, new teammates, and a new attitude converged in Pittsburgh. Murtaugh and General Manager Joe L. Brown decided to give the Pirates a new look. Slugger Frank Thomas and Bob Purkey, a talented and well-liked starting pitcher, were traded to Cincinnati, where Purkey would continue his fine career (full disclosure: I played Little League baseball against Purkey's son, Bob Jr., who died from heart failure as a teenager. The baseball field at the high school from which I graduated is named after Bob Purkey Jr.). The Pirates got third baseman Don Hoak, left-handed pitcher Harvey Haddix, and catcher Forrest "Smoky" Burgess, who would become Law's roommate on the road.

The club also had a cocky and super-talented new right fielder named Roberto Clemente. Born in Puerto Rico, Clemente was blessed with a whip-fast bat, foot speed that rivaled any Major Leaguer, and a rocket for an arm that could gun down a runner from the darkest corner of the park. These four newcomers formed the nucleus of the team that would propel the Pirates out of the cellar in 1959 and beyond their wildest expectations the following season.

Clemente, endowed with all the tools of baseball, was

Courtesy Pittsburgh Pirates

The Great One: Clemente and the fans didn't get along at first.

also a whiner. He wasn't feeling well. His arm hurt. He had a cramp. Pittsburgh was a little town too small for a star like him. He was better than Willie Mays and Hank Aaron but didn't make as much money. The fans didn't like him because his skin was black. Or because he could not (*would not* was more accurate) speak English. And on and on.

Word gets around the Major Leagues quickly. Clemente got a reputation not only for complaining but for bailing out of the batter's box if a pitcher buzzed him. In Philadelphia one night, Law recalls, Clemente was laid out flat by a pitch aimed right at his head. "After grounding out weakly, he came back to the dugout cursing and screaming at the top of his lungs. I said to him, 'Roberto, shut up, I'll take care of this.' So when I took the mound, the first batter went down, the second went down, so did the third. I didn't actually hit them. If I'd wanted to, I'd have thrown just behind their waist. A batter doesn't know what to do when you throw there. So I just threw high and inside. After the third batter hit the ground, the umpire told both benches that if there was another brush-back pitch, both teams would be fined. From that time on, we had no trouble with pitchers throwing at Roberto, and he went on to have a great year."

Law's composure amid his teammates' turmoil, his quiet retaliation without actually hitting and potentially hurting anyone, and his modest recounting of the incident were emblematic. He knew how to scare hitters, knew where to throw if he had wanted to hit them. But he achieved his goal—intimidation—without unsportsmanlike conduct.

He also knew how to turn his squeaky-clean image to his advantage. Because he was known throughout the league as a religious man, he was a favorite of Pittsburgh's Catholic nuns, many of whom also happened to be die-hard Pirates supporters. "The Catholic sisters were our best fans," Law told me. "They could tell you what you ate for breakfast, that's how knowledgeable they were. I guess it was a real outlet for them,

Courtesy Pittsburgh Pirates

Nuns were Law's secret weapon at home. Murtaugh knew it.

and the club would open up the ballpark about three times a year for the nuns. They would come and shout out, 'Deacon, Deacon, won't you come over and sign my notebook?'"

Because they were getting in free, the nuns were relegated to the center-right field stands, far from the pitcher's mound but also directly in the line of vision of a right-handed batter. The white bibs that nuns wore at that time contrasted strikingly against the rest of their black habits and veils. Today, baseball parks have a so-called batter's eye, where seats have been removed and the backdrop painted black so that hitters are not distracted by spectators' movements or clothing and the whiteness of the ball is not obscured. But at

Forbes Field, the nuns, jumping up and down, their bibs caught by the occasional breeze, created a visual blind spot for batters. If Law knew this and pitched slightly higher on those days, so that the ball blended with the moving bibs behind him, he never admitted it. But he pitched very well when the nuns were there, cheering him on.

And he was wildly popular with Pittsburghers of faith, who knew nothing about the Mormon Church, but who knew Vern Law was a great pitcher and a good guy (I was one of them). After one seesaw game, Mary Oceak, the devout Catholic wife of the Pirates' third-base coach, saw Law coming out the clubhouse and, still fingering her rosary, said, "Boy, Deacon, did I have to make speed with the beads for you today."

There may or may not have been some divine help involved, but the Pirates were now a fundamentally better club than they had been for decades. While some fans missed Frank Thomas's bat, the trade with the Reds gave the Pirates an experienced infield and, with Clemente's rapidly developing superstardom, an outfield of renown.

The infield was anchored by shortstop Dick Groat, the Pirate captain, and second baseman Bill Mazeroski, whose baseball immortality would come with one swing of the bat. With his innate talent, Groat could have been the model for *The Natural.* Although at Duke University he was known more for his basketball skills than his baseball prowess, Groat was drafted by the Pirates in 1952 and immediately joined

Deadly double-play duo: Mazeroski and Groat.

the big team without spending a day in the minors. After a hitch in the army—where he *did* play both sports—he became the starting shortstop in 1955. He was not a big man—5–11, 180—nor particularly speedy, but he seemed always to know exactly where to stand in the field. He and Maz turned into one of the best double-play combinations of the era. At the end of 1959, the Pirates' front office wanted to trade Groat to the Yankees for Roger Maris, but Manager Murtaugh nixed the deal.

Like Groat, Bill Mazeroski was a star in both baseball and basketball. Unlike the more cerebral, Duke-educated short-stop, Mazeroski, a native son of Wheeling, West Virginia, never spent a day at college. He signed as an amateur free agent with the Pirates in 1953 at the age of 17 and honed his skills in the minors. Originally a shortstop, Maz was con-verted to second base to replace Curt Roberts, who played nearly every game in 1954 and got into only six contests after Mazeroski arrived. The same height and within a few pounds of the same weight, Groat and Mazeroski were perfect book-ends in the middle of the infield. Groat was the better hitter of the two; Mazeroski was the superior fielder. In fact, Maz's .983 career fielding average earned him the nickname The Glove. So smooth and dependable was Mazeroski's defense, usually executed with a wad of tobacco stuck in his cheek, that some baseball essayists and statisticians have estimated he saved the Pirates an average of 57 runs a year during his career.

If Groat and Mazeroski were the team's precision tandem up the middle, first and third base provided the passion and often unasked-for suspense. Dick Stuart, a tall, handsome first baseman, who batted right-handed, was half of a pla-toon system with lefty Rocky Nelson. Stuart could slam the ball with authority and set a minor league record with 66 home runs in one season. Stuart was also so possessive of his beautiful wife, Lois, that when she became pregnant, he pre-vented her from seeing a doctor until she could find a female obstetrician. When the baby was finally born, Lois fretted to VaNita Law before her husband entered the hospital room, "Dick's never seen me without my makeup on before." Later in his career, Stuart set another mark—the negative kind— with 29 errors at first, earning him the nickname "Dr. Strange-glove," a play on the title of Stanley Kubrick's 1964 antiwar movie, *Dr. Strangelove,* starring Peter Sellers and George C. Scott.

Perhaps it was significant that Don Hoak, the Pirates' third baseman, was born in a Pennsylvania town named Roulette. If luck had not intervened, Hoak might be best re-membered as Jackie Robinson's backup at third base for the 1955 champion Brooklyn Dodgers. A former professional boxing palooka—he lost seven fights in a row—Hoak, like Nelson, played ball in Cuba for a while before breaking in with Brooklyn. After the Dodgers beat the archrival Yankees in seven games in the World Series (an experience Hoak would repeat with the Pirates), the third baseman was traded first to the Cubs, then, after one disappointing season, to the Reds.

Hoak played with the same ferocity with which he boxed—but with superior results. While playing with the Reds in 1957, Hoak contributed to a rule change in baseball. In an April 21 game against the Milwaukee Braves, Hoak was on second base when his teammate Wally Post grounded to short. Hoak broke for third, then bent over, picked up the bouncing ball with his bare hand, and flipped it to the

Nobody played with more ferocity than The Tiger, Don Hoak.

Milwaukee shortstop, Johnny Logan. Hoak was called out, but Post was credited with a single. To discourage base runners from touching batted balls, or allowing themselves to be hit by them to break up double plays, Major League baseball ruled that if a batted ball touches a runner, both the runner and the batter are automatically out.

When Hoak arrived in Pittsburgh in 1959, he was the only member of the team who owned a World Series ring.

Hoak's unorthodox baserunning caused the rules of the game to change.

He was also the team's enforcer. If an opposing pitcher threw at a Pirate, Hoak could be counted on to jam his spikes into the heel of the next runner to slide into third. Once, when a runner slid into him with his spikes high—which might have injured Hoak—the Pirate third baseman took the ball from his glove, held it in his right hand, and used it to bash the runner in the mouth. Hoak's profanity was legendary even among hard-bitten veterans. He blamed his vocabulary on the time he had spent in the U.S. Marine Corps, and after he retired from baseball and became an announcer, he had to constantly monitor himself to avoid making obscene outbursts on the air.

When facing right-handed pitching, the Pirates relied on first baseman Glenn Richard "Rocky" Nelson, a hard-luck, left-handed hitter who always had power but not consistency. Nelson knocked around with several teams in the '40s and '50s before settling in with the Pirates in 1959. He could belt the ball, but he also struck out a lot. While Nelson was playing winter ball in Cuba, Reggie Otero, the manager of the Havana Sugar Kings, taught Nelson a new way to stand at the plate and probably set the stage for his eventual heroics with the Pirates.

Bob Skinner was a California kid whose level swing was the envy of every hitting coach and the bane of right-handed pitchers. At 6–2, he was big enough to reach the ball anywhere across the plate or to haul it in from his domain in left field. He moved as fast as a man his size could. In 1959, he ran smack into the left-center field wall at Milwaukee. Though his injuries were never known, Skinner did not recover for the rest of the season.

To backstop Skinner in 1960, the Pirates traded starting pitcher Ron Kline to the Cardinals for a right-hand hitting, San Francisco–born outfielder named Gino Cimoli. His first name was exotic enough sounding, and his looks Latin and dramatic enough that Cimoli became an instant heartthrob in Pittsburgh. His father, Abramo, would come to Forbes Field and, in almost stereotypical fashion, when his son came

Left field meets right: Skinner and Clemente.

to bat, stand and announce to the rest of the paid audience, "Atsa my boy, Gino!"

Between the rotating left fielders and the mercurial Clemente, the Pirates planted a pillar of stability in center field. If he did not change into a baseball uniform when he went to work, Bill Virdon could easily have been mistaken for a visiting chemistry professor or an executive at an insurance company. His wire-rimmed spectacles gave him the look of an intense academic in a game that was then more familiarly characterized by tobacco stains and dirt-encrusted fingernails. Signed by the Yankees, Virdon was traded to the Cardinals' minor league system before he got to wear pinstripes. He joined the Cardinals in 1955 and was named Rookie of the Year. That apparently meant little to the club, which dealt him to the Pirates during the next season. As soon as Virdon arrived, he claimed the gaping central outfield grounds of Forbes Field for his own.

Virdon was not the strongest Pirate or the fastest. But he may have been the smartest. He got incredible jumps on fly balls; that knack, along with his native speed, usually put him under the batted sphere when it came back to earth. The same qualities of anticipation and quickness made him an ideal leadoff hitter in front of Groat. Virdon was a career .267 hitter, and he was often on base when the Pirates needed a rally. His quiet intensity made him the cerebral force of the team. Hoak was its heart. Law was its soul.

And Clemente was its sparkle. By far the most talented member of the Pirates (then and now), with natural skills that set him apart as clearly as Alex Rodriguez stands out from his contemporaries in the twenty-first century, Clemente was a typical mix of genius and malcontent. Born in Puerto Rico's Carolina Province, Clemente caught the first of many breaks when Pedrín Zorilla of the local Santurce Crabbers saw him playing sandlot ball and offered him a pittance of a contract. Clemente liked to say in later life that he had started by playing without a glove; this may or may not be accurate. It is true that he rode the bench in his first year as a professional. In his second year in Puerto Rican ball, he caught the attention of scouts from the Brooklyn Dodgers who signed him and sent him to their Triple-A club in Montreal, the Royals.

The change of venue nearly soured Clemente on baseball and North America. Had not a teammate named Joe Black been able to communicate with the moody Spanish speaker and help him adjust to life in French-speaking Canada, Clemente might have returned to his homeland, never to fulfill his enormous potential. In 1954, Pirate scout Clyde Sukeforth suggested the club try to acquire Clemente from Brooklyn. The Pirates selected Clemente in the rookie draft that November, and the Pirates had their first superstar since Ralph Kiner.

It was fitting that Clemente's Major League debut with the Pirates came against the Dodgers, who had failed to see his potential. But then, for a while, it seemed the Pirates would not realize what they had acquired, either. Clemente's first season with the club was tense. He did not speak English. Though there were black players on the club, there were none who were both as dark-skinned as Clemente and who spoke only Spanish. And his high-octane style of play led to injuries, about which Clemente complained vociferously to anyone who could, or chose to, understand him.

In his first year, he was involved in a car accident that injured his lower back and left him occasionally unable to straighten up. When he begged off playing, he was called a

*Even when his back was turned, runners knew better than
to test Clemente's arm from the outfield.*

malingerer. When he played with pain and performed
poorly, he was accused of dogging it. And all these charges
came in a language he did not understand and to which he
could not respond adequately.

When he was fit, and motivated, Clemente answered
criticism with accomplishment. His batting stance was unusual and probably learned on the hard dirt fields of Puerto
Rico. He challenged pitchers with an arrogant wave of his

head, as if daring them to throw the ball past him. When they threw close to him, he instinctively bailed out of the batter's box, and it quickly became known through the league that a buzz pitch would unnerve Clemente and rob him of his aggressiveness at the plate. For that reason, he was also known as a first-pitch hitter.

In right field, his arm quickly gained the force of legend. Clemente could cut runners down at the plate, on the fly, from more than 400 feet away. His unorthodox basket catch of fly balls let him get into position for the throw home more quickly. Runners soon learned that while he might complain about his injuries, Clemente was silently lethal when he uncorked one of his prodigious throws.

With the twisted logic of life and baseball, the teammate of whom Vernon Law was initially the most suspicious turned out to be his best friend. Forrest Harrill Burgess brought with him from the Reds the nickname Smoky, and Law feared the rotund catcher might be a user of tobacco, which Latter-day Saints shun. Law was even more alarmed when he learned that he would be Smoky's roommate on the road—dual occupancy of a hotel room was a universal custom in the majors in the 1950s but would be ridiculed by Big League players today as hopelessly antiquated. But two men to a room cost less than giving each player his privacy, so roommates they were.

As it turned out, Smoky was the other Pirate in 1960 who neither smoked nor drank, by edict of his devout

Courtesy Pittsburgh Pirates

*When he wasn't crushing the ball, Burgess would
talk about anything to anyone.*

Baptist faith. A native of Caroleen, North Carolina, Forrest
acquired his nickname from his father, a semipro baseball
player who was said to be "smoke" on the base paths. No one
would say that of the younger Burgess. After a stint in the
army in which he was relegated to base postal service, Smoky
carried 190 pounds on a 5–7 frame. His lumbering gait from
first to second base was every infielder's guilty pleasure at the
beginning of a double play.

Pitchers had another view of the rotund backstop. Smoky Burgess was a flat-out great hitter. He made contact on almost every at bat. "He doesn't care what you throw up there," said his former teammate on Cincinnati, pitcher Tom Acker, "just so there's a pitch on the way. I threw to him—too high to be a strike—and he hit it out."

And hitters hated to step into the box, only to hear Smoky's voice coming from behind his catcher's mask, already in full flow. Smoky talked to batters about anything: the weather, their wives, a good restaurant he'd just found (and there were many), the noise from the crowd, the sermon he'd listened to at the last Baptist service he'd attended, what kind of pitch the batter was likely to face. His constant banter was infuriating, like a cloud of gnats enveloping a picnic party. Some batters told Smoky to shut up. Some stoically ignored him and tried to concentrate on hitting. And some, like Willie Mays and Henry Aaron, managed to still Smoky's tongue by blasting long home runs, then asking Smoky what they'd missed of his commentary on their return from around the bases. "Them two hit pretty good when I talked, so I stopped talking," Smoky noted sagely. But not many people hit the way Aaron or Mays did.

With little fanfare, Law and Burgess became not just roommates but friends. "The only difference between how we saw things was I was Mormon and he was Baptist," Law says now. That overlooks quite a few theological collisions, but Law's point was obviously about temporal preferences.

They shared an abstemious lifestyle, though Smoky spent more time and effort at dinner than did the lean pitcher. Burgess also liked to "lobby sit," as Law called it—parked in the entrance of whatever hotel they were staying in, waiting to strike up a conversation with someone, anyone.

That did not mean they had no excitement. During the 1959 season, after Law had beaten Milwaukee by pitching a complete game and adding two hits of his own, Burgess was once again camped out in the lobby, and Law was asleep in their room when the phone rang. "On the other end of the line was this sweet little voice that congratulated me on my win and asked what I was doing. My answer was I was in bed. She asked if I'd like to go for a ride. My answer was negative, so she said how about coming down for a drink. I said, I'm sorry, I don't drink. Then she said, well, what do you do for fun? I said, 'Beat the Braves.'"

The Pirates' pitching rotation included Bob Friend, who might have been a Hall of Fame pitcher if his career had started with a more promising team. But Friend went from Purdue University to the pathetic Pirates in 1950, the same year that Law broke into the Bigs. Friend was the hard-luck story that personified Pirates pitching in the '50s. He was talented and often compared to Warren Spahn, the Braves' ace lefty, for his craftiness on the mound, and to Cardinals pitcher Bob Gibson for the way he fooled hitters by changing speed. But while both Spahn and Gibson now have plaques in Cooperstown, Friend was never a serious Hall of Fame candidate.

One game probably made left-handed starter Harvey Haddix more famous than all his others, and it was a game he lost. On May 26, 1959, Haddix hooked up against Lou Burdette of the Braves (the same pitcher against whom Law began his 18-inning marathon) and took a perfect game into the 13th inning. Haddix had mowed down 36 consecutive hitters, until a fielding error by Hoak with two outs broke the streak and the perfect game. After that, Haddix understandably was unnerved and served up a home run to Joe Adcock. So he lost a game in which no one reached base against him until the 13th inning. That piece of bad luck aside, Haddix, who along with Law and Friend represented the core of the team's starting pitching, was a reliable, if underpowered pitcher on whom the Pirates would come to rely when their season of magic began.

The best closer in the history of baseball is Mariano Rivera of the Yankees, whose dominance began in the late 1990s and continued into the twenty-first century. But the *first* full-time closer was ElRoy Face, Law's Pirate teammate in the 1950s and through the World Series year. Face came to the Pirates in 1951, armed with an adequate fastball and the only pitch he really needed: a forkball that seemed to drop from a batter's belt to his shoe tops within the last few feet of its delivery. Even Face admitted he seldom knew

Courtesy Pittsburgh Pirates

Mr. Reliable and Mr. Unhittable: Law and Face.

where the forkball would go. "Sometimes in, sometimes out, mostly down," was how he described it.

The pitch was so effective that for most of the 1959 season, Face had a perk that few baseball players then received: free parking. Face normally parked his car at an Esso service station near Forbes Field for a dollar a day. But after he had racked up five wins in relief appearances, the owner of the station told him he could park for free until he lost a game.

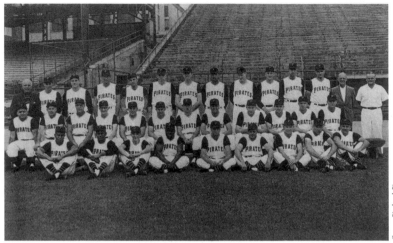

The team to watch.

Face's record that year was 18–1, still the highest winning percentage for a reliever, and it boosted not just his reputation but his finances. He didn't lose again until September. Face had a slight build, 5–8, 155. But he was wiry, strong, and seemingly tireless. He told an interviewer, "Everyone asks me the same question: are you tired? I always say, no, I've pitched so many times, once more isn't going to make any difference."

There are 25 players at any given time on a Major League roster. Each, in some way, affects the outcome of the season, whether it is by dazzling or dreadful play, or a clubhouse demeanor that heartens his teammates or makes them despise him. There were also Joe Christopher, Bob Oldis, and Dick Schofield on the Pirates in 1959. They and the others named above constituted the team that was preparing for the 1960 season—the season that would propel the Pirates, and Pittsburgh, from the backwaters of public opinion to the pinnacle of baseball's promise.

Eighth Inning

"Many have the will to win on the day of the contest.
Few have the will to prepare to win."

(From Vernon Law's *Words to Live By*)

I T COULD BE SAID THAT Vernon Law's career in professional baseball got started because of cigars. Bing Crosby encouraged Pirate scout Babe Herman to bring a box of stogies for the other scouts waiting on the Laws' porch. The smoke and smell of the cigars so disturbed Vernon's Mormon parents that they were perhaps unduly influenced when Herman, representing Pittsburgh, came in without a cigar in his mouth, clutching instead chocolates and flowers for Mrs. Law.

So there was no mistaking the omens in 1960 when the team arrived in Fort Myers, Florida, for spring training. At Chuck's Cigar store, the owner welcomed the club to town with a homemade banner reading "1960 World Champions." It was premature, of course, but the Pirates that year had a mystique, almost a sense of destiny, hanging over them. No longer were they the snake-bit cellar dwellers.

At spring training, the Skipper told his team 1960 would be different.
He was right as usual.

Referring to that magical season, Groat said, "We didn't
think we were ever supposed to lose." With Hoak, Burgess,
and most of all, Clemente, swinging the bat well the season
before, Pittsburgh's management believed it had finally put
together the lineup that could take the Pirates to the World
Series.

Vern Law also believed it. Typically, he had worked
harder than ever to ensure that he would be able to give the
club his best that hope-soaked year. He began running in the
frigid Idaho winter months, building up to six miles at

Courtesy Pittsburgh Pirates

Who can relax more? Prince and Murtaugh at spring training, 1960.

full-out effort. He and Evan went through the same fraternal routine they had employed for more than two decades:
Vern throwing carefully at first, then harder, then at full
speed; Evan crouched behind a makeshift plate in the relative warmth of their church cultural hall (most LDS chapels
contain a gym, commonly referred to as the cultural hall),
telling his brother where the pitch had entered his mitt, com-
menting on his delivery. Not every brother can catch a Major

League pitcher throwing his hardest. In his memoir, Vern credits Evan, his first battery mate, his first and best friend, with helping get him in optimum shape in 1960.

Manager Danny Murtaugh also felt this was his best shot at the brass ring. His manner with the players was different in the spring of 1960. He was both more direct and more collegial. There were fewer clubhouse lectures and almost no angry outbursts. He was in this fight with them. Like a trainer with a superbly conditioned boxer, he told his pitchers he did not want them to have sex the night before they were scheduled to throw. Reliever ElRoy Face objected, "Hell, Danny, I might be pitching every day. Am I shut out for the whole season?"

It was probably a price Face and the others would have paid if it guaranteed success. The Pirates had finished 78–76 in 1959, nine games behind the pennant-winning Los Angeles Dodgers, and trailing the second-place Braves and third-place Giants, now of San Francisco. The addition of Burgess, Haddix, and Hoak had given the club depth, power, and reliability. But Murtaugh had not figured out how to make it click in his first full year as manager. Now, in the spring of 1960, everything seemed ready to coalesce.

Law's first exhibition start was against the Yankees at the Pirates' compound in Fort Myers, Florida. The buzz about the team was loud and growing and even spring training games were sellouts. Remembering that exhibition match against the Yankees, Law wrote: "They were a piece of cake

A Prince, a Singing Sensation, and an Innovator:
Prince, Crosby, and Murtaugh.

and a lot of people had the feeling we'd be meeting each
other again that fall."

The regular season opened against Milwaukee at County
Stadium. Though he had expected to be the starter, Law was
bypassed for Bob Friend, the Purdue-educated right-hander
who had gone 8–19 the year before, as opposed to Law's 18–
9. The Pirates opened with a 4–3 loss, absorbed by reliever
ElRoy Face. With one day off for travel, the Pirates then
began a four-game series against Cincinnati with a 16–4
blowout in which Law pitched the complete game and got

the win. He would win three more times before his first loss, 13–6, on May 6, in San Francisco.

For most of the month, the National League was unsettled, with the Pirates, Milwaukee, San Francisco, and St. Louis jostling for the lead, each forging ahead for a few games before dropping back. Then in June, the Pirates were scheduled to make a West Coast trip, with an exhibition game—*in the middle of the regular season!*—in Salt Lake City against the Bees, a Pirate farm club. Before he left with the club for Salt Lake, Law was contacted by Marvin Ashton, then the president of the Mormon Church's Young Men organization. Law, to his surprise and delight, was invited to lunch at the Beehive House. The Beehive House, located at 67 East South Temple Street, was erected in 1865 to house Brigham Young and his sizeable family when he was president of the Church. It is still one of the city's leading tourist attractions, the Mormon equivalent of Mount Vernon.

For an everyday Latter-day Saint to be the guest of honor there was singular recognition. Law of course, was not an everyday Mormon. "They escorted me to the Hotel Utah, where I checked in, and we immediately went to the Beehive House to a beautiful dining room. To my surprise, many of the Church authorities were there. I was a bit nervous with all the dignitaries—I was afraid I'd use the wrong fork or say something wrong. After the luncheon, Marvin presented me with an All-Church award for Excellence in Athletics, for setting an example to the young people of the country. From

In his prime: the Pirate ace, 1960.

that point on, we started winning ball games that we had no business winning, like being down three runs in the ninth with two out and before they could get the third out, we'd score four runs to win. This happened not once but thirty-some times through the season. So I've always contended we had to go to Salt Lake City to get inspired. At least we played inspired baseball after our visit."

Come-from-behind wins were a trademark of the 1960

team, a phenomenon that several surviving team members—Groat and Virdon among others—recall as the single most important ingredient leading toward the championship. They got fine pitching and timely hitting, but it was the indomitable will to win, or perhaps the cheeky determination not to lose, that drove them forward. That and, in Vern Law's opinion, the blessings received from that luncheon at the Beehive House made the difference. Increasingly in his memoir, beginning with 1960, Law credits divine intervention for his success in baseball. As a player, he said he often called upon the Almighty, not to help him throw a strike, not for his club to win. "I prayed for strength," he said. "I prayed that I would do my best. I prayed that no one would be hurt in the game. Just praying to win would have been selfish."

One cloistered fan of the Pirates, and of Law in particular, was Sister Mary Edna, a medical records librarian at the New Castle Hospital, just outside Pittsburgh. Sister Mary Edna entered the convent as a teenager in 1928 and had lived all her life in and around Pittsburgh, and the Pirates. "I've always liked sports," she told a reporter for the Pittsburgh *Post-Gazette* in 1960. "Particularly baseball. It seems like such a clean sport." And Law personified the morals she hoped prevailed in that athletic environment.

Sister Mary Edna was typical of the nuns who occasionally found the time to get to Forbes Field, especially when The Deacon was on the mound. In her office at the hospital, she kept a bulletin board with a list of descending numbers on it—the number of games the Pirates needed to win to clinch the pennant. Despite her day-job clerical duties, she was a veritable authority on batting averages and the particular qualities of Vernon Sanders Law.

It was one thing to pray, another to be the beneficiary of another's prayers and spiritual attention. Perhaps because his personal code of conduct forbad bragging, Law passed the credit for his achievements on to heaven. Perhaps he truly believed that God was the difference between a fourth-place team and a world champion. To Pirates fans, who had seen so much failure and who had endured season after season of disappointment, the reason was less important than the result. The Pirates were winning.

Since the All-Star mini-scandal of the 1950s where fans packed the ballot boxes at Crosley Field to benefit Cincinnati players—only to have the vote taken away from them and given instead to sportswriters—Major League Baseball had been trying to figure out how to select the best of the best to play in what became known as the Midseason Classic.

For a bizarre three-year period, from 1959 to 1962, Commissioner Ford Frick hit upon the notion of having *two* All-Star games per year, on the theory that if fans liked one, they would love two. In 1959, the leagues met on July 11 and 13, in Pittsburgh and Los Angeles, both National League cities. In 1960, the venues were Kansas City and Yankee Stadium. Part of the motivation was to provide badly needed cash for the baseball players' pension fund, which Major

League Baseball had underfunded. But Frick also believed fans wanted to see more All-Star games. It turned out he was only half right.

With sportswriters selecting the teams, it was perhaps not surprising that the Pirates, finally ripe with talent and surging in the standings, would be overrepresented. In all, there were eight Pirates on the National League team that year: Law, Bob Friend, ElRoy Face, catcher Smoky Burgess, outfielders Roberto Clemente and Bob Skinner, second baseman Mazeroski, and shortstop Groat. Friend started, and won, the first game, in Kansas City, with Law coming on in relief. Law began and won the other contest, at Yankee Stadium. His reward: a sterling silver punch bowl.

The two-game format lasted only three years. Fans decided that two All-Star games were one too many; the Yankee Stadium game of 1960, for example, drew only 38,000 spectators to the 67,000-seat capacity cathedral (the Stadium was later downsized). But now, Vern Law, who ten years earlier had been awed by Forbes Field, knew what it was like to pitch at the House That Ruth Built. It was knowledge that would soon come in handy.

Today, the notion that players would be required to play two All-Star games, thousands of miles apart, within 48 hours, and then return to competitive pennant races, sounds absurd. Managers would rebel. Players would decline the honor. Reaching the playoffs and winning the World Series is what matters today. Playing the game well, doing the best they could to bring honor to their teams, and giving fans pleasure, were what mattered in 1960.

For a few hours, on July 23, the Milwaukee Braves edged ahead of the Pirates by a few percentage points to take first place in the National League. Other than that, the Pirates either owned or shared the top spot all season. By August, they knew the pennant was theirs to lose. Murtaugh, the tobacco-chomping skipper, seemed placid enough, but inside, he was churning. He expected to face the Yankees, who had won ten of the last twelve American League flags, and he was already working out matchups in his head. Would Friend or Law start the first game? Would Burgess or Hal Smith catch each of his aces? How long would he wait before bringing in Face in relief? Would it be Skinner or Cimoli in left field? Who, between Stuart and Nelson, at first? The questions had no answers, only angles to be considered. Angles in the Outfield, for a change.

Just as any player on a winning team, then or now, Vernon Law was a public figure, an object of intense scrutiny, and much in demand by groups in and around Pittsburgh who hoped to trade in on his celebrity. Over the course of the nearly six-month season that year, Law figures he spoke to or appeared at one hundred group gatherings and events. That is more than one event every other night. Many were church-sponsored. Law would always have an interest in the weakest, persons of faith, and the disadvantaged. His visits

Law was a frequent visitor to Children's Hospital. Here with sons Veldon, Veryl, and baby Vance in 1957.

Law estimates he spoke at 100 events during the 1960 pennant race.

to the Children's Hospital of Pittsburgh went largely unpublicized and undocumented.

He did not try to convert cancer-stricken kids to Mormonism. Instead, he talked boldly and unabashedly of the need to believe in God. "I remember one boy in particular who had open heart surgery," Law writes. "His name was Robert Stringer. He was a real fan of mine. I guess he was having a very hard time recuperating so his dad called me. I took an autographed baseball and went to see him. Just the look on his face made it all worthwhile. His dad reported afterward that that was the turning point for him, and he made rapid progress after that."

Law was not unique in his charity, nor was the era in which he played necessarily more inclined to promote it. Players today spend vast sums of their vast salaries on personal charities, pet causes, and good deeds. The difference is that Law was going out nearly every night *during the season,* while his team was hot in pursuit of the league flag. He believed in the game that gave him his living. But he believed even more in the principles that gave him a reason *to* live. A player's life was not just baseball in 1960. A superstar (for that is what Vernon Law was in his prime playing days) was expected to take his children to school, to find work in the off-season to supplement his income, to make sure the grass was cut and the windows were clean, the garbage taken out, the lights turned off at bedtime. A player was expected not

Law never forgot what the game was all about.

just to play but to be a man. A *good* man. And then, at game time, to go out *and win*.

Another time, on the road in San Francisco, the Pirates were leaving their hotel to board the bus that would take them to play the Giants, when they encountered a legless man in a wheelchair on the street, begging. Some of the players edged past the man, unwilling to engage him. This was 1960, not 2010, and sensitivity to the disabled was not in fashion. One by one the players boarded the bus. And waited. And waited. They waited because Vernon Law was stooped down, next to the beggar, holding his hand and talking intently.

A few weeks later, in Milwaukee, Law would be the one waiting on the bus for his teammates. And when they arrived, they would bring with them not the outstretched hand of charity, but disaster.

Law had a life off the field, too, and it did not always play out according to script. He and VaNita had, by this time, four sons—Veldon, Veryl, Vance, and Vaughn (Varlin and daughter VaLynda would come later. Their dog, for the record, was named Victor)—and occupied a house at 112 Frazier Drive in Churchill Borough until August. VaNita had planned to return to Idaho then to enroll Veldon in school—children's birthdays come up on schedule no matter what place their father's team is in. However, the family decided to stay together in Pittsburgh to see if this season would end differently from all the others. They quickly became acquainted with their neighbors and could rely on them to watch the boys, or the house, when Vern was on the road.

In August, Vern's brother Evan, and his wife, Joyce, came to visit and lend their support as the team began its final drive for its first National League flag since 1927. As the Pirates bore down on the pennant, each of Law's starts became more crucial. On August 2, Vern was pitching against the Dodgers. Evan accompanied him to Forbes Field early, as was Vern's custom, so he could prepare himself. VaNita usually arrived at just before game time. On this day, she was

Vroom! VaNita, Varlin, Vern, Vaughn, Vance, Veryl, and Veldon.

running late. She was perhaps overstressed since she was taking Joyce with her, as well as the boys. Cleaning up after lunch, VaNita reached up to put a glass in the kitchen cupboard. It hit the ledge and shattered, and a jagged edge of glass went into VaNita's wrist.

She and Joyce went to a nearby doctor, who stitched the wound and pronounced her fine. But as they drove to Forbes Field, her wrist began to throb, and she suspected there was still glass inside. "About the seventh inning," Vern recalled, "it really began to bother her, so she looked up Dr. Joseph Finegold (the Pirates' physician). He looked at it and found

But in 1960, the idea of asking for more money, or asking to be traded, or to participate in decisions about one's career, seemed as outlandish as wearing your baseball uniform with the pants down to the ankles. It just wasn't done. Vern Law, by now a seasoned veteran of ten years, made $35,000 in 1960 and counted himself fortunate, not just for his relative affluence, but for the teammates on whom he could rely every day. He (as well as other Pirates) endorsed a few products, like Isaly's restaurants, locally famous for their ice cream, and the Kroger grocery stores' Tenderay steaks.

A proud carnivore, Law actually did enjoy grilling meat. His family history of heart ailments—which claimed his father, Jesse, and would eventually be the cause of Evan's death in 1989—seemed unconnected in those days to chowing down on a nutritious steak. And Law had his share of steak in 1960. The day after he won his 20th game, both the city's newspapers, the *Press* and the *Post-Gazette,* ran advertisements showing Law at the backyard grill, preparing dinner for his clan. Top-cut tailless porterhouse was on sale for $1.09 a pound.

Law was a leader of the club, but not *the* leader. "The driving force on our ball club was Don Hoak," Law contends. "If he didn't start a rally for us that year, he kept it going. One game late in the season he came up to me on the mound and said, 'If it doesn't look as if I'm hustling for you tonight, I'm doing the best I can. I went swimming last night and cut my foot on the ladder of the pool. I've got seven

Law was a pitchman for Tenderay steaks.
He turned down a chance to sell cigarettes.

stitches between my toes.' I don't know how he did it, but he played that whole game and then emptied the blood out of his shoe afterward." Hoak was, without debate, the fiercest competitor on the Pirates. His fighter's body lunged after every ground ball, regardless of the pain it caused him, and he routinely tried to stretch singles into doubles. He gave the Pirates a manly, intimidating presence.

Balanced with that was the cool, cerebral style of center

fielder Virdon. As the Bucs' leadoff hitter, Virdon was not expected to hit home runs, and he did not. But his more than 100 hits and solid .270 average meant he was on base often enough when Dick Groat came to bat. And Groat knew how to get him home.

Then disaster struck. On September 6, an errant pitch by Lou Burdette of the Braves shattered Groat's left wrist, and with it, seemingly, the hopes of the Pirates. Groat was not just the captain. He was the pace-keeper and playmaker, the cortex to Hoak's heart. Groat and Mazeroski had developed into the most productive double-play combination in the Major Leagues, and it seemed that without Number 24 in the lineup, the club was doomed.

But this was a year of magic, and magicians come in all shapes and sizes. John Richard Schofield broke in with the Cardinals in 1953 and came to the Pirates in 1958—where he was christened by announcer Bob Prince The Duck. Schofield, born in Springfield, Illinois, was 5–9 and 165, and seemed destined to be one of those players who barely dented the consciousness of the Major Leagues—a bench rider, a second stringer, an average utility player of whom the league has seen thousands.

Then Burdette lost control of a pitch. In less than a second, the Pirates' captain had a shattered paw, and the thin, young Illinoisan, who had never played more than 65 games in a Major League season, was put to the test.

Always an adept fielder, Ducky Schofield slotted into the

double-play combination with Maz as though he, not Groat, had invented it. In the last, pivotal month of the season, the switch-hitting shortstop batted .330 and, though there was no doubt that Groat would return to the lineup when his wrist healed, Schofield briefly became the talk of the town.

"I never really felt the pressure," he told me nearly 50 years later. "If you're scared, you're really in trouble. For some reason, that team, I think we knew we were going to win. We figured this was our year. I was always the kind of player who could go in and play for ten days and you wouldn't miss the guy that much. I was pleased to get to play. There were some nice guys on that team. I always knew I was good, and I was waiting for my chance to prove myself. Nobody wanted to see Groat get hurt, but when it happened, I was ready."

Although it seems that in those innocent days of the early '60s baseball was more a game for grown-up boys than the multibillion-dollar industry it is now, there was pressure on the Pirates, and every other Major League team, to perform. Some of the bench players' biggest contributions to the team were off the field. Bob Oldis, a third-string catcher, was the unofficial chairman of entertainment for one gaggle of Pirates. Now a scout for the Florida Marlins, Oldis recalls one time when he decided to enlarge the group. "Mazeroski was a very quiet guy," he told me. "We were in L.A., and Maz had been hitless for a couple of days, and he said to me, 'Hey, Bob, can I come out with you guys after the game tonight?' It was ElRoy Face, Fred Green, and Rocky Nelson and me. We went around together all the time. So Maz came out with us, and we went and had a few beers and a few laughs. It loosened Maz up. The next day he got two hits."

Vern Law might not have approved and certainly would not have experimented with Mazeroski's method of loosening up. But at that crucial moment in the pennant race, it seems likely he could have overlooked a few glasses of hops in favor of results.

There is a rhythm to winning. It comes first as a pleasant surprise, then becomes normal, then an expectation, finally a habit. The Pirates expected to win in 1960. The stray cats that Danny Murtaugh and General Manager Joe L. Brown assembled became a pack of panthers, exploiting opponents' mistakes and picking one another up.

The city felt the excitement and by early September, Pittsburgh was alight with optimism. Radio stations had begun playing a ditty by Joe Negri and Sy Bloom that over the course of the summer seeped into the collective Pittsburgh consciousness:

The Bucs are going all the way, all the way, all the way.

Yes, the Bucs are going all the way, all the way this year.

Beat 'em Bucs!

The song had been recorded by a group called Benny Benack and his Iron City Six and was popular with Pirate fans, if not all the Pirates themselves. Clemente, for one, was superstitious and believed that every time the group played

Courtesy Pittsburgh Pirates

Murtaugh got all the players, including Hoak, to dig deeper for wins.

inside Forbes Field, the Pirates lost. As a result, the Iron City Six and their front man were banished from the park.

Women such as my mother, who cared little intrinsically for baseball, and her friends would cart their irons, ironing boards, and wrinkled wash to one another's houses and perform the duties that most housewives did in those days, together, to the accompaniment of Bob Prince's voice on the radio, or, occasionally, to the television if the Pirates were on the road. Little League teams assigned their players the same numbers as the Pirates for the positions each kid played—the catcher was 6, the first baseman was 7, second base 9, shortstop 24, third base 12, left field 4, center 18, and in right, The Great One, Clemente, 21.

I played first base that year but wanted to wear 32 because it was Vern's number. The coach said no, so I drew that number on a piece of yellow material my mother allowed me to have and wore it inside my baseball uniform. Such was my and every kid's devotion to the Pirates as they marched along the path to what we thought we knew (but really only *hoped*) to be certain victory.

There were other things going on in the world that year, of course. But for all Pittsburghers knew or cared, they were taking place on another planet. Some, literally, were. In September 1960, President Dwight Eisenhower told the Russians he would work with them to ban the installation and use of weapons in outer space. Since the Soviets had launched *Sputnik,* an unmanned space probe, in 1957, and then put a dog named Laika into orbit a few months later (the dog died shortly after launch from stress and overheating), the American president was scrambling to get his nation into the game while simultaneously protecting the country against a doomsday scenario in which the technologically superior Russians could rain down death on the U.S. from space. Indeed, on September 24, 1960, a U.S. attempt to put an unmanned rocket in orbit around the moon failed. *Pioneer VI* burned to a crisp only a few minutes after takeoff, turning to ashes not just the craft and American dreams of equaling the Soviets, but also the $9 million invested in the project.

For his part, the Soviet leader, Nikita Khrushchev, was in New York to address the United Nations General Assembly. On September 21, New York police told the Russian delegation that Khrushchev would have to stay in his country's consulate rather than meet and talk with American citizens, as he had planned. The police, it seems, had discovered two plots to assassinate Khrushchev, one with a gun disguised as a camera, the other with a massive bomb. Khrushchev complied but groused that he felt as if he were being held under house arrest (as though that was not what he was doing to tens of millions of his countrymen). Later in the week, at the U.N. itself, Khrushchev objected to remarks made by British Prime Minister Harold Macmillan. The irate, red-faced Russian began pounding his desk and was soon joined by his lickspittle foreign minister, Andrey Gromyko. The display of undiplomatic manners confirmed the view of many Americans that the Soviets were untamed beasts who would have to be dealt with, sooner or later.

Khrushchev was not the most disruptive visitor to New York that week. Fidel Castro, Cuba's then-young dictator, flew with his comrades and cigars to New York only to have the U.S. government threaten to confiscate the plane to settle an unpaid sum owed by the Cuban government to an American advertising agency.

When Castro and the Cuban delegation were housed in a

rundown hotel in midtown Manhattan, he fumed for a few days before decamping for Harlem, then a neighborhood best known for poverty and crime. Castro said he felt more at home among Harlem's black residents, who he assumed also nurtured grievances against the U.S. government. The midtown hotel that Castro deserted complained that the Cubans had trashed their rooms, burning cigar holes in the carpets and furniture and strewing them with chicken feathers. The Cubans, it seemed, had done some home-style cooking at the hotel.

The hometown players weren't the only buccaneers on the front page of Pittsburgh's papers in September of that year. The *Post-Gazette* reported that "modern day pirates, armed with submachine guns and carbines, rowed silently along[side] the anchored freighter *Dona Luisa* in Manila Bay last night, held up the crew, and ransacked the ship."

And politics, which has since replaced baseball as the national sport, was also alive and well in 1960. Vice President Richard Nixon and U.S. Senator John F. Kennedy of Massachusetts were vying to succeed Ike. The Pittsburgh *Press* ran a front-page series called "The Great Debate," in which the two candidates were asked the same questions. Their answers were printed, side by side, on the two leftmost columns of the front page, allowing readers to decide for themselves who would make the best leader. The two were also preparing to debate each other live, on television on September 26, a face-off that would demonstrate, forever, the power of television to reach the electorate in a way newspapers never would again.

Politics were indeed on people's minds, but it was a gentler age for democracy when argument did not necessarily devolve into acrimony. An advice column in the *Press* by Molly Mayfield that week was headlined, "Politics, Love Don't Mix" and admonished a woman identified as Marsha that her boyfriend, a Republican, should keep his political opinions to himself when he had dinner with Marsha and her staunchly Democratic family. "Where did you ever see a dyed in the wool Republican, or Democrat, change his views because of love?" wrote Molly Mayfield. "Your best bet is to suggest that the subject of politics not come up when he visits your house."

The same newspaper that week made it official: Plastic dishes are fine to use at birthday parties, since they are unbreakable and easily washed. Next to that happy announcement was the sobering news that tax cheats were often turned in by those they least expected to turn on them—unhappy wives and girlfriends, presumably not at the same time. Estranged spouses, the article noted, were entitled to 10 percent of any additional funds the Internal Revenue Service collected as a result of their anonymous tips. Spiteful ex-girlfriends had to settle for the satisfaction of seeing their former lovers justly impoverished.

Richman's, a local Pittsburgh men's clothing store, offered a new innovation—a suit with two pairs of trousers, for

$39.95. A higher-tier tailoring company, Brooks Brothers, though it was headquartered in New York, ran advertisements in the Pittsburgh papers to exploit local sentiment (and sales): "Like everyone else in Pittsburgh, we have a bad case of pennant fever. We're proud of the Bucs and are rooting mightily for them to go all the way. We're proud, too, to be part of Pittsburgh at such an exciting moment. As one pacesetter to another, Good Luck, and let's take the World Series too." The company presumably amended that copy when it ran ads in the New York *Times*.

Perhaps the most talked-about, non-Pirates news that week, the event that touched the most hearts and brought a few tears, was the announcement that Ted Williams, The Splendid Splinter, and arguably the best pure hitter in baseball, would retire at the end of the season. The Red Sox's Number 9, the last man to hit .400 through a season, was a living legend in baseball and America. Williams would eventually return to baseball as a manager, but many thought the game would never again see his equal in the batter's box. All these things and more were going on in September 1960. But in Pittsburgh, the talk was of the Pirates and the nearly too-good-to-be-true prospect that tiny Pittsburgh, and its Mutt-and-Jeff baseball heroes, would face the mighty Yankees: Mantle, Maris, Berra, Kubek, Skowron, Richardson—names that had already earned a place in the pantheon of the game. Might they truly descend on Pittsburgh, armed only with the same lumber and leather that the town's top nine had at their disposal? How would the locals match up to these giants?

"On paper, the Yankees appear to have a wide edge over the Pirates in power," opined UPI sportswriter Fred Down. "But the vast reaches of Forbes Field, where four of the seven games are to be played, may prove the equalizer."

Encouraging words. The center field wall in Pittsburgh was, after all, 467 feet from home plate. But the Yankee bats had been known to send balls dizzying distances before.

Yankee fever may have been premature. Still, as the Bucs bore down on the National League pennant, their sense of destiny was underlined by the final games of the regular season. On September 23, in Milwaukee, the Pirates sent George Witt, a middling pitcher who was never happy as a Pirate, to the mound for only his tenth start of the season (Law had already won 20 games). Witt was outpitched by the Braves' Bob Buhl, who scattered five hits and came out the winner in a 2–1 squeaker.

Meanwhile, the Cardinals, in second place and the only team now truly challenging the Pirates, were on a hot streak. They swept a doubleheader against the Cubs in Chicago. The magic number for Pittsburgh remained at two—any combination of two wins by the Pirates or two losses by the Cardinals would give the Pirates the pennant. The Pirates fared no better the next day against Lou Burdette, losing 4–2. But as the Pirates made their grim way into the clubhouse, they heard welcome news: the Cardinals had lost to the

Cubs, 5–4. They had only to win one more or the Cardinals to lose again, and they would be the champions. "Tomorrow, we do it sure," enthused Roberto Clemente in his broken but brave English. "We be happy on the plane, I tell you."

The marvelously talented right fielder was proven right. The Pirates did nothing to help their own cause the next day. Playing in Milwaukee, they lost their third straight to the Braves, 4–2, with the Braves' future Hall of Famer, Warren Spahn, taking the tie game into the ninth before he was relieved by Ron Piche. Eddie Mathews homered in the bottom of the tenth to end the game. But it didn't matter. Because during the seventh inning of the game, word came that the Cardinals had lost to the Cubs, 5–0. By default, and despite losing, the Pirates were champions of the National League.

The end of their own game set off a celebration that the Pirates' players, coaches, sportswriters, and anyone else lucky enough to be admitted to the visitors' dressing room would long remember. Al Abrams, the *Post-Gazette* sports editor whose description of foot-deep pools of celebratory liquid in the Pirate clubhouse probably was not an exaggeration, decided three days later that things had not been so hedonistic. "To begin with, only two dozen bottles of champagne were set up for the affair," he wrote later in the week. "Half of them, possibly more, were poured over the heads of anybody silly enough to venture close to one of the players. I was among the silly so-and-sos," Abrams admitted.

Perhaps Abrams was trying to rewrite the history he

Courtesy Pittsburgh Pirates

*The Deacon and the Manager could afford to smile
as the season came to an end.*

himself had witnessed. A video of the visitors' dressing room
clearly shows more than 24 bottles of bubbly. That the
Pirates and their retinue were drinking after the pennant-
clincher is indisputable. How much they were drinking, who
drank more, and who, if anyone, was inebriated are different
questions that will never be answered. Nor, until now, has
the question of who is most responsible for the injury that
Vernon Law suffered on the bus outside County Stadium in
Milwaukee been squarely addressed.

Pittsburgh *Press* sportswriter Roy McHugh went some

way toward solving the mystery in a column, valedictory in tone, that he wrote on September 9, 1965, two years before Law retired from Major League Baseball. "There was nobody better than Law in 1960, his 20–9 year. But a good-natured catcher named Bob Oldis, playfully celebrating the capture of the pennant, yanked a shoe off Law's foot and because of the sprained ankle that resulted, Law had to change his delivery. It put a strain on his shoulder and though he won two games of the World Series, the muscles may have been torn even then. He is sure they were torn the next spring."

End of story, right? Now we know what happened aboard the bus. Now we know who caused Law the injury that damaged his body and quite possibly shortened his career.

Not exactly. No mystery that has endured for 50 years is ever quite so simply unraveled.

With pained and plain reluctance, Vernon Law told me what had happened to him, in response to repeated prodding from me as I was writing this book. Why was I bothering this man, my lifelong hero, to recount something he obviously wanted to let go? Part of it, of course, was to get to the truth. I wanted to know who to blame for the demise of my paragon. But there was something more to my dogged resolve. I needed to turn an emotional page in my own life, a page written forty-some years before, when I was a little boy asking my father why Vernon Law no longer pitched as well as he used to. My father—in those days a tower of strength and authority to me, as he is now, even as I myself cross the finish line of middle age—told me the story of what had happened to my hero.

We were, of all places, in Baltimore, where my father's aged mother was living with his unmarried sister and brother. My grandmother had been diagnosed with melancholia and had been taken by her son and daughter—my father's siblings—to Baltimore so she could be treated at Johns Hopkins. Occasionally, my mother, my father, and I would drive to Baltimore, where my grandmother would sit, inert, sometimes unable or unwilling to recognize her own son who had driven six hours from Pittsburgh to see her. Sometimes it was worse. "I know why you're here," she greeted him once. "You want to send me away again. You're no damn good." My father looked at her aghast, as afflicted by sadness as I had ever seen him.

Baltimore was a long way from Pittsburgh, far from all that I knew and loved, far from my Pirates. Baltimore didn't love the Pirates. It had its own team, the Orioles, and its own field, Memorial Stadium (in those days) that sat on the edge of Lake Montebello. During one of our trips to Baltimore, my father and I walked the circumference of the lake, and I aimed my chin toward the stadium on its far side and asked snidely, "Why would anyone root for *that* team?"

My father never went to college. After serving in World War II, he married my mother and began working at a newspaper in western Maryland as a proofreader. It was a

Courtesy Author

New to Pittsburgh, my parents strike a pose.

dead-end job, but his sense of self-worth had never been high, at least until he met Mom. He might never have emerged from the proofreader's pool in Cumberland, Maryland, if fate (and Mom) had not prodded him. By good fortune, he got a chance to try his hand at writing headlines, then going out to report on a story. He had crossed the invisible barrier from technical to editorial. He became a journalist.

Dad may have lacked self-esteem, but he knew enough

to recognize that Cumberland was not the big time. He would not consider himself successful until he was reporting big-time stories in a big city. And to my father, that confidence-deprived native of a small town in western Maryland, the big city he wanted to conquer was Pittsburgh, 102 miles and a world of importance away.

After five years on the Cumberland paper, my father had come to know some reporters at the Associated Press, the wire service that nearly all American newspapers (and a growing number of radio stations) used as the source for their national and foreign news. He knew what he wanted: He wanted to be a foreign correspondent, to report from far-away places with exotic names. Because he was a hard worker and a dedicated reporter, he finally got a chance to join the AP, as a reporter, in Pittsburgh, in 1950. My mother, from the same small Maryland town, had no desire to leave the place she knew and the family she loved. But she followed him because she loved him and because in the 1950s that is what wives did. My father never became a foreign correspondent because in 1953 his wife told him that they were expecting a child—me. And so he stayed where he was, to provide his son with a safe and secure childhood.

Over the course of his career in Pittsburgh, my father became the nation's leading reporter on labor unions and their efforts on behalf of working men and women. The Pittsburgh where I grew up, the Pittsburgh where until 1960 it seemed nothing interesting ever happened, the Pittsburgh

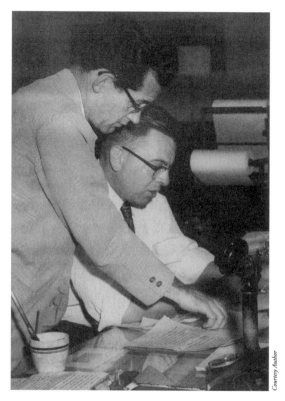

The chance he always wanted: at the Associated Press, Pittsburgh.
(Author's father is standing, left.)

I could not wait to get out of when I became a teenager—
this tired city of smoke and steel was, to my father, a land of
promise and professional advancement.

When he heard me denigrating Baltimore and its baseball team and its baseball team's stadium, my father knew he
had a little wisdom to impart. He usually began such missions by putting his hand on my neck as we walked. In his

other hand was often, as there was this day, a Camel cigarette.

"You know, old buddy," he said to me, "you love the Pirates and Forbes Field, I know. And that's fine. But not everyone lives in Pittsburgh. Somewhere nearby here, there's another little boy who's growing up in Baltimore, and he loves the Orioles, and he loves going to this stadium to see them play. Remember, old buddy, it's a big world."

That short lecture probably shaped my worldview as much as any I heard later on college campuses or from church pulpits or in great debates between scholars or politicians. It made me realize that I had a lot to learn, and do, and places to see and people to meet. It made me start to grow up.

I also asked my father that day about Vernon Law and why he could no longer get batters out with the grace and ease that he had in 1960, that most magical year. My father said: "When they won the pennant that year, some of the other players got a little out of control and they hurt him. They didn't mean to hurt him. They were being stupid. They hurt him because they were being stupid. And he forgave them."

"He forgave them? Why? I'd have punched them in the nose."

"He forgave them because he's a good man. Jesus told us to forgive each other for the things that hurt us, even bad things. There are a few things for you to learn here, old buddy. First, don't let yourself get out of control. Don't do stupid things. Nothing good comes from it. And, when someone does something bad to you, I want you to forgive him, too. Okay? Just like Vernon did." And I nodded my little boy's head and felt my father ruffle my hair with his hands, strong and smelling of tobacco, hands with which he caught the baseballs I threw to him, hands that had always been there to hold me when I needed—still need—his comfort, his support, his love.

The story of Vernon Law's willingness to forgive, as told me by my father, would stay with me all my life. It also allowed me to see who my real hero was—is—and why he always will be.

The thrill of cheering a sports team to victory is something unlike any other emotion. It is a mission for the fan, almost as much as for the players, to have that team win. Of course, the fans are powerless to affect the outcome, save for their enthusiasm, their faith in their idols, and their ability to generate noise. The relationship between player and fan is intense and sometimes soul-searing. But it is also a relationship with a fence or foul line to separate them.

Nothing separated me from my father that day in Baltimore, or any other day we were together. I was of him, and with him, and would succeed him. And his cheers for me, his support and wish for victory, were separated by no fence, no foul line. I entered the same profession in which he had made his living. I was a foreign correspondent, as he had

Courtesy Author

*With my father at Forbes Field, during the bad years.
It didn't matter if they lost.*

once hoped to be. I was successful and respected by most of my colleagues. My father's cheers for me, his love of me, had not been unrequited. Indeed, what he wished for me is what I became, and how many fathers can say that?

All that remained was to ferret out the truth of what had happened to the man who wore the uniform I so adored. And so, when I had the chance to coerce a first-person account from the victim of this sports tragedy, I could not resist. And here is what Law told me:

"To name names for the unfortunate horseplay really has no purpose at this time. I suppose many were to blame and not just one person. The person who twisted my foot has had enough disappointments in his own life. All of us were a close-knit bunch of players, and I believe all the players would lose a great deal of respect for me if this person was named. The players involved literally picked me up and tried ripping my shirt off, but because I resisted so, it might have been my fault as well.

"Bob Prince, our TV and radio announcer, probably was more of an instigator than anyone, as he was in front of me leading the pack on. There were about five or six of them, and it could have been any of them. Certainly Bob could have stopped the whole thing if he'd wanted to. There never were any hard feelings towards anyone for putting me through three years of misery. The important thing is, I was able to continue my career. I loved what I was doing and wanted to go out of the game on my own terms.

"The day the pennant was clinched in Milwaukee is like having your name carved in stone. All of us remember it as if it happened yesterday. The excitement was exhilarating and caused the adrenaline to flow as the game against Milwaukee drew closer. By the time the bus arrived at the ballpark, it was quite a different feeling that came over all of us. We knew what we had to do and what was ahead of us if we could etch out a win. This, for many of us, would prove to be a life-changing experience" (for no one more than Law).

"Every one was wishing each other luck and trying to get everyone up for the challenge. For those of us not playing that day, we were really pushing our players to be at their best and bring history back to Pittsburgh by getting to the World Series. During the game, as it moved along, I was up and down the bench as the hitters went up to hit, encouraging them and wishing them luck. I wasn't one to sit and be quiet and just hope things went well. I wanted to be involved any way I could in the game, and so I guess I was a designated cheerleader. Maybe I had too much energy and had to get rid of it the only way I knew how—by cheering and encouraging my teammates.

"A lot of us on that team were like that. We rooted for each other and wanted all to succeed, even those who didn't have major roles. We hoped when they were called upon, they'd come through with a big hit or play for us. Everyone on that team contributed in one way or another to our championship that year.

"It was in the seventh inning that word came down from our broadcasters, Bob Prince and Jim Woods, that the Cardinals, who were chasing us in the pennant race, had lost their game. We couldn't wait to get into the clubhouse and start the celebrating. We did share a few handshakes and hugs on the bench, but the celebrating wasn't complete until we got into the clubhouse. To me it was interesting to see grown men turn into little boys as they cut loose with the different ways they celebrated. Some poured champagne on each other between sips.

"I wasn't about to stay in the clubhouse any longer than

necessary, so my roommate, Smoky Burgess, another non-drinker, and I showered, dressed, and got out of there as quickly as we could.

"Most of the others came pretty soon after we did. I think most of them were anxious to get back to Pittsburgh. They were pretty lit up, loud and doing crazy things. So was Bob [Prince]. All of us had to get our suitcases off of the bus, get new shirts, ties, whatever. We practically had to undress right in the parking lot because there were guys that had had their shirts torn off and their ties cut off. They'd gotten into the trainer's bag and taken his scissors. When Bob and Jim Woods were onboard they had to get their share of the celebrating done, as they were as much of our team as anyone else. Both of them joined in cutting our ties, ripping shirts off, and all the other stuff. Bob grabbed my shirt and popped the buttons right off of it. Then he put his hands on my underwear, and I said, 'I wish you wouldn't do that.' And he said, 'Ohhh,—' He recognized what it was, he knew a bit about my church and what we believe, the undergarment we wear and what it means to us. But by then, it was too late, the damage had been done. So yes, it's true, he was the one more than any other who was responsible for the things that happened to me.

"I'm going to write a bit more concerning the act of forgiveness as all of us, during our lifetimes, will have people who will take advantage of us and who may even offend us, even try to hurt us or our family. Indeed there are people who are downright ornery and go through life trying to make trouble for others. In my case I've had people take advantage of my being a Major League player. One person I ran across wanted to use my influence and good name for whatever good it may have been to advance a special cause he was promoting. There were others also who cost me a good deal of money getting me involved in a business that showed good promise but went south because he used much of the funds for his self-interest and personal use. I won't belabor this as all of us run into these kinds of situations during our lifetimes, and sometimes we have to learn some hard lessons.

"Now, what to do with these people? Should we forget and forgive or do we try to get even, destroy their lives, or do we let the Lord judge these people and their actions? We know in the scriptures it says to all of us, 'Wherefore, I say unto you, that ye ought to forgive one another.' A common error is the idea that the offender must apologize and humble himself to the dust before he is forgiven. I agree the offender should apologize, but the offended one must also forgive the offender regardless of the attitude of the other. There are people who get satisfaction from seeing the other person on his knees and groveling in the dust. But that is not what the Savior or the gospel teaches.

"The best advice I've received and have given to others, if there are misunderstandings, is to clear them up, forgive and forget, don't let old or new grievances become cancers to your souls and destroy your lives with malice and hatred. If you want peace in your lives, do as it says in Matthew 6:14–15, 'For if ye forgive men their trespasses, your heavenly Father will also forgive you: But if ye forgive not men their trespasses, neither will your Father forgive your trespasses.'

"Even the Savior on the cross said, 'Father, forgive them; for they know not what they do.' Are we above the Savior? I say not! We know the Lord Jesus Christ suffered every indignity and yet spoke no word of condemnation. So what manner of men ought we to be? His answer to us is 'Even as I am.' If we fail to forgive those who trespass against us, we are told, we stand condemned before the Lord and in us is the greater sin. It is also stated, 'I, the Lord, will forgive whom I will forgive, but of you it is required to forgive all men.'

"This forgiveness is not just lip service, which to me doesn't show real forgiveness. This has to be done in a heartfelt way. Forgiveness also means forgetting. I remember the story of a woman who had a quarrel with someone and then decided to reconcile. She even went to this person and expressed forgiveness, but afterward remarked, 'I will forgive you, but I have a memory like an elephant and I'll never forget!' So her act of forgiveness was valueless and void. All of us should lead a life that shows we are kind, merciful, and forgiving and leave to the Lord the judgment of those who trespass or hurt us in any way. If we are harsh, we should not expect other than harshness. If we are merciful with those who injure us, He will be merciful with us in our errors. If we are unforgiving, He will leave us weltering in our own sins.

"The Lord can and will judge men by their thoughts as well as by what they say and do, for He knows even the intent of their hearts, but this is not true of us as humans. We hear what people say, we see what they do, but being unable to discern what they think or intend, we will most assuredly judge wrongfully if we try to understand their meaning and motive behind their actions.

"Now back to Milwaukee and what happened to me. Indeed I did get hurt, my career was in jeopardy, and I lost three good years that cost me a good deal of money. Even more maybe, just maybe, it cost me a chance of getting recognition at Cooperstown. I really was blessed to just be able to play again the game I loved and to once again be able to compete against some of the greatest players that ever played the game. For that blessing, I'll ever be grateful."

Though it stunned me initially to learn it, it should have come as no surprise that Bob Prince, the voice of the Pirates, had played a major role in the hijinks. As devoted to the club and its players (and fans) as he was, Prince had a wild side. In his earliest days as a sportscaster, Prince accused a Pittsburgh-born prizefighter, Billy Conn, of being afraid of tough opponents. Conn cornered Prince and threatened to thrash him. In later years, when he was boarding a plane with the team for San Francisco, an attendant offered to relieve him of the bulky reel-to-reel tape recorder he was carrying. Prince declined, saying, "I handle this thing more carefully than a bomb." Even twenty-five years before 9/11, that remark got Prince removed

Courtesy Pittsburgh Pirates

"And you can kiss it good-bye!" Bob Prince at work.

from the flight. If there was horseplay going on in the Pirates'
bus, Prince figured to be somewhere near the saddle.

None of which takes away from Prince's central and
beloved role as the Pirates'—and Pittsburgh's—cheerleader-
in-chief. Prince believed in rooting for the home team. When
the Pirates won, especially with one of their many come-
from-behind victories in 1960, it was Prince who would
crow his trademark line, "We had 'em aaaaaaallllll the way!"

Prince also contributed time and money to numerous charities around Pittsburgh, none more so than Children's Hospital, which was also one of Vernon Law's favorite destinations for celebrity appearances. The Pirates' broadcaster was a sure show at charity golf tournaments and had a special affinity for the Allegheny Valley School, a nonprofit organization that he cofounded to serve mentally disabled children. But Prince was always controversial with his bosses. He criticized Pirate trades on the air, made fun of advertisers who were brought into his broadcast booth to listen to him announce the games, and was constantly making up new nicknames for new players, whether they liked them or not. His style of calling games, one-sided and unabashedly pro-Pirate, had its critics. And truth be told, when he worked the 1960 World Series on NBC television with Mel Allen, the Yankees' equally prominent radio voice, Prince sounded like a rube from the hinterlands in comparison. He could not openly root for the Bucs as he wanted to and as a result was sometimes tongue-tied. But when, in 1975, the Pirates' advertisers convinced Westinghouse Broadcasting, which owned the Pirates' flagship station, KDKA, to fire Prince and his sidekick Nellie King (the relief pitcher who was sitting with Law during the one game from which Vern was ejected), there was a fan revolt. Boycotts of Pirates' sponsors were planned, and Prince fans demonstrated in the streets. But the power of a corporation determined to make a change rarely succumbs to public opinion. Prince and King were out.

The bard of Pittsburgh found other work; he was too talented not to. But Prince's new employer was the Houston Astros, a club he regarded as inferior to the Pirates and their hometown a world away from the city he loved and that loved him back. Just a year later, Prince moved from calling Houston's games to ABC where he, Warner Wolf, and Bob Uecker did tag-team broadcasts of *Monday Night Baseball*. Unable to warm to or root for any particular team, and constricted by Wolf's and Uecker's own brand of humor, Prince found himself the odd man out.

Wolf, however, thought Prince was charming. "He knew the game backwards and forwards," Wolf told me. "He had a great radio voice. I had never met him before until 1976. We'd each do three innings of the *Game of the Week*. I was really a novice compared to those guys. But Prince had done the Pirate games forever, and Uecker had done the Brewers' games. The style, though, didn't work for Prince. On radio, you're your own man, but in TV you have a producer talking in your ear. That interrupted him and broke his train of thought."

Wolf also recalled: "One of the Monday night games, we went to Pittsburgh. Now Prince had been fired by KDKA. It was my turn to do the three innings. And during those three innings, the Pirates put up on the scoreboard that Bob Prince was here doing the game for *Monday Night Baseball*. Well, 20,000 fans stood up and started applauding Prince during the game. They had to interrupt the game. That was the only time I'd ever seen a game suspended because fans were applauding an announcer."

Always a heavy smoker, Prince died in 1985 of cancer, but his memory lives on in Pittsburgh. He was, and to those who remember the 1960 championship season, will always be, The Voice of the Pirates. He had us, aaaaaaalllllll the way!

Prince's daughter, Nancy Thomas, who lives in the suburbs of Pittsburgh, is intensely proud of her father. It was not always so. "When I was a little girl, everyone knew my father. He was the most famous man in Pittsburgh. And everywhere we went, people would be talking to him, saying, 'Hey, Bob,' or 'Go get 'em, Gunner,' and it was incredibly intimidating. I was very shy as a young girl and so I figured if I didn't learn anything about the sport that my father was involved in, no one would bother me. So I didn't learn about baseball until long after Dad died."

She did not, however, fail to learn about her father and his legend in the Steel City. Bob Prince was one of the most in-demand after-dinner speakers in Pennsylvania in those days of his glory. Often, after speaking, he would read a poem that he had written—Prince wrote, but did not publish, many poems—to inspire his audience. Nancy sent this one to me:

> The thing that makes a champion is obvious enuff
> It isn't any mystic prestidigitator's stuff
> It's nothing more than giving to whatever be the chore
> The power that is in you and a small scintilla more.

There isn't any wizardry, it's not a magic gift
It's merely lifting honestly the load you have to lift
Or in the game you're playing, it's using all your store
Of gut and nerve and energy and just a trifle more.

  The thing that makes a champion is simple, plain,
    and clear
It's never being almost, just about, or pretty near
It's summoning the utmost from your spirit's inner
  core
And giving every bit of it and then just a little more.

That little more, how much it is, as deep and wide
  and far
As that enormous emptiness from dunghill to a star
It's the gourd between the earthbound and the eagles
  as they soar
The champions who give their best, and ONE IOTA
MORE.

So how to assess Prince's saintlike status in Pittsburgh against the cold fact that he, more than anyone, was responsible for Vernon Law's injury? Law himself never discussed the incident with Prince again. And he forgave him instantly. In later years, he would encounter Prince in planes when the Pirates were flying to and from away games, and Prince would offer recommendations on Western novels for Law to read. "Don't read this one, Deacon, it's not for you," Law would remember Prince telling him. "Little too much cow-girl action, if you get my drift." Bob Prince was a good man who, like all of us, occasionally made mistakes.

By overcompensating for the injury to his ankle, Law changed his pitching motion in a way that strained and eventually tore his rotator cuff and left him unable to pitch with the force and accuracy he had once taken for granted. For his part, Law put the incident behind him, though it is apparent from his discussions with me that he still—fifty years later—wondered whether, if he had not been injured, he might have been a candidate for the Hall of Fame. The signs, at least as compiled by baseball statisticians like Bill James, are not encouraging. Law, injured as a result of the September 25 foolishness on the team bus, was never the same pitcher. In his next start, on September 30, against Milwaukee at Forbes Field, he was lit up in a 13–2 drubbing.

The difference was clear: He was favoring his ankle. "With me, I pitched as much with my lower body as I did my upper. Normally, I'd drive off the mound with the back foot and stride right out there. My theory was the closer you could release the ball to home plate the faster it's going to get there." Deprived of the ability to push off full force, he resorted to falling off the mound and trying to make up the difference in arm speed.

The injury also played a key role in Murtaugh's decision to lift Law from Game 7 of the World Series while the Pirates were ahead. Certainly, he never again won 20 games in a season as he did in 1960. The closest he came was in 1965, when he went 17–9 and was named Comeback Player of the Year. Two years later, he knew he was washed up. He had compiled a 17-year career in the Majors (including the two spent in military service). His record was 162–147, a winning percentage of .524, and a lifetime ERA of 3.77. And, given the circumstances in which the Pirates found themselves before and after 1960, these are honorable numbers. But do they rate him a plaque in Cooperstown?

By comparison, Robin Roberts, who broke in to the Majors two years before Law and retired a year ahead of him, in 1966, was inducted into the Hall in 1976. Roberts pitched for the Philadelphia Phillies from 1948 to 1961, and for Baltimore, Houston, and the Chicago Cubs for the balance of his career. He pitched two World Series games against the New York Yankees in 1950, and lost one of them. His career record was 286–245 (41 more wins than losses as opposed to Law's 15-game margin); his ERA was 3.41.

Another contemporary of Law's, Lou Burdette, whose appearance and style nearly mirrored The Deacon's, played during the same 17 years as Law (Burdette did not serve in the armed services while he played in the Majors) and finished with a career record of 203–144, a winning percentage of .585 and an ERA of 3.66. Burdette, while an outstanding pitcher, who pitched in a total of six World Series games for the Milwaukee Braves against the Yankees, was never a serious candidate for the Hall.

Let's assume that Law had been healthy after the 1960 season and that he had won 20 games in each of his seven remaining seasons with the Pirates (though the rest of the club was not the same as it had been). Instead of the 60 games that Law won from 1960 through 1967, let's assume he won 140 more, for a total of 242, and that he lost the same number as he really did, 147. That would put his winning percentage at a highly desirable .622—if he had been healthy and if he hadn't lost any more than he actually did. There is, of course, no way to guess what a healthy Law's ERA would have been. Those kinds of numbers would have put him in the realm of Juan Marichal, the San Francisco Giants' Hall of Fame right-hander, whose career record was similar, 243–142 over 16 years.

Speculation, of course, is pointless. Law was the ace of the Pirates staff in 1960, a premier pitcher who spent the last seven years of his career trying to match the glory that had been his and his club's. As Law and the Pirates prepared to play the Series against the Yankees, they had no idea that they had already changed Pittsburgh, and Pittsburghers, in a way that would distinguish it for generations to come. He has forgiven those who caused him suffering. And, for what little it matters, I have also kissed it good-bye.

Ninth Inning

"Believe in yourself and what others think won't matter."
—*Theodore Roosevelt*
(From Vernon Law's *Words to Live By*)

THE CITY FOUNDED AS A FORT to safeguard two rivers so that they could converge into a third; the city that allowed its inhabitants to choke on soot and smoke for decades so those same people could afford to feed their children, who would also choke on smoke; the city that barely survived a flood in 1936 that filled its streets with water and waste; the city that watched as its downtown was torn down, then rebuilt, in a renaissance as determined if not as finely detailed as anything in Italy; this city finally had reason to celebrate. The Bucs were back in town.

The Pirates learned that they had clinched the National League pennant at 4:43 P.M. Eastern time on Sunday, September 25. Less than six hours later, at 10:25 P.M., the Pirates' charter plane, a United Airlines four-engine propeller craft, touched down at Greater Pittsburgh Airport in Moon Township, 16 miles west of the Golden Triangle. This,

remember, was late on a Sunday night, the night before the
workweek began anew, when men would have to let the
weekend's momentous events fade, and return to their offices, their plants, their trucks, their real lives.

Pittsburghers were having none of it.

By the time the aircraft had finished taxiing, the players
inside were aware that their day was a long way from being
done. Although radio and television newscasts told
Pittsburghers who wanted to celebrate to gather in the downtown area, some 4,500 were at the airport to be among the
first to get a glimpse of the National League's conquerors. A
bus awaited the players who climbed, stiff and some still
sloshed, off the UAL plane. Forty convertible limousines had
been requisitioned to carry them downtown in style.

As might be expected at that hour of the night, after a
plane ride, on a Sunday, few of the Pirates were wearing ties.
Front-page pictures that appeared in the Pittsburgh newspapers the next day show the emotion on the men's faces.
Craggy-faced Murtaugh, who might not change expressions
for a whole game, unless it was to spit out his tobacco,
planted a passionate kiss on his wife, Kate's, mouth. Groat,
the captain, raised his right hand in acknowledgment of the
adulation. He would soon be back in the batting cage, and
pronounce himself ready for the Yankees. Vern flashed a V
with his right hand from the open-top car in which he and
VaNita rode.

*September 25, 1960. The V could have stood for Vern,
VaNita, or any of their children. Behind Law's smile, the ankle
that had been twisted hours earlier was hurting.*

As the celebratory motorcade made its way east along the
Parkway, cars pulled to the side of the road and honked their
horns in tribute to the passing celebrities. It was unlike anything that had happened before, a celebration more spontaneous and joy filled even than the V-E Day and V-J Day
tumult of 1945. It seemed as if the deadly haze of boredom
and ennui that had settled over Pittsburgh for so long had

been lifted in the middle of the night. This was Pittsburgh, the place to be.

The Mount Lebanon High School marching band, complete with its 70-girl dance corps, the Rockettes, had been mobilized and sent to Gateway Center. So had the Wilkinsburg Starlet Drum and Bugle Corps and the musical unit of the National Guard. Volunteer fire units from the suburbs raced into town, lights flashing, not to douse a fire but to add to the extravaganza. Whole Little League teams were assembled, in uniform, to see their grown-up role models. Everyone wanted to show the Pirates how much they meant to Pittsburgh. The city's skyscrapers came into view and, for the first time anyone could remember, the lights in the U.S. Steel building's top floor had been arranged to spell out *BUCS*. "You see those words in the building lights," said Charles Levey, vice president of Local 29 of the Building Service Employees Union. "Well, they reflect our membership's feeling. This team has captured the imagination of everyone, and that includes the little charwoman, too."

Some politicians couldn't wait to link their name to the new league champions. David Lawrence, who had ridden the success of the downtown renaissance project as mayor of Pittsburgh to the governor's mansion, yet remained a Pittsburgher, said, aptly: "This victory dulls the memory of more than three decades of disappointment for the Pirates and loyal Pittsburgh fans."

It was just as well Lawrence released his statement on

David Lawrence, architect of Pittsburgh's renaissance, throws out the ceremonial first pitch.

paper. No one could have heard him had he tried to give a speech. The cacophony of car horns rendered Pittsburgh a quiet-free zone, nearly as soon as the Cardinals failed to score in the ninth, and continued deep into the blackening night. In Gateway Center, Joe Morrone's guitar band played "Take Me Out to the Ball Game." The Clan Douglas bagpipers wheezed out "Blue Bonnets over the Border," for whatever reason. Long after the Pirates themselves had been cheered and idolized and finally allowed to go home to their families and their beds, Pittsburgh roared on. This was a night unlike any other night. And no one in Pittsburgh wanted it to end.

Mornings after are often terrible things, a turbulent, tardy discovery of the hiccups that follow the night-before's evanescence. Pittsburgh had nine days to get ready—"red up," as Pittsburghers say—for the World Series that would open at Forbes Field on October 5. By 7 A.M. the day after the parade, the streets had been cleared of the mountain of confetti, litter, and other refuse that the revelers left behind. Frank Ambrose, the superintendent of the bureau of highways and sewers, had realized what 100,000 celebrants would do to the usually spic-and-span streets and told all his employees to be prepared to work all night.

Unlike New York, which had won ten pennants in the previous dozen years, Pittsburgh was unaccustomed to hosting baseball's high mass. Forbes Field itself underwent a good bit of hasty repair, even as the Pirates finished out their regular season. Who would get to see the Pirates and Yankees? Tickets to a potential World Series had been offered weeks in advance, with 130,000 applications pouring through the mail. Only about one in sixteen applications would be honored, so great was the demand. Lucky winners of tickets (priced from $3 for bleachers to $11 for box seats to mark the momentousness of the occasion) received long brown envelopes by return mail with their tickets inside. Less

Bing Crosby made good on his pledge to bring Vern's mother to Pittsburgh if her son pitched the Pirates into the World Series. She and Vern's stepfather, Leo Kelley, attended the opener.

fortunate applicants got their own envelope returned to them with a red stamped hand pointing to their return address and the words "Return to Writer: Sold Out." Originally, the Pirates had planned to open each application and respond individually. When the volume of incoming requests outstripped their wildest dreams and the post office explained that the club could return unopened mail without paying postage, the team's plans for a courteous, personal response went by the wayside.

Even the fortunate ones who could get tickets faced

logistical problems. Forbes Field was located in the Oakland section of Pittsburgh, a three-mile ride up the Boulevard of the Allies from downtown. To handle the expected throngs, Pittsburgh Railways Co., which ran the city's buses, put extra vehicles on call. And People's Cab and Yellow Cab hired part-time drivers. At $1.50 a ride, each way, the companies figured to profit handsomely from the games.

So did owners of the parking lots that dotted the streets around Forbes Field. The word *gouging* was quickly added to Pittsburghers' vocabularies when they saw the signs that had sprung up overnight. "Day Parking: 75 cents. Special Events: $5," declared one on Bouquet Street, near the park. Edwin Klein, who ran a parking lot at 3525 Forbes Street, jacked his rates from $1 to $5 and didn't take any guff about why. "We sit out here all summer with twenty cars on the lot all day, but we pay $11,000 a year rent," he snorted.

Because there were so many restaurants and soda fountains around the park, purveyors had to be careful how much they jacked up food prices and keep an eye on the competition. Hot dogs sold for 25 cents. Hamburgers and kielbasa sandwiches were a dime more. A plate of soup: 20 cents. If the Pirates were good for Pittsburgh, they were a tonic for Pittsburgh businesses.

These days, the run-up to the World Series features constant speculation on sports channels, online, and in newspapers. What matchup will favor which team? Does home field advantage matter? In 1960, it took the local papers

Restaurants near the ballpark jacked up prices for the Series.
No one complained.

exactly five days to push the Pirates off the front page. The *Post-Gazette* headlined Khrushchev's misbehavior at the U.N. and the actress Brigitte Bardot's recovery from a suicide attempt. The sports pages, though, were replete with details, most designed to keep up the spirits of Pirate fans. "Stengel respects Pirates," said one headline, followed by the shaky assurance, "Yanks Can't Match Their Defense." Matchups of the likely lineups bore out the claim. The Pirates had a better overall fielding average.

Power, however, was something else. This was one of the finest Yankee teams ever to take the field: the incomparable Mickey Mantle in center; Roger Maris (who a year later would make asterisked baseball history with his 61 home runs); the always underestimated Yogi Berra trading off catching duties with Elston Howard, who had injured his finger during the regular season; the aptly nicknamed Bill "Moose" Skowron at first base, always a threat to flick a pitch into the stands; and the middle infield duo of diminutive Bobby Richardson and agile Tony Kubek, a double-play combo to rival the Pirates' own.

The Series began in Pittsburgh. If anyone wondered who the favorites to win were, they had only to look at who (or what) was supporting the Pirates. Outside Forbes Field on Opening Day, a young man in a red jacket led a jackass along Bouquet Street. The burro was wearing a straw hat with its ears sticking through two cut-out holes. A sign on the hat said, "Beat 'Em Bucs," and cardboard panels on both the beast's flanks read, "Spank the Yanks."

With the commissioner of baseball, Ford Frick, in the stands, and both league presidents wagering the customary barter bet, the atmospherics were all in place. Forbes Field, which seated 35,000, had been getting its share of sellouts as the Bucs bore down on the pennant, but no one could remember the old park being as full as it was on this

Read all about it. His ankle in a whirlpool, Law read the newspaper speculation that his injury would keep him from pitching the Series opener. That wasn't going to happen.

Wednesday. In fact, 36,676 souls had jammed their way in, not counting the "knothole gang" of kids and adults who stared, one-eyed, at the proceedings through gaps and holes in the outfield fences.

Unlike the season's opening day, there was no debate about who would start for the Pirates. Law was the club's only 20-game winner that year. Moreover, his style of controlled power and deception played well against the Yankee lineup. Prior to the game, Law spent hours with his ankle in a whirlpool, hoping to ease the pain. "Yeah, we knew Law sprained his ankle when we clinched the pennant," said Bob Oldis, who had been one of the players grabbing at the pitcher on the bus, egged on by Prince. "But we knew he would take that mound with no excuses. He was a real gamer, and he showed it."

Casey Stengel, for reasons that are still debated among Yankee historians, chose to go with Art Ditmar, a right-hander with good stuff and 15 wins. But why not start with the Yankee ace, Whitey Ford? Casey never explained himself to fans' satisfaction.

Law's first pitch to Tony Kubek was a ball, and the Series was under way. On the second pitch, Kubek rapped a ground ball sharply down the third-base line. It hit the bag and spun high in the air, leaving Don Hoak with nothing to do but grab it as it returned to earth. The leadoff batter was on. The auguries for this series in which one team was so obviously superior—on paper, anyway—were terrible for the home team. Hector Lopez, the second batter, tried to bunt but missed. On Law's next pitch, Lopez sent a shrieking ground ball under the pitcher's outstretched glove. A good thing, for Bill Mazeroski was there to grab it, tag out the sliding Kubek, and throw to Dick Stuart to complete the double play. Law had a satisfied look on his face as he watched the 4–4–3 play.

He knew he was facing Roger Maris next. Better to do so with the bases empty.

And that proved to be the case. After taking a ball and swinging at a high fastball, Maris connected with the third pitch and sent the ball well into the right-field stands. There was never any doubt that it was gone. Pirate fans looked at each other and said, or thought, *what did you expect?* But Law got out of the inning without further damage, and the Pirates came to bat.

It was not that Bill Virdon was a great hitter. But he had judgment, precision, and the calm required of a leadoff hitter. Ditmar never zeroed in on the plate that inning. Virdon walked to lead things off, then stole second on the first pitch to Groat. Yogi Berra, always underestimated as a catcher, came up with the pitch like a cat and fired it to second base where Bobby Richardson . . . was nowhere to be found. The ball sailed into center field, and Virdon, who had seen what was going to happen, never hesitated. He took off for third and slid in, unnecessarily. The Pirates were 90 feet from scoring, with no one out.

Groat knew how to spray the ball and he did so on the next pitch, whacking a double into right field that Maris had to play off the wall. Fans, some in sunglasses, almost all of them smoking either cigarettes or cigars, rose up as one to cheer. The Pirates could, after all, score against the killing machine from the Bronx. Stengel could sense that Ditmar would not have a good day. Virdon had hardly crossed home plate with the Pirates' first run before Casey was calling for his bullpen to start warming up, then limping to the mound, trying to settle his starter and buy some time. Bob Skinner, the lanky left fielder with a sweet swing that made him a fan favorite in Pittsburgh, waited only one pitch to send a single up the middle, scoring Groat from second. Stuart struck out, and then The Great One, Roberto Clemente, stepped to the plate. Watching Clemente on tape now—the arrogant way he made himself at home in the batter's box, the challenge on his face as he jerked his chin up at the pitcher as if to say, *put it right here, see what I do*—still causes me to wonder what, with his prodigious abilities, he might have done if he had lived longer.

Sensing that the 35-year-old Yogi's arm was not what it had once been, Skinner streaked for second on the first pitch. Berra's throw was high and wide, and Skinner stood at second, his hands on his skinny hips, then nodded to Clemente. Whatever signal passed between them worked because Clemente shot a two-bouncer right over second, with Skinner already in motion. Skinner lanked all the way home. The Pirates had a 3–1 lead, and it was only the first inning.

Stengel came back out now to lift Ditmar and bring in Jim Coates, who ended the rally. But the damage was done, and more importantly, the psychological onus of facing the mighty Yankees was broken. The Yankees got back into it in the second. With one out, Berra singled and moved to second on another hit. Then Bobby Richardson slapped the ball into left. Berra thought it would drop and began chugging to third. He had underestimated Bob Skinner's speed. The left fielder gloved the ball and zipped a throw to second that Maz caught on the fly, doubling Berra and ending the threat.

The Pirates went quietly in the second, and though the Yankees scored their second run in the third, Virdon's over-the-shoulder catch of a Yogi Berra drive—in which the Pirate center fielder nearly collided with Clemente—saved Law from further trouble. In the Pirates' fourth, a walk to Hoak brought up Bill Mazeroski. Coates got one strike past him, but his second pitch was too good, and Maz—foreshadowing the most famous hit of his or any Pirate's career—launched a 400-foot home run over the left-field scoreboard and into Schenley Park.

Though his ankle was bothering him (he was already, unknowingly, damaging his shoulder with an altered delivery to favor that leg), Law was dominant for seven innings, allowing only the two runs. In the sixth he struck out Mickey Mantle and Moose Skowron, then made his way gingerly off the mound. In the eighth, Law gave up a single to Hector Lopez and another to Maris. Murtaugh noticed Law favoring the ankle and with his trademark "who, me hurry?" trudge to the mound, pulled the starter for ElRoy Face. As Law walked to the dugout, the cheering crowd could not miss his uneven walk. His ankle was killing him. Face shut the Yankees down, getting Law off the hook. In the ninth, with Richardson on first, pinch hitter Elston Howard lofted a Face fastball the opposite way and into the right-field stands. With the lead cut to 6–4, Face went into his emergency routine of all forkballs, all the time. With one out, Tony Kubek scratched a hit up the middle, but Face induced Lopez to ground to Mazeroski. He flipped to Groat who tossed to Stuart to complete the double play and the game.

So Pittsburgh learned the Yankees could be beaten, and out-powered at that. Law's gutty performance was noted; the extent of his injury was not. Typically, in his memoir, he minimizes his own role in the win and credits "the other guys" on his team with earning it.

The next day, Thursday, October 6, was a different story. The potent Yankees, who everyone had expected, finally turned up that day to face hard-luck starter Bob Friend. Even the weather gods tried to tell Pittsburgh what was coming. A steady rain through the morning had fans in their seats under umbrellas ("bumbershoots" as Pittsburghers liked to misname them), but the sky cleared enough by game time to start on schedule. The Yankees scored twice in the third and again in the fourth, chasing Friend, before the Pirates got on the board. But the day belonged to the Yankees, especially Mickey Mantle, who hammered a two-run homer in the fifth off reliever Fred Green, making it 5–1. It was Mantle's twelfth Series home run, moving him past Duke Snider for the all-time lead in that revered category. Elston Howard led off the sixth with a towering triple to the 436-foot mark in right-center field that Virdon chased until he ran into the

After winning Game 1 of the Series,
Law came home to a neighborhood surprise party.

wall. It was a spot Virdon would revisit later in the game. Clemente retrieved the ball, but Howard was safely on third and not inclined to challenge the right fielder's already legendary arm. Bobby Richardson then doubled in Howard. That was all for Green, who Murtaugh lifted for Clem Labine.

A former Dodger when the club was in Brooklyn, Labine had faced the Yankees in the 1955 and 1956 Series. He promptly gave up a single to Berra. Skowron kept the slaughter going with another hit. By the time Murtaugh lifted

Labine for George Witt, the Yankees had a 12–1 blowout going. And still they were not finished. With left-hander Joe Gibbon (a future Pirate starter) on in relief, Mantle, batting from the right side of the plate, uncorked a tremendous drive to right center. Virdon was standing just to the right of the 436-foot mark when the ball sailed above him. It was, up until then, the longest recorded home run by a right-handed hitter in Forbes Field. With one more run tacked on, the Yankees had a 16–1 lead. Turley, the starter, had allowed 13 Pirate hits, but only one run in 8⅓ innings. The Pirates scored twice in the ninth, and Stengel brought in Bobby Shantz, who had made 46 relief appearances during the season. On his first pitch, Don Hoak tapped a comeback ground ball to the mound. Fielding the ball, Shantz whirled around and started a double play that ended the contest. The Game 2 crowd of 37,308 filed out, for the most part disappointed, but also a bit terrified.

This was the kind of merciless domination the Yankees had been expected to demonstrate. The quirky Pirate victory in Game 1 was put off to Opening Day jitters, something odd in the much-reviled Pittsburgh air. The Yankees would surely take care of business in the Bronx and dispose of these pesky Pirates in the sanctified confines of Yankee Stadium.

There was nothing new to the Yankees about hosting World Series games. During Stengel's twelve years at the helm, the Yankees had won ten AL pennants. That the championship of baseball was routinely played in the Bronx,

Game 2: The Yankees' relentless bats finally came alive.

however, did not dampen fan enthusiasm. The House That Ruth Built was bulging with 70,000 fans (the center-field bleachers were later closed off and draped in black to create the so-called "batter's eye" so the hitter can see the ball better) and at long last—well overdue, many thought—the Yankees were starting their ace, the chairman of the board, Whitey Ford. For years afterward, Stengel would be pestered with questions about why he started Ditmar in Game 1 instead of Ford. The future Hall of Famer had last started on September 28, though he had pitched two innings of relief on October 2, more as a tune-up than out of necessity.

Casey answered the question inconsistently, sometimes arguing that he never expected a seven-game series, sometimes claiming vaguely that Ford wasn't ready to start Game 1.

Whitey was more than ready for Game 3 and so were his teammates. After Ted Williams—whose retirement as a player had overshadowed the Pirates' clinching of the pennant on September 25—threw out the ceremonial first ball, the Pirates went down in order in the first. Then the Bronx Bombers resumed the slaughter they had started in Pittsburgh. The Pirates' starter, Wilmer "Vinegar Bend" Mizell (the nickname recalled the town in Alabama where he had grown up) looked as though he was pitching with his eyes closed. The Yankees scored six runs in the first, including a grand slam by Richardson, only the seventh in Series history, chasing Mizell before he could get two outs. The rout had recommenced. Mantle hit his 14th Series homer, over the 402-foot mark in left field. Ford took a no-hitter into the fourth before Virdon got a double, but no Pirate would cross home safely that day. The final score: 10–0. Ford went the distance, gave up only four hits, and struck out three in as dominating a performance as Yankee fans could have hoped for—and which they fully expected.

The Pirates were facing extinction. Two games, 26 runs. Two consecutive games in which the starter couldn't get out of the first inning. The persistent thwack of bats by Maris, Mantle, Richardson, Skowron. In response, the Pirates were batting a collective .241 against Yankee pitching. A third loss would put the Series out of reach. Murtaugh, the chaw-chewer, the sage silent one, the manager who got his way by getting others to do what he wanted anyway, was faced with a crucial choice. Should he pitch Law on three days' rest, hoping his gimpy ankle would hold up? What Murtaugh needed was a low-scoring game, so that the Pirates' skimpy offense would stand a chance against Ralph Terry. Murtaugh knew that Law was throwing from a different angle, more three quarters than the classic overhand motion that had characterized his career. The Pirates manager may even have realized that the overcompensation could not be good for Law's shoulder. If he did, and if he allowed Law to throw on short rest anyway, who could blame him? For baseball men, a World Series championship ring is worth nudging the limits of sanity, thinking outside the confines of logic.

And Murtaugh may have also factored in that Law knew Yankee Stadium better than anyone else on his staff. On July 13, Law had started and won the second of the All-Star games played that summer, in that venue.

Yankee Stadium is an intimidating piece of real estate. With a capacity of 67,337, in those days, the noise that came from the stands could, literally, cause the ground to shake. The short right-field porch was a left-handed batter's dream. The Pirates had scored only three runs in the last 21 innings. The decision was easy: Murtaugh tapped Vernon Law. And the Mormon who had once insisted that his contract exempt him from pitching on Sunday would do just that in Game 4.

What neither Murtaugh nor any other baseball pundit had anticipated was that Law's bat would prove the difference.

Law had first-inning jitters, there was no doubt. Bob Cerv whacked a single to center on the first pitch of the game. The next batter, Tony Kubek, doubled to left. Law had thrown three pitches and put runners on second and third. He struck out Maris. But the next batter was Mantle. Law had always hated giving intentional passes. He felt the integrity of the game demanded that pitchers match their skills against hitters. But these circumstances were extraordinary. A Mantle home run would start another free-flow of scoring from which the Pirates might never recover. He purposely walked Mantle.

With only one out, and the bases loaded, Yogi Berra tapped a slow ground ball down the third-base line. It was Don Hoak, The Tiger, who had played with stitches in his foot, whose foul mouth and indomitable will had urged his teammates on all season, who showed the bravery of his nickname. Hoak gloved the ball, stepped on third, and threw a BB to Dick Stuart at first. First-base coach Ralph Houk (who would supplant Stengel as Yankee manager the next season) argued the call, and Yogi literally jumped up and down in frustration. The play was extremely close and after multiple reviews of the tape of the game, it could be argued either way. But Berra was called out, and Law had escaped the fate of Mizell the day before.

After that threat, the game settled into a pitchers' duel.

Law gave up a solo home run in the fourth to Bill Skowron who pumped the ball convincingly over the 344-mark in right center. As Law watched the ball clear the fence, he winced and lifted his weight off his ankle.

Terry, who mixed a fastball, slider, and sinker, was on top of the hitters from the beginning, and had a no-hitter going into the fourth. Gino Cimoli, the Latin lover from San Francisco, finally cracked a single to right to break the string of zeroes in the Pirates' hit column. Smoky Burgess, Law's roommate and fellow teetotaler, dribbled a slow grounder down the right-field line. Skowron, who had hit a home run in the previous inning, decided to show that he could stand out in the field as well. He tried to force out Cimoli at second, but his toss to Kubek was high and Cimoli slid in while Kubek was in the air. It was the second disputed call to go the Pirates' way in the game. That was when the number-nine hitter, Vernon Law, stepped into the batter's box.

Law was one of baseball's better-hitting pitchers, a fact the Yankees knew. But Terry had been shaken by the breakup of his no-hitter. He laid a fastball over the heart of the plate, and Law slashed it into left field, where it caromed around the curving green wall of Yankee Stadium. Cimoli scored, the chug-chugging Burgess stopped at third, and Vernon Law had done what his teammates had been unable to do for 25 innings—knock in a run.

The next batter, Virdon, blooped a single into center. On tape, it appears Mantle could have dived for the ball. Instead, the center fielder took it on a bounce, allowing Burgess and Law to score. The Pirates led 3–1.

There would be no more scoring until the bottom of the seventh, when Skowron opened the inning with a ground rule double that bounced into and out of the right-field stands. Gil McDougald, a Stengel favorite who was playing third that day, dumped a little single into right. Skowron might have tried to score, if the outfielder collecting the hit had not been Roberto Clemente. The Puerto Rican's arm was gaining in reputation but had not yet been tested in the Series. Clemente, perhaps unnecessarily, unloaded a bullet throw into home that Burgess caught on the fly. Skowron would have been dead at the plate.

Murtaugh came out to the mound to ask Law about his ankle. The Mormon pitcher, who lived by his honor, used some twisted semantics and said it didn't feel any different than it usually did.

It didn't matter. Bobby Richardson tapped a ground ball to Mazeroski, who flipped to Groat to force McDougald. But Skowron scored, making it 3–2, Pirates. Johnny Blanchard, pinch-hitting for the pitcher, slugged a single to right field. Again, Clemente's arm slowed down the Yankee runners. Richardson, who had reached first when McDougald was forced out, stayed put at second. The tying and go-ahead runs were on base.

This time, when Murtaugh came to the mound, there was no discussion. He brought in Face. And again, Law

Courtesy Pittsburgh Pirates

Virdon's circus catch saves the day.
He never got enough credit for his talent.

limped as much as walked off the mound, after handing the ball over to the relief ace.

Face's first pitch to Bob Cerv was blistered into center field. It was at least a double, which would have scored both runners and put the Yankees ahead. That was what Bill Virdon was also thinking, as he raced toward the 407-foot mark in right center, leaped in front of an onrushing Roberto Clemente, and caught the drive over his shoulder. It was a catch to match Willie Mays's legendary grab, but never got the same publicity.

With the Pirates still leading in their half of the ninth, Mantle returned the favor, spearing a Don Hoak drive to exactly the same spot as Cerv's. The tape of Mantle, in his prime, racing the ball down, is a relic of baseball beauty.

Deprived of a sure double, Hoak went out to third in the bottom of the ninth still steaming. He put his anger to good use. Face's pitch to Skowron was blistered down the third-base line. With no time to think, only to react, Hoak somehow got his glove down and backhanded the drive off the ground. The white chalk of the third-base line flew into his face, but The Tiger, untamable, unstoppable, completed the miracle play with a bullet throw to first baseman Dick Stuart.

Next up was the Yankees' Dale Long, who, while with the Pirates, had once hit eight straight home runs as a pinch hitter. Hoping for a similar outcome with two outs, he launched a drive to right field. But once again, the Yankees were not dealing with just any outfielder. Clemente got beneath the drive, gloved it with his infuriatingly casual, palm-up basket catch, and the game was over. On the tape of the game, a young fan in a dark shirt is already standing next to Clemente on the field as he makes the final out. Baseball was a very different game in 1960. The Series was tied, 2–2.

Friend needed four days' rest between starts and couldn't be used. Mizell had proven ineffective. So Murtaugh gave the ball to Harvey Haddix, the left-handed curveball artist who, along with Hoak and Burgess, had come to the Pirates from Cincinnati. Haddix's 12 innings of perfect baseball on May 26, 1959, which nevertheless resulted in a Pirate loss, was still the stuff of legend. The Kitten, as Bob Prince called him, was a deceptive pitcher, whose skull still carried in it pieces of buckshot, the result of an accidental shooting while

Courtesy Pittsburgh Pirates

*Game 4, Yankee Stadium: Fans had no trouble
getting in touch with the winners.*

rabbit hunting with his father and uncle. A wag once teased
Harvey, "They didn't have very good aim, did they?"

"I don't know about that," Harvey replied, "but it's a sure
thing they didn't hit the rabbit."

Haddix would need more run support than the Bucs had
given Law. His control was not as fine-tuned as the right-
handed ace. Too many of his curves twisted off course, over
the heart of the plate. To give him another chance to show
his stuff, Stengel let Art Ditmar start the last game that
would be played in Yankee Stadium that year. He got

through the first inning this time, but not much was going Ditmar's way. In the Pirates' second, Dick Stuart singled to left. Gino Cimoli hit a ground ball that forced Stuart at second, but the handsome outfielder avoided a double play. That was fortunate, since the next batter, Burgess, walloped a double down the right-field line. Maris came up with it quickly, holding Cimoli on third.

Next up was Don Hoak, the roaring heart of the Pirates. He slashed a grounder to Kubek at short, who assumed he could get the lumbering Burgess out at third. Kubek speared the grounder—knowing that Cimoli would score easily— and threw to McDougald at third to tag Burgess. But the third baseman in whom Stengel put so much hope dropped the ball and Burgess hook-slid in safely, while Hoak scrambled to second. The Pirates were set up with runners for Bill Mazeroski. The second baseman lanced the first pitch to third base. McDougald should have had no problem grabbing it, until it took an odd bounce off the dirt and flew over his head, into left field. Burgess and Hoak scored and Mazeroski had a stand-up double. The Pirates had an early 3–0 lead and Stengel had seen enough of Ditmar. The Yankee manager quickly called in reliever Luis Arroyo, who put out the fire, temporarily.

Haddix gave up a run to the Yankees in the second. But the little Pirate left-hander was putting his pitches where he wanted them, preventing the Yankee power machine from ratcheting into high gear. In the top of the third, Dick Groat

Courtesy Pittsburgh Pirates

Game 5: Burgess hook-sliding into third.

led off with a double and Clemente singled him home. The Yankees fought back. Haddix threw a hanging curve to Maris, who would never win the hearts of Yankee fans the way Mantle did, even during the next year when he hit 61 regular-season homers. Maris deposited the pitch in the right-field seats, making it 4–2.

And that is how it stayed, even when Haddix let two Yankees on base with one out in the seventh. Murtaugh decided his starter was out of gas and called on Face, who had worked the day before. So fine was Haddix's performance that even the overwhelmingly pro-Yankee crowd gave him a warm ovation as he left the field. Face, The Baron of the Bullpen, never minded how often he was called upon. As he put it, "I'll have all winter to rest." He got the Pirates out of the worst jam they faced in Game 5 and shut down the Yankees for the next two innings as well. As with the day before, the last out was a fly ball to right, which Clemente cupped in his glove. And as they had on Saturday, the raucous Yankee Stadium crowd was swarming the field before the last out had been made.

With the Pirates leading the Series 3 games to 2, the teams would return to Pittsburgh to finish their grudge match. The Pirates needed to win only one of the remaining two games to be played at their home park. They were on the cusp of greatness. And the city they had put in the spotlight knew it and loved them for it. The Pirates' plane arrived at Greater Pittsburgh Airport late Monday night, but the teams had a day off before Game 6.

"Upon arriving in Pittsburgh, we were met by thousands of fans and the excitement was very high," Law recalls. "I had many of my friends who personally came out to greet me and wish us the best in the next games. They wanted a win as badly as the players." Law was hoping that Bob Friend would finish off the Yankees on Wednesday. He didn't want the burden of an all-or-nothing game hanging on him. Besides, his ankle was hurting more, not improving, and he already felt soreness in his right shoulder from overcompensating with his delivery.

Fate had other ideas. With the prospect of clinching the Series, Forbes Field was packed with 38,580 fans, nearly all of whom wanted the Bucs to go all the way that day. Friend, the hard-luck loser of Game 2, was determined to reverse his fortune.

The day did not begin well, as far as Law was concerned. "When I arrived at the park and was getting dressed for the game, I received a phone call from an advertising agency in New York wanting me to endorse Marlboro cigarettes. I was really taken aback because I'd been so outspoken about tobacco. I certainly had no qualification, other than sort of being from Marlboro Country out in Idaho. I explained that I didn't use tobacco and couldn't endorse something I didn't believe in. They said that was all right—that a lot of people let them use their names and they didn't smoke. My answer to that was, 'With my association with the Church, and with the standards I think athletes ought to maintain, I'm sorry I can't endorse your product.' Well, his answer to that was, 'Is there anyone else there I could talk to?' I said, 'There's Dick Groat, but he's already signed up with Camels.' I finally called over Bill Virdon, our fine center fielder, and told him who it was and what he wanted and handed him the phone. As I was walking away, I heard Virdon saying, 'I can't endorse something I don't use.' I felt sure he'd give that answer, otherwise I wouldn't have called him over."

With fifty years to think about it, Law is not entirely sure the call was not an attempt by someone in New York—

whether or not they represented Marlboro—to rattle him. Everyone knew that unless Friend won Game 6, Law would take the mound the next day for the decisive, climactic face-off. Psychological warfare, dumbed down to the term "head games," might not have been perfected in baseball in 1960, but it was not unknown, either.

Friend was luckless in his only World Series. The Yankee hitters ganged up on his flat fastball and his roundhouse curve. Years later, Friend would still recall the anguish he felt in each start, realizing he was letting his team down and pushing the responsibility for victory to someone else—in this case, Law.

The Pirates were hungry for action, anxious for the contest to commence. For them, victory was not just a possibility. It was destiny. And when the Pirates took the field, the largest-ever crowd at Forbes Field roared like warriors in pitched battle. One game to go. But first, Friend had to tame the bats from the Bronx.

He did—for one inning. The Yankees scored once in the second (it was all they would need). Could Friend keep the dike from splitting open, so his team might have a chance to score? In the third, he hit shortstop Tony Kubek with a pitch, and Maris followed, slashing a double into the right-field screen that missed being a home run by about three feet. Kubek got as far as third. Then Mantle, who was having an MVP series, singled them both home. The Yankees had a 3–0 lead. When Berra singled Mantle to third, Murtaugh decided to try to stem the damage. He lifted Friend for Tom Cheney, the right-handed power pitcher who Pittsburgh had acquired that year from St. Louis along with Cimoli. Cheney could do no more than Friend to mute the Yankees. Bobby Richardson blasted a double to the base of the scoreboard in left field. New York scored two runs apiece in the sixth, seventh, and eighth innings. Whitey Ford, meanwhile, scattered seven hits across his second complete game, a 12–0 shutout. Summed up Murtaugh: "They beat the heck out of us."

Yankee power could not, it seemed, be kept under control.

Except, perhaps, by a man whose religion had taught him to always be in control of himself. Vernon Law had to call on all his experience, from the earliest of his memories, when he was entrusted to do something, and to do it when it was required. He had fed chickens, milked cows, hoed rows of vegetables, earned extra money for his family, and played every sport with the intensity of a winner. And so, as he tried to put himself in the mind-set to fulfill the latest (and greatest) challenge of his professional life, he felt he had the tools to get the job done.

There was one last-minute distraction. The night before the game, the Laws' home phone rang. On the other end was Ezra Taft Benson, who was not only President Eisenhower's Secretary of Agriculture and one of the country's highest-ranking Mormon public servants, but also a member of the Church's Quorum of the Twelve Apostles. The Secretary was in Pittsburgh and wanted to know if Law could provide him with four tickets to the seventh game. Even for the starting pitcher of the tiebreaker, four tickets on short notice were not easy to obtain. After several frantic calls, Law obtained a promise that the tickets would be held for the Secretary. Only then could he relax. Or try to.

"Let me tell you, it was the hardest thing in the world to try to get some sleep that night," Law recalls. "I tossed and turned the whole night, and every time I'd turn, I'd go over the hitters thinking how I'd pitch to them tomorrow. I was ready to get up at six o'clock but stayed in bed until eight. We had breakfast and then I took off for the park. I wanted to get there before the crowd, but I found some of the fans had slept there that night in their sleeping bags. A few of them grabbed me and wished me good luck. I felt as if I had the weight of the world on my shoulders and it was all up to me to see if we were going to be champions or also-rans.

"I knew if I did a good job, we'd win. It was that simple. I tried to keep it in perspective rather than dwell on the millions of people looking in [or allowing myself to think], what if I lost? I put those negative thoughts out of my mind and thought only of winning and getting people out.

"By now I had a good idea of how to get Mantle, Maris, Berra and the rest of the lineup out. Now I just had to do it. Time before the game was really heavy, but it finally passed and it was warm-up time. I was glad for that, for now I could get rid of some of the nervous energy that had been building up. After the first out, it was pretty much just another ball game."

Just another ball game. By 1960, Vernon Law, age 30, was the longest-serving member of the Pirates. He had been with the club ten years—years in which the Pirates had mostly been atrocious. His ankle was killing him. His right shoulder was betraying the signs of stress that would later reveal he had torn his rotator cuff. That was for later. Now, on Thursday, October 13, 1960, he was the one player who, more than any other on the field, could write the fate of the team, and to a large degree the city, for which he toiled.

In his moving and thoroughly researched 2007 book, *The Best Game Ever: Pirates vs. Yankees, October 13, 1960,* Jim Reisler writes: "Striding to the mound to begin Game 7, Law knew what was at stake. Murtaugh may have wanted his ace to go at least five innings, but Law intended to go longer—maybe six or seven—to make ElRoy Face's relief job a little easier. Even with a sore ankle, Law had been effective to date . . ."

But would he be effective in this, the biggest game he and his teammates had ever played? Law's first pitch to Bobby Richardson, the leadoff hitter, was a curve that veered outside. Law later remembers wincing as he released the ball. It felt, as it left his hand, as if it might hang, giving the hot-hitting Richardson a chance to get the game off with a bang. But the Yankee second baseman was trying to get Law to throw as many pitches as he could. Typically, leadoff hitters try to extend the count as far as possible, to see what the pitcher is throwing well and to figure out how his weaknesses might be exploited.

Richardson liked the second pitch and swung at it, lining out to Groat. One up, one down. Shortstop Tony Kubek fared no better, lifting a pop fly ball that Mazeroski swallowed in his glove. Maris, the third batter, also popped up, to third baseman Hoak. Law had distributed three put-outs to three different infielders. He had done his part in the first. Now it was up to the Pirates hitters to make baseball history.

Bob Turley, the Yankee starter, had seen better days. In 1958 he had gone 21–7 and won the Cy Young award and the World Series MVP. So popular was the Illinois-born "Bullet Bob" at one point in his career that he was chosen to make a commercial for Gillette razors with Yankee announcer Mel Allen. The dreadful acting performance turned in by both men is almost too painful to watch. In 1960, Turley was only 9–3, but his victory over Friend in Game 2 made him the obvious choice to start the determining match.

Turley got Virdon to fly out to Yogi Berra, who was playing left field while Johnny Blanchard was handling Turley behind the plate. Groat, who was still feeling the effects of his broken left wrist (courtesy of Lou Burdette), lifted a harmless pop behind second, which Kubek easily handled. Bob Skinner, who batted lefty, worked a walk, bringing up Rocky Nelson, the left-handed first baseman who platooned with Stuart. Nelson had set batting records in the minors but never quite achieved stardom in the Big Leagues. That changed on the 2–1 pitch from Turley, which Nelson cracked almost on a straight line into the right-field seats over the head of a racing Roger Maris. Clemente then took some of the buzz out of the Forbes Field air by popping out to Richardson. But the Pirates had already done more in one inning of this monumental game than they had the day before: They had scored on the Yankees and were leading the game.

Law went back to work. He would have to face Mantle, Berra, and Skowron. No big deal. Just two future Hall of Famers and a slugging first baseman who had already torn Pirate pitching to shreds. Law was pitching with a fluid motion—one that effectively camouflaged the pain he was feeling. With Mantle at the plate, he tried two fastballs, then a curve, then resorted to the changeup, which pulled at his shoulder even more painfully than throwing heat but got the switch-hitting Mantle to pop up.

Berra, underestimated as an offensive threat throughout his career (though he would chalk up more World Series time than any other twentieth-century player), slapped a foul down the third-base line, then straightened out his next swing and stung the ball in the same direction, this time inside the line. Hoak, playing a step closer than normal given that Berra was batting from the left, had to throw himself on the hurtling ball to prevent its escape into the outfield. Knowing Berra could not run well, Hoak took his time getting up, but threw from a crouch that caused him to fall down again. The throw, however, found its mark—Nelson's first-baseman's mitt. Two down.

Moose Skowron would never receive the same kind of accolades as his more celebrated teammates. Even his nickname was misunderstood. He stood only 5–11 and weighed less than 200 pounds. "Moose" referred not to the noble woodland beast but was a shortened reference to the World War II-era Italian dictator Benito Mussolini, whose close-cropped hairstyle Skowron's was thought to resemble as a youth. Skowron took a strike, then a ball, then, perhaps too eager to make contact and rally his team, met a fastball and sent it bounding to Groat, who made short work of the challenge. The Pirates had held their lead for two innings.

Skowron had a chance to redeem himself almost immediately in the Pirates' second. Smoky Burgess drilled a pitch down the first-base line. It hugged the inside of the bag, got past Skowron, and caromed off the box-seat railing and into the dark right-field corner of Forbes Field. No fleeter of foot than Berra, Burgess managed only a single. Still, Stengel had seen all he could take. With all the marbles up for grabs in this game, he could not afford to stay with Turley. Clearly irked to be pulled this early, Turley committed a gross breach of pitcher's etiquette. As reliever Bill Stafford strode to the mound to take over, Turley flipped the ball to him and stomped to the dugout without a word of advice or encouragement.

Stafford was 21 years old that day in Forbes Field, a talented rookie, but a rookie who had been called up midway, late in the season. Anyone who is not nervous pitching in the decisive game of the World Series probably doesn't know anything about baseball and certainly doesn't belong in that situation. Neither applied to Stafford, who looked, and later said he was, petrified. He walked Don Hoak on four pitches. That brought Bill Mazeroski up. Though he had already hit the first, and least notable, of his two World Series homers that year, Maz was still regarded as a light-hitter by Yankee scouts. But to guard against an extra-base hit, third baseman Clete Boyer had backed up an extra step. Which was just what Maz wanted. He laid down a textbook bunt along the line and launched his stocky body toward first base. Boyer had no chance to make the play and Stafford knew it. The pitcher reached the ball and threw a BB to Richardson, who was covering first. As before, the tape of the play is inconclusive, but it was ruled that Mazeroski beat the throw. So the Pirates got the call, loading the bases for Vern Law.

In Game 4, Law had helped his own cause with a double that got his team started. This time, he batted more like the pitcher he was. He one-hopped a pitch back to Stafford, who threw to catcher Blanchard to force Burgess. Blanchard then whipped the ball to Skowron at first to complete the double play on Law.

"I was so disappointed," Law recalled. "There, I'd had a

chance to really make things happen, and I didn't. But I knew someone would."

That someone was Bill Virdon, dubbed The Quail by Prince and a man who, of all the Pirates that year, may have had the most strategic baseball mind. Certainly Virdon's aptitude would be tested in later years as he managed the Pirates, the Astros, and, less successfully, the Yankees. In the second inning that day, however, Virdon's only goal, with two outs, was to put the ball in play. He did, driving the ball hard to right field where it bounced once in front of Maris. Hoak, who had moved over to third on the Law double play, scored easily. First Maris bobbled, then completely dropped the ball, then needed three tries to finally pick it back up. Mazeroski turned on whatever speed he had and also crossed the plate, while Virdon scurried to second. Groat then grounded out, but when the inning ended, the Pirates had a 4–0 lead. Pittsburgh fans, who hadn't quite believed their team could pull off this miracle, who had turned out in greater numbers for the sixth game (38,580) than for the decisive seventh (36,683), were beginning to hope.

Law was tiring. That should have been obvious. He was pitching under enormous pressure and in pain. His ankle was throbbing as it had on the plane ride from Milwaukee back in September. But when Murtaugh asked him about it before he took the mound in the third, the Mormon from Idaho shrugged like the tough farm boy he had once been and said, "It's fine." And it seemed to be just that. Law shut down the Yankees in both the third and the fourth.

He never had any intention of coming out of the game. With a 4–0 lead, why should he? Murtaugh had hoped for six innings from the ace of his rotation. Law, who always thought of games as consisting of nine innings of effort, *by him,* had decided before the game to do, or say, whatever it took to remain on the field. Going the distance had become, for the humble man from Meridian, a quest of honor. He remembered the game in 1955 when he had gone 18 innings, only to hand the ball over to someone else to etch the win in the next inning. He also thought about Harvey Haddix, who had been perfect for twelve and lost. This year, he had been the go-to guy when things got rough. Twice, the Bucs had lost four games in a row; each time, the team called on Law, who ended the skids.

So far in the seventh game, Law had thrown 39 pitches. The plan that he had formulated in his own bed during the previous wakeful night—after scurrying around to fill the last-minute ticket request—was working. Keep Maris looking at curves and changeups, give Mantle nothing to take out of the park, keep Berra high, where the rotund catcher liked to swing but where he often met only failure. Law says he can't remember what he worked out as a battle plan against the first baseman, Moose Skowron. Perhaps his forgetfulness is selective. We don't like to remember when our plans begin to unravel.

Ninth Inning

For Law, that day, the first sign of an errant string beginning to come loose—was Moose. Law's first pitch to
Skowron was a strike. His ankle hurt but, he had concluded,
it would hurt a lot more if he were sitting in the dugout
watching someone else control the Pirates' destiny. On the
next pitch, a fastball, Skowron, acting on his own, tried to
bunt down the first-base line. The ball crossed the chalk and
into foul territory. A bunt was so uncharacteristic of Skowron
that, had it stayed fair, he could have trotted half-speed to
the base and made it. Rocky Nelson was playing well behind
the first-base bag, respectful of the right-hand-hitting
Skowron's ability to push the ball to the opposite field.

Increasingly, in an effort to mitigate the pain in his ankle,
Law was throwing pitches three quarter or sidearm. He could
plant his foot less authoritatively that way, the ball already
having left his grip. That was what he did on the 0–2 pitch
to Skowron, hoping to ease his pain momentarily with a
cheater. And as with so many attempts to cheat, he paid for
it. Skowron was looking for something outside, and that was
where the ball crossed the edge of the plate. Skowron let rip.
The sound of the bat on the ball, as it sailed quickly into
right field, was unmistakable. Major League hitters of suc-
cessive generations insist they know when one is gone.

Skowron said he never even ran hard, that sure was he
that the ball was leaving the playing field. Clemente, seeing
the ball come his way, turned his back to the infield and
began to charge for the wall. But as he reached the warning

track, the Pirates superstar slowed, stood momentarily on his left foot, and made an odd gesture toward the ball that was now in the seats. It resembled a little bye-bye wave. The Yankees were on the board, and the dramatic events that would be forever remembered in Pittsburgh were starting their inexorable roll-out.

In the stands, nervous men sucked harder on their cigars. Women in sunglasses who had earlier exhibited carefree smiles now pursed their mouths as if someone had told them they had lipstick on their front teeth. The mood changed, in that instant, from celebratory to cautious. And the game was only just reaching the halfway mark.

Law was looking down at the mound more often now between pitches, the body language of someone in doubt, or perhaps just in deep reflection. Was he thinking of the bus in Milwaukee, the drunken grins of these men around him, of what they had done to him on that day? Whatever they had done, they were the men with whom he shared his life and on whose abilities his livelihood depended. Law says he was only thinking about Johnny Blanchard, the next batter, and how to get him out. But did he think the answers were buried beneath the pitcher's mound?

Perhaps. He induced Blanchard to pop to Virdon in center. Clete Boyer, the third baseman, was not known for his hitting, and after fouling off a bunt attempt, Boyer grounded to Maz. That left the relief pitcher, Bobby Shantz, who had taken over for Stafford in the third. Stengel had decided to let him hit, on the grounds that the Pirates had Law due up first, then the left-handed leadoff hitter, Bill Virdon, who had been a nemesis of Yankee pitchers throughout the series. Shantz got the count to 1–2, then took his first swing and sent the ball high in the air between first base and the Pirates dugout, where Rocky Nelson circled under it. The Pirates had given up a run, but retained the lead.

Law was tired. More tired than even he wanted to acknowledge. But his body language in tapes of the final game shows a young man—he was just 30—fighting against adrenaline drain, pain, and exhaustion. Later in his career, Law would give interviews suggesting that had he known how difficult the Major League was for pitchers, he might have tried to play third base and hone his always-respectable hitting skills. Law was no sure out, as many National League pitchers are nowadays. He had already doubled and singled in the Series. But batting put even further strain on his ankle. He hooked Shantz's 2–2 pitch into the left-field canyon of Forbes Field, and the crowd was instantly alive, until they saw it bend into the seats beyond the Yankee bullpen. The effort seemed to drain Law, and he hit a one-hopper to third for out number one.

Perhaps the Pirates had hit an emotional lull. They were ahead, but the Yankees had just tightened the score with Skowron's homer. The energy they felt at the beginning of the game had given way to the physical wear and mental fatigue that every game, be it spring training or the last one of the World Series, demands of professional athletes. Whatever the reason (most grown men in 1960 did not discuss their inner feelings), the Pirates were flat in the fifth. Virdon grounded out to second and Groat, The Captain, the man to whom teammates looked for strength and inspiration, could only line out to Shantz. Then it was back to the field for the sixth and the top of the Yankee order.

The 5-foot-9 Richardson had been a pain out of all proportion to his physical stature. His statistics at the end of the Series would earn him the Most Valuable Player award, the first time it went to a member of the losing team. In later years, Richardson, somewhat larger of girth, would remember the 1960 Series as a terrible event. But as he was playing it, Richardson seemed determined to make it one of New York's, and certainly his, finest moments. As the sixth inning began, Richardson wasn't interested in hitting a home run. His grand slam in Game 3 was, after all, an aberration. All he needed to do was get on base. He was the spark; the heart of the order would provide the gasoline. On an 0–1 pitch, Richardson slapped, more than punched, the ball into center. It wasn't much of an offensive display. But it got the Yankees started. Kubek, the number-two hitter in the lineup and the inning, thought he saw a difference in Law's delivery. He was planting his left foot differently as he came off the mound, and the ball was cutting to the right side of the plate. Kubek took the first pitch. It was a ball.

Now Law had to pitch from the stretch rather than from

a full windup. It usually made no difference to him. He simply adjusted his delivery. Now, however, the stretch made him put even more pressure on his shoulder, which, he now acknowledges, was slowly wrenching itself out of its socket because of his different stride. Out of character, he was behind 2–0 on Kubek. Don Hoak came to the mound. Law recalls that when other pitchers were out there, Hoak's visits were things to dread. He would tell Friend, in stark anatomical detail, what he was going to do to him if he didn't start throwing strikes, dammit. With Law, the third baseman took the opposite approach. "Deacon," he said, as Law remembers it, "you've done a great job so far. Just throw it in there. We're behind you. We'll take care of things."

Were two men ever more different in demeanor? Hoak was the product of the streets and the grungy boxing clubs of the Northeast—a man who used threats to intimidate and was not afraid to back them up with violence. Some years earlier, when he was with the Cincinnati Reds, Hoak had become smitten with a nightclub singer named Jill Corey. After he was traded to the Pirates, she began to see the rough-hewn ballplayer showing up, unannounced, and at first, unwanted, at her performances. His tactics worked, but only after he had chased off Corey's then-beau with some colorful suggestions about what could happen to him. Yet, with Vernon Law, Hoak behaved as though he were one seminarian encouraging another. The transformation of Hoak's personality was so startling that Law put his uncharacteristic behavior down, quite seriously, "to the influence of the Lord."

Buoyed by Hoak's pep talk, Law returned to the task of dismissing Kubek. There was no denying that his stuff had faded. In fact, he was drained. He threw ball three, then a strike, then his worst pitch of the at bat, low, and Kubek trotted to first with a walk. There were two Yankees on and none out.

What happened next may be the three minutes of his baseball career about which Law least likes talking. Murtaugh was out of the dugout before Kubek had reached first. In the past, when Murtaugh approached the mound on which Law was standing, it was for a discussion. Opinions were exchanged. Views were traded. Law was a participant in deciding his fate. Sometimes, Murtaugh's visits were merely to stall for time so that the era's premier closer, Face, could continue warming up. More often, they were genuine skull sessions with a pitcher whose talent had earned him the right to be heard, to have a say in whether he could continue or not.

The tape of Game 7 is an unforgiving historical document. By the time Murtaugh had reached the mound, Groat and Burgess were already there. Law was looking at neither of them, talking with neither. He was dragging his right foot over and over the dirt in front of the rubber, as though looking for a dime that he had dropped and hoping that repeated digging with his spike might unearth it.

When Murtaugh arrived, with his pigeon-toed walk, the

sparring commenced. Law insisted, though plainly untruly, that he was fine, that the last pitch to Kubek had just gotten away from him. Murtaugh nodded, as one does to a child who's arguing why he should be allowed to stay up late. In coming years, Murtaugh's versions of what he told Law would vary. In one version, he warned him that he might do his arm lasting damage if he kept pitching in his modified delivery due to the ankle injury. In another, he claims not to have spoken at all. And there are other versions where the now-deceased manager says he was unsure what he was going to do until he looked into the whites of Law's eyes.

He was, as was Law, probably fitting the truth to the situation. This was the biggest game in Murtaugh's, in Law's, in any of the Pirates' lives. It all hung on the results of the next three and a half innings. A victory would dull the ache Law felt at being lifted. A loss would leave them all shriveled, forever wondering, what if? Murtaugh looked at Law, then to right field where the Pirate bullpen was located. He stuck out his right hand, palm down. It was the signal he used when he wanted the little one, ElRoy Face.

Vernon Law's season was over.

"Danny saw me favoring my ankle too much," Law recalls. Through the haze of five decades, the pain of being pulled has dulled, but Law insists, even now, that he could have carried on. Reflecting on the disappointment of being pulled, Law wrote: "One thing I'll always appreciate was Hoak, who came in to the mound while they were making the change. 'Listen, Deacon, you go out of here holding your head high. You did a great job.' Coming from him that was the best thing anyone could have told me at the time. I had my head up but my eyes were down, and as I reached the dugout, I knew the fans were giving me a standing ovation, which eased the hurt."

In the end, the horseplay in Milwaukee had done more than rip his clothes and shred his tie. It had torn his muscles and cost the Pirates what might have been a straightforward victory in the most important game any of them had ever played.

Unlike today's closers, who sprint across the field, Face's custom was to walk from the bullpen to the mound when he was entering a game. "What the hell," he once said, "they can't do anything until I get there, can they?"

In calling on Face in the sixth inning, when his club was still ahead by three runs, Murtaugh may have felt he was doing the prudent thing. Face was a dominant closer, really the first specialist singled out for the specific purpose of shutting down an opposing team for the final inning or so. The sixth was early for Face. Though the violent drop of his forkball did not diminish as his pitch count rose, batters coming through for the second time were ready for it. Face smoked two packs of cigarettes a day, sometimes puffing on one while waiting to be called into a game. In the off-season, he was a union carpenter, using drills and awls and power saws that could have cut or pounded his valuable pitcher's hands to ribbons. No club today would permit it. But this was 1960, and ElRoy Face had, for the moment, just one job: get twelve Yankees to swing over his forkball.

The first one was Roger Maris, who a year later would stun the baseball world when he, with a few more games at his disposal than Babe Ruth had, would break Ruth's sacred mark of 60 home runs in a single season. On this day, though, Maris was still a mortal, as Face proved when he hummed a strike over the inside corner. A second pitch missed, but the third Maris made contact with. Harmlessly, as it turned out. He lofted a fly into foul territory along third base. Hoak was there. One out.

No pitcher in 1960 liked seeing Mickey Mantle come to the plate. The switch-hitting center fielder from Commerce, Oklahoma, was only then beginning to display his mastery of the game. Still young and relatively free of the injuries that would dog him throughout his career, Mantle was a blond, smiling, immensely talented ballplayer—at the plate, on the base paths, and in the field. He was, that year, perhaps the most dangerous Yankee in the lineup, matched now against a little man who could make a pitch drop a foot in the last millisecond of its flight from the mound. The first pitch was all Mantle needed. He screeched it past Face's right, past a diving Groat, and into center field. Richardson scored easily, Kubek dashed to third, and the Mantle legend had another paean added to it. The Yankees now trailed, 4–2, but they had two more outs before they would be finished.

Face's hard good looks seldom betrayed emotion. Mickey Mantle had gotten a hit. How surprising was that? The answer was that to Face, it was *incredibly surprising*. He expected to get everyone out, every time he faced them. To the 36,000 fans, however, Face looked like a business executive who had been told his next meeting was delayed. Peeved, nothing more.

He would take out his frustration on Berra, better known as a catcher, though on this day playing left field. Berra was playing in his eleventh World Series and deserved respect. But he was no Mickey Mantle. Face's first pitch was right over the plate, and Berra hacked. It sped down the first-base line, then took a sudden bounce and kicked foul. Face had decided to go after Berra, to throw strikes and see what happened. His next pitch was a tad high, just where Berra liked it. The hitter snapped his bat around with a speed and coordination that his size, build, and nickname did not portend. But Berra, for all his malapropisms, all his clowning, was a *hitter.* And this ball had found the sweet spot on his bat. It sailed above Nelson's head, on its way to right field, gaining altitude at an alarming rate. Clemente, as he had with Skowron's drive, turned and started to run for the wall. Even before he got to the warning track, however, he stopped in his tracks. The ball was in the seats. Running to first, Berra later said, he could not tell whether the ball was going to land fair or foul. Then the first-base umpire, Nestor Chylak, pointed emphatically toward the inner part of the field. Fair ball.

Berra actually jumped like a kid, his right hand pointing heavenward, when he saw what he had done. No one ever claimed Berra was a speedy runner. Now he did not have to be. He lumbered around the bases, taking the outstretched hand of third-base coach Frank Crosetti, then, as he crossed the plate, tapping fists with Richardson and Mantle. The man who in later years would become the living symbol of Yankee tenacity and invincibility had done it. The Yankees were in the lead, 5–4, for the first but not the last time that day.

Face never flinched. He signaled for a new ball as if the last one had merely been misplaced and prepared to face Moose Skowron, who already had a home run that day. Skowron popped up the first pitch he saw, first over the third-base line, then into foul turf, near the seats. Hoak had been tracing it with his angry eyes since it left Skowron's bat and made the catch. Two down. Catcher Blanchard, with not much to show for his day against Law, did no better with Face on the mound. He bounced to Nelson, who handled it nicely and put the Yankees away. Just not soon enough.

The Pirates were deflated. They had blown the lead. Shantz, the crafty left-handed pitcher who had nearly been lifted for a pinch hitter in the fifth, was now in line to win the Series-clinching game. He had not given up a hit since entering in the third, and the Pirates did nothing to hurt him in their half of the sixth. Skinner flied out, Nelson grounded to first, and Clemente tapped back to Shantz, an excellent fielding pitcher, who threw him out. The Pirates' inning had lasted five pitches and approximately three minutes of playing time. It was back to work for Face, who gave up a single to Shantz, but nothing else.

When the Pirates came to bat again in the bottom of the seventh, there was one small—then again, not so small—surprise. Smoky Burgess, the pear-shaped catcher who kept abstemious company with his roommate and friend, Vernon Law, got a hit off Shantz, who had kept the Pirates at bay for five innings. Almost reflexively, Murtaugh replaced the team's worst runner with its best, Joe Christopher, a talkative utility player from the Virgin Islands whose main reason for being in the Major Leagues was neither hitting nor fielding but speed. Christopher would replace Burgess on first, and Hal Smith would come in to do the catching.

Christopher took a healthy lead off Shantz, only to be chased back to first. In the tape of Game 7, Pirate fans can be seen staring tensely—one man has a handkerchief draped over his head, while he chews on a cigar, hoping the hometown heroes with thirty come-from-behind victories have just one more in them this season. But Hoak flied out and Mazeroski grounded into a 5–4–3 double play, wasting Christopher's speed and at the cost of Burgess's bat later on. If the number-six hitter came up again against the Yankees, it would not be the hard-hitting Burgess. It would be the man taking his place behind the plate, Hal Smith.

When the Pirates took the field in the top of the eighth, they seemed to charge from the dugout like soldiers on a take-that-hill mission. Clemente, Groat, and Virdon were all kneeling on the top step of the dugout, anxious to be out doing what they had done all year. Face, ever intense, ever sure of himself, nearly completed his part of the mission. He got Maris to dribble the ball down to first base and Mantle to line out to shortstop. Then he came up against the man who had cost him the lead, Yogi Berra. It was not a pleasant encounter. Berra was on a roll that day, and Face decided before he threw the first pitch that he would rather walk him than let him swing the bat with authority. Face's pitches were all around the strike zone, but not in it. After six pitches, Berra had earned a walk.

Skowron had been first-pitch swinging a lot, and this at bat was no different. With Berra on first, Skowron chopped the first pitch—a fastball—toward Hoak at third. The ball bounced high, forcing Hoak to wait for it before he bare-handed it and tossed to Maz at second. Even Berra, no speed merchant, could beat that throw. The Yankees had two on and two away, with the catcher, Johnny Blanchard, coming up.

Face was only human. He was getting tired. He got Blanchard to foul off his first pitch. But the second one was a little too good, and the left-hand-hitting catcher poked it just over Mazeroski's head for a single that scored Berra—suddenly running faster than his reputation—and sent Skowron to third. Six to 4, Yankees.

Cletis Boyer and his brother Ken were, as were the DiMaggios (Joe and Dom) and the Deans (Dizzy and Daffy), one of those brother combinations that seemed to divide their talent. Clete was a fielding wonder who often came in for defense late in the game. Ken was a hard-hitting St. Louis Cardinal. As Clete came to the plate with two on, the mood in Forbes Field had chilled to that of a reception room in a funeral home. Three men, two in blue suits and one in brown, one chewing a cigar and one with sunglasses, seated along the third-base line, resemble in the game tape a triptych of gargoyles, the horror on their faces reproduced three-fold. The Yankees were taking command of the game and fulfilling what appeared to be their diabolic destiny.

Face took Boyer's measure and threw an off-speed pitch, which Boyer lifted over Hoak's head into the left-field corner for a double. Skowron scored to make it 7–4. For the Yankees, everything was going according to plan. The next man due up was the pitcher, Bobby Shantz, whose performance on the mound had been such that if MVP awards were given out for each game, he would be the obvious choice. Now Stengel could pinch-hit for the veteran with one of his heavy bats on the bench. It was the obvious move. But Casey Stengel, who had turned 70 that year and figured he knew the auguries of the game as well as any man who ever wore the uniform, went against the grain. He let Shantz bat for himself, on a hunch that the lefty still had enough stuff to keep the Pirates at bay in the eighth.

Like many of his hunches, this one has been debated by cognoscenti of the game for half a century. Unlike many others, this one may have, ultimately, chased Casey from the game he loved.

Shantz made Face go to a full count, then lifted a high fly ball to right, which Clemente put away with his arrogant basket catch. The inning was over, but how could the Pirates come back now?

The game is played differently today. Pitch counts are sacrosanct. Matchups are determined by career stats. Right-handed batters seldom meet left-handed pitchers late in the game. Science and probabilities have supplanted manliness and unquantifiable qualities such as grit. ElRoy Face, the greatest closer of his era, had done all he could against a team that, one year later, would often be called the greatest ever to take the field. Could Law have gutted out the sixth inning and held the Yankees down? Would his ankle, his shoulder, the rest of his screaming body, have held together long enough to continue the bravura performance he had begun? There are no answers. There is only opinion, speculation, the stuff for a beer-fueled argument late into the evening, followed by shrugs and who-knows? And more beer.

Face was done. Bob Friend would have to take over in the ninth to keep the damage to a minimum. But what could the Pirates do now in their half of the eighth? To whom could they turn? Murtaugh chose the San Francisco lover boy, Gino Cimoli, the right-hand-batting utility outfielder and ladies' man. Cimoli played a credible left field and had subbed for Virdon and Clemente on rare occasions. He was not a Hall of Famer. He was a fill-in specialist. And he could hit, which was all Murtaugh cared about now as he sent him up to the plate in Face's spot.

Cimoli was not naturally gifted. He had worked hard and simply found ways to get on base—82 times in the season so far. He had subbed for Skinner in left field in the Series and acquitted himself well, so far, with four hits. As he waited for Shantz to deliver, Gino may have thought of his father, Abramo, and how he told anyone around him, "Atsa my boy, Gino!" He perhaps thought of the teams for which he had played—Brooklyn, St. Louis, and now the Pirates. He undoubtedly thought of who he was and what his team expected of him.

The Pirates had helped Shantz by swinging at too many first pitches. Shantz's curve and screwball sent a hitter's reactions into overdrive and therefore into error. And so Cimoli let the first pitch, a curve, go by for a strike. He did the same with the second pitch and with the same result. A ball outside kept him alive, and now, seriously behind in the count, Cimoli was looking for something to drive. He finally found it on 2–2 and lifted the ball over second base and into right-center. Maris cut in front of Mantle to field the ball, and

Pittsburgh was back in the game. Or so it seemed until Bill Virdon, the leadoff hitter, who knew better than anyone how to get on base to get things started, hit Shantz's 0–1 pitch into a seeming, classic 6–4–3 double play that would let the air out of the Pirates and drive a final, fatal spike into the club's balloon.

Kubek set himself to receive the ball as it bounced twice in front of him. The first hop, on the grass, set Kubek up for the easiest of conversions. But the second bounce, immortally, hit one of the many spike clods in the rough infield of Forbes Field and spun, out of control or reason, into Kubek's Adam's apple—one of the more remarkable accidents in Major League history. Kubek took the ball square in the throat, without a chance to raise his hands to protect himself. Chuck Thompson of NBC Radio described the Yankee infielder as having "flipped over like a fish out of water."

It was one of the most extraordinary bloopers in World Series history, though injurious to Kubek. The Yankee shortstop, blood trickling from his mouth, lay on the infield as Richardson retrieved the ball—Cimoli was on second, Virdon on first—called time out, and quickly signaled to the Yankee dugout that medical attention was needed. The Yankee trainers, as well as Pirate medical director Dr. Joseph Finegold, were all on the infield in a matter of seconds.

Danny Murtaugh, realizing there was nothing he could do except silently rejoice in the Pirates' good fortune, remained in the Pirate dugout. Casey Stengel did come out

Courtesy Pittsburgh Pirates

All choked up: Kubek wasn't badly injured but the Yankees were.

onto the field. He cast an unsympathetic look at Kubek, like someone who did not want to get too close to a sick person, and continued walking as if he might tour the outfield, before finally turning on his right foot and coming back to the injured player. Kubek finally rose to his feet, spat once, then twice into the dirt, and made his case to stay in the game.

Remarkably, Kubek was going to be lifted one way or the other. Stengel had already ordered relief pitcher Ralph Terry and Joe DeMaestri, who often spelled Kubek, to warm up in the Yankee bullpen, to be ready to come in for defensive purposes.

The serendipity of Kubek's injury, the Pirates' sudden reversal of fortune, had stunned and confused the crowd at Forbes Field. Who Fate was pulling for versus who was winning seemed, suddenly, to have two different answers. The next batter was The Captain, Dick Groat, who had not made his way in the Majors as a power slugger but rather as an opportunist, who saw his chances and took them. Right now, the best chance looked like poking a ball into right field. But Groat knew his weaknesses. He did not run particularly well. And a shot intercepted by the fleet Richardson could turn into a double play. So he measured Shantz for a curve on which he could turn.

It came with the count at 1–1. Groat stepped into the pitch and made contact, sending it between Boyer and DeMaestri. Cimoli hustled home and Virdon, the fortunate batter whose luck had resulted in the end of Kubek's season, stopped at second.

Stengel was watching a slow-motion nightmare but was getting no rest as it happened. After five innings plus, Shantz had done magnificent work, but Casey now wished he had pinch-hit for the pitcher. He trod to the mound and brought in Jim Coates, who had done credible work in the previous Series games. Stengel assumed that the next batter, Bob Skinner, would bunt to advance the runners and hoped that a fresh Coates, a sinker ball pitcher, would foil the plot.

Skinner did as expected. He laid a nice bunt down the third-base line, which Boyer fielded and sent to first to get Skinner. But Virdon had moved to third and Groat to second. The Yankees still had command of the game, but for how much longer? Rocky Nelson had hit home runs all during his minor league career and was aware of what one now would do. Nelson, a left-handed-hitting first baseman, was one of those players who always had the abilities to do good things but seldom the opportunity to do great ones. This time, on a 1–0 pitch, Nelson aimed for the fences, but undercut the pitch, a slider, and lofted it to Maris in right field. From his position on third base, Virdon was not about to challenge the right fielder on such a softly hit ball. Two out. Could the Pirates do anything to make a difference now?

"*Arriba!*" began the chant in the stands on the first-base side. "*Arriba!*" answered someone in the third-base box. "Rise up," might be a fair translation from the Spanish, but to be precise, one should ask the man who was coming to the plate.

Roberto Clemente did not much care for Pittsburgh when he got there, and Pittsburghers initially returned the sentiment. He was different, and spoke Spanish, and well, come on now, he *was* black. And it was the 1950s. But over the years, Clemente had won the crowd over with his flamboyant play. He could catch balls that other outfielders could not get to, and he did so with that casual, signature basket catch—a method of hauling in fly balls that seemed almost careless, dismissive of the hitter's prowess.

When he was on the field, Clemente thought, and the Forbes Field crowd had come to believe, that *he* would decide how plays went. He would decide if a ball fell for a hit or was cancelled by his brilliant defense. And the unthinking base runner on third who dared to challenge him—that was a most unfortunate individual. It seemed that Clemente had a rocket launcher attached to his shoulder. So fast did the horsehide leave his possession and with such velocity that the runner was only hitting full speed when he saw the opposing catcher ahead of him, holding The Great One's airmail present, a smile on his face.

The book on Clemente was that he was a coward. Buzz him up by the skull and he had the manner of a pup who'd just been whipped. As noted, when it had happened in a game that Vernon Law was pitching, Vern, the Mormon, the God-fearing man, had told Clemente, "I'll take care of it," and had sent three consecutive batters to the dirt with inside pitches—without hitting any of them.

So when Coates, aware of the scouting reports, sent two consecutive pitches high and inside, Clemente swung at both, not just thinking he could hit them, but also in self-defense. Where, after all, was Vernon Law to protect him now? Clemente was enraged. His manhood was being questioned, and he wanted revenge. He swung at the next two pitches, both of them high and in, and fouled both. On the last swing, his bat cracked in half. Clemente walked back to the Pirates' dugout and chose a new Louisville Slugger.

Armed with new lumber, Clemente let the next pitch slide by—a ball. On the next pitch, Clemente took a hard swing, but barely made contact. The ball danced down the right side of the infield, where first baseman Skowron had it measured. He moved to his right and scooped it up, ready to toss to Coates, who should have been covering the base. For the Pirates, disaster loomed, as it had when Virdon hit his ground ball to Kubek for the certain double play. This time, there was no odd bounce to save the Pirates.

This time, it was human error. Coates had seen the ball bounding along between him and Skowron and decided *he* had the best chance to field it. He followed it off the mound, toward first base, away from the plate, and found to his horror that Skowron had the ball in his mitt and was looking for Coates to finish the play by covering first. But the pitcher was out of position, the Major League equivalent of being caught *in flagrante delicto.* Clemente's speed meant that there was no recovery. Virdon scampered home, Groat went to second, and Clemente, running like the superstar he was, easily crossed the unattended first base. The Pirates were staging one of those late game rallies that had defined the 1960 season, but could they hope to continue that string of luck against this mighty Yankee squad?

If Hal Smith thought he was lucky to be in the game, after Burgess had been pinch-run for, he acted just like a starting catcher who had every right to be at the plate. Hal Smith was a likable man. He played the guitar and favored country music and did it so well he had a semipro group that played at Holiday Inns for extra cash. Smith was not a demonstrative fellow. He knew the game, played it well, but also knew there was no wall space awaiting him at Cooperstown. With a 2–2 count, he expected, against baseball's normal calculus, Coates to throw him something decent. He was not disappointed: The pitch came down the center of the plate. Smith wasn't surprised, he wasn't stunned, he didn't thank God for his good fortune. He just wheeled on the pitch, a fastball, and drove it to left. Would it be a hit, would it be caught, would it score a run? He didn't know. He just started running. He heard, rather than saw the result. The ball took off on a trajectory that might have led it to another planet. It settled instead for the friendly confines of Schenley Park, over the red, ivy-covered brick wall in left field. Bob Prince estimated that the ball cleared the wall by a good 15 feet near the 406-foot mark.

"The Pittsburgh fans have the steel girders throbbing like tuning forks with thunderous cheers," Prince shouted into his microphone. And it was true. The stadium reached a stage of anarchy that would hardly be imaginable now. Groat leapt and threw his arms about his head. Clemente danced, literally *danced,* home. And both slapped Smith as he crossed the plate to put the Pirates officially in the lead. Hal Smith, the guitar-strumming fill-in for Smoky Burgess, had put the no-name Pittsburgh Pirates ahead of the legendary Yankees, 9–7, in the bottom of the eighth. The Pirates had answered the New York team's comeback with five runs of their own.

To quell the onslaught, Ralph Terry, who had lost Game 4 to Law, came in to get the last out—a Don Hoak fly-out

Beauty and the Beast, but which is which?
Murtaugh and Hal Smith, the forgotten hero of Game 7.

to left. But the Pirates had retaken the lead. What could possibly go wrong now? All they needed to do was to prevent two runs and get three outs.

This is expected now of every closer who comes into the top of the ninth with a home-team lead. If you can't do that, you won't stay in the Majors for long. Do your job. Shut them down. Be a closer. It was the spot for ElRoy Face, but Face had left the game for a pinch hitter, Gino Cimoli, in the last inning. To whom should Murtaugh turn? Vernon Law would have been a good choice, but he was already in the clubhouse. Harvey Haddix was a crafty southpaw, the kind of pitcher who might confuse the mighty bats of the Yankees. He had been warming up and was available. The whole club was available, of course. The only thing any man had to plan for was the winter break.

Murtaugh chose Bob Friend. There is no one who can say that Friend had not done his share that season of 1960. He was a power pitcher, the kind of right-hander who shut down batters on both sides of the plate when he had his stuff. But he had pitched two-plus innings the day before in a painful loss, his second of the Series. Was this his moment of redemption or final damnation? Murtaugh had Haddix warming in the bullpen and added another Pirate lefty who had not fared well in his Series start, Wilmer "Vinegar Bend" Mizell.

The mood in the stands had oscillated like a gyroscope on drugs—from desolation, to hope, to giddiness, to sick despair, to jangled anticipation. Had anything like this ever happened in Pittsburgh before? It had, but not in the lifetime of most of those in Forbes Field. *All* Friend had to do was retire the top of the order: Richardson, a probable pinch hitter for DeMaestri, and Maris. Richardson, the eventual MVP of the Series, seemed to be a gnat on steroids, prior to such things having been invented.

Not surprisingly, Richardson took Friend's 0–1 pitch into left field for a single. Virdon came up with the ball and tossed it into Mazeroski. The Friend curse was alive and well. No one expected DeMaestri, a light hitter, to bat for himself. Instead, the Yankees brought on Dale Long, the former Pirate. Long was a professional hitter, not an athlete. He took Friend's third pitch and, with practiced ease, lobbed it safely into right field. Clemente handled it with care, as he had a thousand times before. But this was the ninth inning of the seventh game of the World Series. This couldn't be happening.

What's going on, Murtaugh wondered as he headed for the mound. Friend had been a reliable starter through the season. Some thought of him, rather than Law, as the true ace of the staff, the guy who overpowered hitters when he had to. But in this situation, Friend was floundering. The pressure—whatever it is that takes over men when they are up against a wall, with either life or death, success or failure, survival or drowning about to descend upon them—had gotten to him. Bob Friend was one of the great Pirate pitchers. But he was not up to the task in the 1960 World Series.

As he strode to the mound to yank Friend, Murtaugh couldn't help remembering Harvey Haddix's 12 innings of perfect baseball. Haddix was not a power pitcher, nor a particularly glamorous one. But he knew how to get outs. And so he signaled with his left hand, a bit lower than if he had been calling for the larger Mizell. The game would depend on The Kitten.

As Haddix approached the mound, he picked up a handful of dirt just behind the pitcher's rubber, crushed it with his pitching hand, and tossed it away. A kind of lucky charm.

The Kitten, The Deacon, and The Captain: Haddix, Law, and Groat.

He would need it. Roger Maris was the first hitter. Anxious himself, Maris swung on the second pitch, in on the fists, and popped out to Smith behind the plate. Mickey Mantle had no nerves. It is the difference between great and the greatest—the invisible wall between impressive and immortal. Maris was a capable hitter who knew it. Mantle was a true legend in the making and acted as such. After letting one ball go by, Mantle showed the sweet swing that would make the Yankees retire his Number 7 and Major League Baseball induct him into the Hall of Fame as soon as the rules allowed.

The drive went past Mazeroski, who had no chance at it, and into right field, where Clemente grabbed it quickly but knew he could not prevent Richardson from scoring. The Pirates' lead was now just one run, 9–8, and Yogi Berra was coming to bat. Could the Pirates turn a double play that would end the threat and make Pittsburgh a place to be proud of?

That was all that was on Haddix's mind as he threw one low and inside, then another even lower. Berra's swing wasn't much good. It only drove the ball to Nelson at first. All he had to do was throw to Groat at second to force Mantle and then get back to the bag for the relay throw that would end the inning, the game, and the Series. The Pirates were about to be Champions of the World!

Instead, as he gloved the ball, Nelson inexplicably stepped on first before throwing to second, retiring Berra but making it necessary to tag Mantle for the out. Mantle knew he had no chance to get to second and started back to first. Nelson, who was left-handed, reached his glove across his body to tag Mantle and end the game. But Mantle, superb athlete that he was, eluded the tag and slithered back to first, like an Oklahoma rattler evading a diving eagle.

The skill that Mantle demonstrated on that play is something that base runners are still shown in training films. In avoiding the tag, Mantle did what few other ballplayers of his era could do. And as he did so, Dale Long scored the tying run from third. The Yankees were even again, 9–9, and Pittsburgh fans sank back into their seats with looks of "C'mon," and "What the hell?" on their faces.

"He was out," opined one fan with a cigar clenched between his teeth. But a clear-eyed viewing of the tape of Game 7 reveals that Mantle was not. He was simply the better athlete on that particular play.

Coming to the plate was Bill Skowron, who had been a player of record in this Series—two home runs, key hits, some important fielding plays. Finally, after years as an also-ran among the storied Yankees, Skowron felt like an equal on this squad of superstars. Now was his chance to break the Series open, give the Yankees their win, and take his place as part of the pinstriped legacy.

Fate is not kind to every man. Skowron, who would have a proud but not a stellar career, bounced Haddix's second pitch down to third where Hoak, the heart of the Pirates, who had made at least two other remarkable fielding plays and kept his team in the Series with his alternate viciousness and consolation, grabbed the grounder and tossed to Nelson, whose unthinking play had let the tying run score, for the final out.

The Pirates had given up their lead—twice. The mood in the stadium, as the Longines clock in the left-field scoreboard inched past 3:30 P.M., was approaching enervation. Fans can get juked up for a home team again and again. But when the advantage goes the other way, when misplays and misfortune gather, they retreat into the confines of their seats, benumbed, diminished psychologically and sometimes physically. A woman in the third-base box seats, wearing an orange hat and almond-shaped sunglasses, smoked disconsolately as the Yankees took the field for the bottom of the ninth. Earlier in the game, she was shown on television wildly cheering Hal Smith's home run. Now, she was a portrait of indifference.

Out in the left-field bleachers, Drew Balog, a high-school sophomore from Duquesne, about twelve miles from Pittsburgh, had cut school and gone to Forbes Field to try to sneak in. City kids often watched as the Forbes Field ushers accepted small bribes to let people into the left-field seats. On this day, there were no spare seats, nowhere to sit at all. So Balog stood. "I couldn't see over the heads of the people in front of me. All the men had hats on. So I had to jump up and down. I had just jumped up and caught a look at the plate and the next thing, I heard the bat hit the ball and then I saw Yogi Berra . . ."

Mazeroski was the first batter, and he was determined not to repeat his mistake of the seventh inning. He felt he had swung too hard, trying for the fences, when what he should have done was hack for a single. He was no home-run hitter. Terry had a good slider; it was his out-pitch, the one he threw with the most confidence. But as Terry was warming up in the Yankee bullpen in right field, the pitching coach, Eddie Lopat, was concerned with what he saw. Terry's slider was not scuttling across the plate the way it should have. Before Terry entered the game to close out the eighth, Lopat gave him some advice: Don't throw your slider; it's not working.

Blanchard crouched behind the plate. It was 3:35. He set his mitt low—he didn't want Mazeroski to get a good pitch. The Yankees had grudging respect for the stocky second baseman, who had already hit one home run in the Series and usually made contact. The first pitch was high, not at all where Blanchard wanted it. The catcher came out of his squat, walked partway to the mound, and peppered the ball back to the pitcher.

"Down, dammit!" he ordered.

He resumed his position behind the plate, in front of umpire Bill Jackowski. His mitt was set low, again.

Mike Hayden, the Pittsburgh taxi driver who liked to impress first-time visitors by having them behold the transformed downtown as they emerged from the Fort Pitt Tunnel, would go on to have a stellar career in the military. Later, he would become the director of the Central Intelligence Agency in the administration of George W. Bush. But on October 13, 1960, Mike Hayden was a sophomore at North Catholic High School, on his way home. He passed a drugstore at the corner of Federal and Lacock Streets (near the Pirates' current home, PNC Park), where a black-and-white television was showing the bottom of the ninth as Maz swung at the second pitch. "It was just the most

"He knew it was gone," said Drew Balog, who was in the bleachers.

unbelievable thing," America's spy chief said, decades later. "It put Pittsburgh on the map, for sure."

Did Terry disregard his coach's advice and throw his slider? Blanchard believes he did. Terry, the only person who knows, has never definitively answered the question. "I don't know what the pitch was," he said years later. "All I know is it was the wrong one." What Drew Balog, now a teacher in Ligonier, Pennsylvania, remembers from his illicit perch in the left-field bleachers was not the ball soaring over the 406-foot mark in left field, not its flight over the red ivy, after which its destination was, and remains, a mystery. "I remember looking down to see where Yogi Berra was. He had already turned his back on the ball and was circling back to the dugout," Balog told me. "He knew it was gone."

You could kiss it good-bye.

Worth a thousand words: Maz could never explain how he felt.

Courtesy Pittsburgh Pirates

Thanks. Now get out of my way.

Courtesy Pittsburgh Pirates

Maz wasn't alone.

After victory, mayhem. The scoreboard was vandalized shortly afterward.

Extra Innings

"Children have more need of models than of critics."
—Joseph Joubert
(From Vernon Law's *Words to Live By*)

IN DOWNTOWN PITTSBURGH," Law remembers, "windows went up, and papers, garbage, everything ended up in the streets. Traffic came to a standstill. Even the trolleys couldn't move because of all the paper in the tracks. There was, literally, dancing in the streets. Coeds were giving out free kisses. Everyone was happy, except the Yankees of course. Our clubhouse was worse than when we won the pennant in Milwaukee. Everybody from the mayor to the dog catcher was in there and all were getting doused with champagne."

In fact, the damage was greater than Law suspected. Out on the field, fans had jumped the barriers and simply outnumbered the thousand police and stadium security guards that had been on hand. The scoreboard in left field was attacked. First base and home plate were dug up and pilfered for resale. Dirt was shoveled up from the infield and sold for $5 a handful to passersby, who could not possibly have

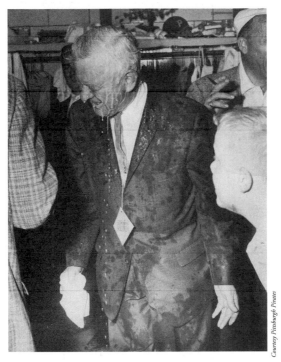

Courtesy Pittsburgh Pirates

Not much honor: Mayor Barr gets a bubble bath. He didn't mind.

authenticated its origin. Several people claimed to have located Mazeroski's home-run ball, and some tried to sell it
back to the club. But there was no way to be certain where
the ball that had ended Pittsburgh's long baseball drought
had rolled to a stop.

Amazingly, for all the chaos, there were almost no serious
injuries reported as a result of excessive celebration. No
doubt, some Pittsburghers woke up with headaches the next
morning, but there were no riots, no gun battles, no looting,
and no pedestrians reported mowed down by errant drivers.

*Maz's home-run ball landed somewhere in
Schenley Park but was never found.*

Not for the first time, Law's faith intervened when he
needed it. Just as he had been able to negotiate, initially, a
contract with the Pirates that exempted him from pitching
on Sunday, just as a fellow Mormon had helped him to avoid
transfer overseas in the army so he could be by VaNita's side
when their first child was born, Law found himself the beneficiary of kindness from someone with whom he shared a
religious affinity. It was Ezra Taft Benson, who was Dwight

Eisenhower's Secretary of Agriculture and would later become the President of The Church of Jesus Christ of Latter-day Saints, who came to the pitcher's rescue. The Secretary had asked Law for tickets to Game 7, a gift the pitcher was happy to provide.

Now, as the team and city were casting caution to the winds, Law just wanted to get away. He found VaNita and the boys but was still worried about walking out of the stadium with his family. "It wasn't safe on the streets, and I didn't know what to do until President Benson saved my life. He had his limousine parked with a driver just outside the door, so we scooted in that, and he drove us to our car."

Law was no longer an Idaho farm boy dazzled by the big city. He knew what Pittsburgh was and was not. He also understood that he, in large part, had made it what it had not been for more than 30 years—a winner. When the local TV station asked the Pirates for someone to come on the eleven o'clock newscast that night, Law volunteered, "seeing as I was about the only one sober," he wrote in his memoir. After that interview, he and VaNita went home where their neighbors were waiting for them with nonalcoholic punch, cookies, and fresh-baked cake. "It was neat," was the hero pitcher's eloquent summation of the day.

Where, you may ask, reader, was the author of this book at that magical instant? Glued to the television? At Forbes Field, elated, perhaps? No such luck. October 13 was a school day, and, World Series or not, I was sent off to class.

Which is not to say that it was a normal day of learning at St. Valentine's. My teacher that year was Sister Mary Raphael, a tall, imposing, and imperious member of the Order of St. Francis, who also happened to be one of those nuns who was a baseball nut. Sister Raphael was, by training, a mathematics teacher, and she put her specialty to good use from the first day of spring training. She could recite the Pirates' batting stats, pitching records, and probably fielding averages at will. An excellent teacher who inspired her students, she nonetheless needed little encouragement to detour from the day's lesson plan to a debate about whether Skinner or Cimoli should start in left, whether Smith or Burgess called a smoother game. Unless she could also throw a curveball, Sister Raphael had only two things in common with Vernon Law: a sincere belief that she was on earth to do God's will—and a passionate desire for the Pirates to be the champions of baseball.

Not surprisingly, perhaps, her dual enthusiasms were sometimes merged. On that Thursday, at about noon, an hour or so before Game 7 was to begin, Sister Raphael went to the metal closet in the front of her classroom where she stored supplies. What she pulled out was a cardboard box that was familiar to her students. It contained rosaries, dozens of them—cheap plastic rosaries knotted together with string.

"Boys and girls," she announced, "we are going to say the rosary." In those days, it was not uncommon for Catholic school students to do just that during class time. After all, we had been sent to St. Valentine's to get a Catholic education. And the prayers were not optional. One did not argue with Sister Raphael if one hoped to live a long and uncrippled life. We each took a rosary from the box that she passed around, stood by our desks, and, in unison, recited the Lord's Prayer, the Hail Mary, and the Glory Be to the Father. Sister Raphael never explained her sudden decision to give her fifty-some students a break from their studies in the middle of the day. But I have no doubt for whom we were asking the Lord's blessings.

Her fanaticism went only so far. When we completed our prayers, Sister Raphael collected the rosaries and continued the day's lessons. She did not keep a transistor radio on her desk, and she did not sneak in a television with rabbit ears to steal looks at the game. She loved the Pirates, but on that day as on other days, her job was to teach us. So she did.

At 3:36 P.M., as Maz's bat made contact with the ball and sent it over the left-field wall, I was ambling home from school. I knew the game was going on, but I was only a six-nearly seven-year-old boy, and congruence of thought and logic are not virtues normally associated with young boys. I don't know of what I was thinking. Probably nothing.

At my home, my mother was ironing. She had not planned to be ironing that day, in the middle of the after-noon. She had other things to do. But after the Pirates fell behind in the sixth inning, my mother's best friend—the mother of my best friend, the kid to whom I had shoveled my way through the snow—appeared at our front door with a load of shirts in her arms.

"Get out your iron!" she was shouting.

"Why?" asked my amazed mother. "Do you need help doing your husband's shirts?"

"We were ironing when they won the last time," said my friend's mom. "If we're not ironing, they might lose!"

And so, they ironed, until Terry's 1–0 pitch crossed the wrong part of the plate and Mazeroski blasted it into history. When I came home from school, only a few minutes later, my mother and her best friend were crying and hugging each other and dancing around like demented launderers. Sister Raphael is no longer alive. Neither is my mother's best friend, my best friend's mother. And so I must take my mother at her word that it was not my pressing the beads of the rosary but her pressing of wrinkled cotton clothes with a heated iron that was responsible for the most remarkable event that had occurred in my life up to that point.

The moment couldn't last forever. And perhaps hallmarks of such intense emotion should not be dragged out. Three weeks later, America elected John F. Kennedy its 35th president, an event that would have far-reaching implications until his assassination and beyond. That tragic event replaced Maz's home run as the "Where were you when . . . ?" question of the young decade.

The 1960 World Series victory was the high-water mark

A streetcar named delirium.

After decades of defeat, what could you expect?

Ten-hut! Ready to take orders, or just raise hell.

A soda jerk's dream: Most of them needed to wet their whistles.

for the Pirates, and, as it turned out, for Vern Law. The injury he incurred at the hands of Prince and the Pirate players would, in fact, turn out to be career-threatening for the man who had won two games in the Series, and, if he had been healthy, might have wrapped up the clincher as well. He had won the Cy Young Award as the outstanding pitcher of 1960, at a time when only one pitcher in all the Majors was chosen (as opposed to the current practice of awarding one to a pitcher in each league). Law had played through enormous pain. He expected to heal during the off-season. But it was not that easy.

"As I was driving home from the Series," Law recalled, "I moved my pitching arm, and it had a funny feeling in it, as though I didn't have any strength at all in it. I didn't pay much attention to it because I had the whole winter to rest. But when I started my pre-spring training, it still didn't feel right. Little did I know that because of the bad ankle and my having to put more strain on my arm, I had torn some muscles in the back of my shoulder during the Series. This would cause me serious problems during the next three years."

Indeed, his record in 1961 was a miserable 3–4. The truth was, Law was chased early from most of his starts and did not figure in the final decisions. The next year, he improved—but only to a listless 10–7. The Pirates were concerned about Law but also about their bottom line. They cut his salary—then $50,000—by 25 percent; worse, on August

9 of the 1963 season, while Law's record was mired at 4–5, Danny Murtaugh suggested voluntary retirement. "I didn't like the sound of that," Law says, "but I could also see they weren't going to use me, so I said, 'If you think that's the best thing to do, perhaps I should.' It was all very emotional for me when the impact of that settled in. To think that my career had come to a disappointing end like this was very hard."

After agreeing to Murtaugh's suggestion, he left a hand-written note in the clubhouse. It read: "Dear Fellows: I hope you'll forgive me for not coming to see each one of you personally and say good-bye, but this is the hardest thing to do. I hope you'll understand.

"I just want you to know it's been fun, and I'll never forget the times we've had together. Every one of you has given me something to remember.

"I want to wish you the best of luck for the rest of the season and for the future. Please tell your wives and families good-bye from me. Godspeed."

The note was signed (unnecessarily): "No. 32 (Vernon Law)"

Vern Law staged a comeback the next season and posted a 12–13 record. He was still not right. The next season, he seemed rejuvenated, and went 17–9, a respectable record but nowhere near the quality of pitcher he knew he had been before that night on the bus in Milwaukee. He was named

Comeback Player of the Year, an award he said he never wanted to receive, "considering the implications."

That season earned him another shot in 1966, when he went 12–8. But the next year, his last, he suffered a groin injury in August with his record at a dismal 2–6. By then, most of the 1960 team had retired or been traded. And some of the players the Pirates had acquired—particularly the flashy, base-stealing shortstop Maury Wills—were not the kind of teammates Law enjoyed being around. Law retired on August 29, returning to Meridian while the team was on the road, in Atlanta, the city that now hosted the Braves, who the Pirates had been playing the night Law's ankle was hurt in 1960.

He left this time without talking to team officials, without leaving any note for his teammates. This time, as it had been before, quitting the Pirates was "the hardest thing to do."

It was hard for Law's fans, too. I know, because I was one of them. But I was not the only one. Ron Thulin, with whom I played pickup baseball and football as a grade-schooler, became a sportscaster for Turner Broadcasting and roamed the country covering sports. He still remembers 1960 with special fervor:

"In my 33 years of broadcasting sports, I have seen how teams can galvanize a city, giving those who live there inspiration and adding pride to the area. There is just something

In Utah, 1967, the year he retired from Major League Baseball.

about your hometown team winning, even if you are not the most diehard sports fan.

"Even before moving to Pittsburgh, I envisioned it as a dirty, smoke-filled, dark place with people only working in steel mills and riding streetcars. That all changed when I saw the highlight of Bill Mazeroski's home run over the left-field scoreboard, giving the Pirates the World Series. Instantly, I became the biggest fan of Maz, Roberto Clemente, Smoky

Burgess, Bob Friend, Vern Law, and ElRoy Face. That is what I wanted to be when I grew up: a Pittsburgh Pirate.

"But to me it was much more than just a winning baseball team. I heard Vern Law speak in 1965 about what it took to win a World Series, and his words have stayed with me during my career. Talent, yes, but it went beyond that. He spoke of a work ethic that typified the city of Pittsburgh. Growing up in Pittsburgh I saw firsthand what Mr. Law was talking about. My dad walked a mile to catch a streetcar early in the morning despite snow, rain, and the typical Pittsburgh winter weather. He did what it took to make a living. Talent, yes, but he had much more than that. He had the Pittsburgh work ethic.

"Winning the World Series in 1960 changed the way the rest of the country viewed the city. It also set the stage for the Steelers winning their NFL titles. Both teams reflected what made the city great. Playing by the rules, playing tough, playing with emotion, overcoming odds, and a will to win that was second to none.

"I can still remember as a sophomore and junior in high school, playing the state baseball championship in Forbes Field. Walking onto the field the first time gave me chills. Standing in left field where Maz's home run cleared the scoreboard, running out to right field where Roberto Clemente made many spectacular plays, all made me realize how proud I was to be from the Steel City.

"To this day, mention the Pirates of 1960, and the locals

The champions: Face, Mazeroski, Law, and Clemente. Clemente later died in a plane crash trying to help earthquake victims in Central America.

will still remember that afternoon with a tear in the eye. It was Pittsburgh's first step to becoming a city of champions. But to me, it was the first step in the pride I have when someone asks me where I am from and I say, 'Pittsburgh.'"

Mike Hayden, the taxi driver turned spymaster, concurs. "After the shouting it still mattered a lot," Hayden told me. "Pittsburgh had never experienced anything like that in the lifetime of most of its citizens. I also think that the celebration was the first of its kind, a kind of public party.

Something that's old hat by now. But it felt great to come from Pittsburgh."

Richard Sebak, the chubby-faced boy in my first-grade class, whose outgoing personality so contrasted with mine, became one of Pittsburgh's finest contemporary storytellers. Rick's annual television documentaries, among them *What Makes Pittsburgh, Pittsburgh?; It's the Neighborhood; Things That Aren't There Anymore;* and *Something about Oakland* are among the highest-rated and most anticipated events on the city's public broadcasting station, WQED. "There's something about Pittsburgh that's really interesting," Rick told me. "It's what I make my living at, trying to figure that out. I interviewed a very accomplished woman who could have worked anywhere in the world but had decided to stay in Pittsburgh. I asked her why, and she said because it doesn't feel artificial here. There's a depth of family, a depth of culture, a depth of feeling. Pittsburgh is the right size. It's knowable, and it's like the much-discussed small city that you can really learn to love.

"I can remember coming home from school that day, October 13th, and seeing my mother crying in the living room," Rick said. "I asked her what was wrong and she said, 'Nothing.' She was just so happy about the World Series. And she was never a baseball fan."

I was somewhat different. In 1967, I graduated from St. Valentine's grammar school and moved on to high school. I was still playing baseball and thought I was getting good at it (I was wrong about that). I still wore Number 32 whenever I could, still followed The Deacon's career, still hoped for his return to form. But other things were going on in my life, and my passion for the Pirates and their players had new competition. I began getting interested in girls, and my new school, and the war in Vietnam, and the changing season of rebellious culture brewing throughout America that would that year be misnamed The Summer of Love. Instead, I think, it was the coming of age of a generation that came to believe it was right about everything: right to oppose war, right to want the country to change, right to want to do away with the prohibitions and restrictions that marked American society as stuffy, suffocating, lacking in spontaneous passion, and artificial in its affections. It would not be the last generation to hold those beliefs.

By then, the Pirates' incredible 1960 run, the youthful naiveté with which they took on and conquered the mighty Yankees, seemed as out of tune with the morally complex times as the simple bumpity-bump rhythm of Joe Negri's ditty, "The Bucs Are Going All the Way," did when compared with the chord-weaving, mind-warp music of McCartney, Dylan, and Hendrix.

I played baseball through high school, usually first base, sometimes pitching. But I knew the parabola that had boosted Vern Law from sandlot games to Forbes Field was well beyond my average ability. I could put the ball in play, and sometimes, very occasionally, out of play, over the fence.

My fielding was exceptional, but only for a teenager. For me, the dream was over, not before I woke up, but before I even shut my eyes to imagine it.

Instead, I became enamored of writing about sports and other events. It was not a stretch. My father never encouraged me nor talked up the business by which he had supported us during my childhood. He left it to me to decide if getting paid for observing and describing events as they occurred appealed to me. It did. I worked at a weekly community newspaper one summer, then, during the next school year, continued to contribute by covering town and village council and school board meetings. I suppose I had some innate abilities; maybe my familiarity with the craft, inherited from my father, helped.

The news business is not easily entered; it has codes and conventions that the general public does not understand. News people like it that way. It sets and keeps us apart. It also causes people to distrust us. People want, and deserve, to know how we come by the information upon which we rely to report the news. They want to know our sources, their reliability, and their potential prejudices. And we news people, on the inside of the information circle, work very hard to keep those things from being divulged to the public at large.

To break into the circle, you need more than a press card. You must pass the test of trust and be invited to join the confraternity of journalists. We share a longing for finding the truth, yes. But we also have each other's backs. Learning that, and learning how to protect colleagues, and benefit from their protection of you, is not automatic. For me, it was easier, because of my father. I was John's kid. I was halfway to being accepted as a reporter before I ever wrote a story.

And the language of the craft came naturally to me, like someone whose ear is attuned to foreign tongues. I knew that reporters (at that time) wrote "-30-"at the end of a story to signify it was finished. I knew that "stet" means to ignore an editing change and to go with the original wording. I knew that when you talk on background to a source, you cannot use that person's name in your story. Like any novice, I made mistakes. But I learned quickly, and, because my father was who he was and did what he had done, I got the benefit of the doubt.

The one aspect of the business that I quickly got to know was the competitiveness between reporters. The thrill of getting a story first (and getting it right) provides the kind of rush that very few people not in the business can understand. It is the kind of thrill that athletes feel when they score or that a Wall Street trader gets when he knows he has just made millions. Reporters like to know things that other people don't. Even better, they like it when others know they knew something before anyone else. Especially before other reporters.

When it came time for me to go to college, I knew one thing: I wanted to leave Pittsburgh. The bubble of excitement that the Pirates had brought to the city had dissipated like the smoke that once choked its skies. The idea of staying in the place where I had grown up felt like a dead-end option, a road to nowhere, or at least to nowhere new. I had no idea what to say I wanted to major in, so, as a sop to myself, I said, "Communications." That could have taken me down a lot of paths. Perhaps because the times and technology were changing so quickly, I ended up on radio, reading and reporting news, instead of in the print world that had pointed the way for my father's escape from small-town Maryland. There was no question of my playing baseball at that level. The players in college towered over me. The big little boy had now become an average-sized-at-best eighteen-year-old.

In the summer of my second year in college, I applied for a job at United Press International, the wire service that competed against my father's former employer, the Associated Press. I was hired, in part, because my father talked to a friend and rival from UPI and asked him to give me a break. He did. My father, by then, worked for the Pittsburgh *Post-Gazette,* the city's morning paper, where he became the country's leading reporter on the labor movement. When a president of the United Mine Workers, running for reelection, was accused of ordering the murder of a challenger, it was a big story for Pittsburgh, where the coal and steel industries, though much diminished from their heyday, were still important. The rest of the country paid attention, too. Had the labor movement, which was all too often associated with organized crime and underhanded tactics, reached the level where murder was an election tactic?

Despite my youth and inexperience, UPI assigned me to cover one phase of the union president's trial for conspiracy in the death of his rival. The AP knew that my father, better versed on the story than anyone, would be there and asked him to let them know the verdict. So there we were, John Moody versus John Moody, sitting in the courtroom press gallery together, filling our notebooks with the details that caught our eyes, the quotes that filled our ears. When the jury's guilty verdict was read, the reporters in the courtroom bolted for the door. There were no cell phones, no Blackberries, no wireless communication. And not nearly enough pay phones to accommodate the crush. I rushed with the others, mindful that my father was behind me. He was reading over his notes, carefully, frowning at what he had written. I couldn't understand why he wasn't moving with the rest of the scrum, wrestling for a pay phone to call in the news.

I was younger, faster, and very determined to make my name in this business, which at that moment, seemed more thrilling to me than anything I had ever done. I dialed the UPI number and shouted the news. "Guilty. Get ready. I'll dictate a lead." I don't know how long I poured details down the phone line, checked information that the editors on the other end wanted, made sure my prose was pure, my facts unassailable. And when I was done, I was glistening with excitement and adrenaline.

I looked around and saw my father ambling up the courthouse hallway, to one of the now-free phones. He dialed the AP's number and calmly told them the verdict. UPI's bulletin had already been on the wire for a minute by this time. It was a clear-cut victory for my summertime employer, over the man who knew the story better than anyone in the country but who had taken his sweet time to get to the phone—because he was competing against his son.

I was good. Good enough, anyway, to get a job with UPI when I graduated from college. That meant moving to New York, in the mid-1970s, when the Yankees were transitioning from garbage to glory. If I'd been asked, I would have said I was still an avid baseball fan, though the Yankees and their heroes of the day—Munson and Murcer, Chambliss, Nettles, and Ron Guidry, aka Louisiana Lightnin'—meant nothing to me. I watched, neutrally, the games that my colleagues kept on the TV monitors in the newsrooms during the nightshift. I sensed the city's grief when Munson died in a plane crash, but did not partake of it. I was more interested in the rest of the world.

What was happening in Iran? Would the Shah really be overthrown? And what about Russia? What did Brezhnev want from the West and why couldn't impotent Jimmy Carter stand up to him? My interest morphed into activity in the office. I was noticed. And before my 26th birthday, the foreign editor asked me to have a drink with him after work and, before I had even brought the glass to my lips, asked me: "Would you like to be our bureau chief in Moscow?"

There are important moments that we recognize as life-changing; others pass without our immediate notice. This was the former kind. I knew then, at the age of 25, that this would be my life, my calling. I would still have called myself a baseball fan—still felt the stomach-tightening excitement of a close game or a big hit. But I would have filtered it through the screen of 1960, the Pirates, and Vern. It was not them, it was not him. And so, I could let it go. I had to let it go. I was going to Moscow.

I had been studying Spanish, at the suggestion of this same foreign editor. He had imagined I might be of use in the Buenos Aires bureau. But the news business has no design except the crazy curves of immediacy and crisis. I was needed in Moscow. Forget the Spanish lessons, kid, and pack your bags.

I got home from my life-changing drink and sat down to think. Moscow in 1979 was not a friendly place for Americans. But the challenge outweighed the uncertainty, and off I went. If Vern found Pittsburgh a different place from any he'd ever seen, imagine my surprise when I landed in Moscow, which reeked of old cigarettes, sweat, and beets cooked too long. A gray sky in the middle of the day—not unlike the Pittsburgh of the pre-renaissance days—and blessed little to smile about. The Moscow of 1979 was a dreary collection of cold, dirty millions of citizens luxuriating in what Lenin had cruelly called the worker's paradise. I was lost there. When I opened one of my shipping boxes and saw that I'd brought my baseball mitt from childhood, I felt tears prick my eyes, just as I had when I thought my favorite ball had been lost. Lost and found. Found and lost.

There was no baseball in Moscow. There were hardly any potatoes. I worked in a dirty, crowded office, reading the Russian *Tass* newswire's numbing accounts of how wonderful everything was in the Soviet Union and how everyone was nearly dying of happiness. That was half right, anyhow—people were dying but more because of alcoholism and harsh living conditions. The mood in Moscow was surly, uncooperative, and definitely anti-American. Within months, the Red Army had invaded Afghanistan and plunged the world into a new level of cold war. In response, the United States said that it would boycott the 1980 Summer Olympic Games to be held in Moscow. So I was responsible for covering not just a political story but a war and an Olympics—at the age of 26.

Those Summer Games were monumentally important to the Soviets. They desperately wanted to show that a communist empire could successfully host an important, worldwide event. New stadiums were built. Roadways were improved. Traffic around the Olympic sites was severely restricted. Items that were never available in Moscow—Polish razor blades, Rumanian wine, women's synthetic stockings from East Germany—flooded the markets and stores. Anyone who looked remotely needy was rounded up and escorted, roughly, out of the capital. Security, always tight, became choking. And when the Games began, it was as though the rest of the world had come to a complete and utter standstill. In the part of the world that the Russians then controlled, there was no other news. To have created a distraction from the Olympics would have been antisocialist.

The opening ceremony was nothing compared to the huge extravaganzas that are now the norm. But for Moscow in 1980, it was a statement of might. Entire battalions of the Red Army were brought to the capital to march in crisply pressed uniforms that they would never get to wear again. Except for the Games, the country—arguably the most important military power in the world, given that it was in the process of taking over a neighboring land—came to a halt.

All television channels were devoted to the exploits of Soviet athletes. Interviews with the coaches emphasized their allegiance to the Communist Party and their gratitude to its leadership for making available the resources to create champions. The visiting countries' athletes were barely acknowledged on television or in *Pravda*, the Communist Party newspaper; *Izvestia*, the government organ; or *Trud*, the labor unions' daily. These Olympics were to be perfect, by decree of the Communist Party.

Of course, the Soviets overplayed their hand. At the track-and-field events, held at the cavernous outdoor Lenin Stadium, on the hillside above Moscow, there were doors at each end of the stadium to allow machinery to be brought in to work on the field. The Russians must have figured that since it was their Olympics, their stadium, and since the Americans were boycotting anyway, they had nothing to lose in trying to ensure their athletes would dominate.

During the track-and-field events, such as javelin throw, discus throw, long jump, or triple jump—where one athlete competes at a time and their distances are then compared— the doors at the back of the stadium mysteriously opened while Soviet athletes were performing, thus putting the wind at their backs. When athletes from other countries were about to compete, the back doors were closed and those at the other end of the stadium swung open, meaning that the athlete was throwing or running into a wind coming at them from the far side.

I was sitting in the press facilities provided by the Olympic Committee. I was up high enough to see both ends of the stadium and the door shenanigans that were going on. I knew what I was seeing.

In 1980, there were no cell phones, no laptop comput- ers, no high-speed Internet connections. To send informa- tion to the home office in New York, I had to type out my story on paper, using a typewriter, then give the paper to a teletype operator. That operator would then retype, or "punch" as it was called, the story onto Telex tape—a yellow paper tape just wide enough for five holes to be punched into it by the teletype operator's machine. Depending on what series of holes were punched, the entire alphabet and the numbers zero through nine could be distinguished when the tape was fed into a Telex machine, which transmitted it to my employer's address.

The sounds of Telex machines binging and banging were my earliest association with the news business. When I would visit my father working at the Associated Press in Pittsburgh, or, later, at the Pittsburgh *Post-Gazette,* the noise was enough to distract casual visitors and cause them not to be able to hear each other. But to reporters, such as my father and, now, me, the ding-ding-ding of a news bulletin coming across the Telex was the reason we existed.

My story was straightforward enough: On the first day of the Moscow Olympics, Soviet officials used windy conditions to unfairly benefit their nation's athletes in the track-and-field events. The words flew off my typewriter easily because I knew what I had seen. It was, in the lingo of my profession (was this really my profession?), "firsthand reporting." I handed the paper to a teletype operator, a stout Russian woman (this description did not narrow the field much when applied to 1980) who appeared unable to speak English but who had been trained to type Latin letters with skill and precision. She began punching the story with hardly a glance at me, and so I returned to my seat to provide more

details to my story. Probably no more than five minutes had
elapsed when four men, dressed nearly identically in badly
fitting suits, tight white shirts, and thin black neckties, came
bustling down the steps of the stadium and into the press
section.

"Up, up!" they all said, as if competing to see who could
get this English word out the most times in the fewest seconds. One grabbed my arm, another got his thumb under
my armpit, a third did the same with the other arm, and, just
as they had requested, up I got. They hustled me, not
gently, out of the press section and into a hidden hallway, beneath the seats and out of sight of the spectators.

There, the finery of the Olympics, overhead and everywhere else in Moscow, was entirely missing. This was the
dank, smoke- and sweat-smelling, neglected Soviet Union
that the hosts were trying to keep concealed from the thousands of visitors to the Games. I, on the other hand, had
worn out my welcome. Nothing was needed to impress me,
except, perhaps, a good old-fashioned show of force. One
bad suit yelled at me in bad English, another in excellent
Russian. I was a provocateur, a liar, a capitalist pig. And then
they got personal. As the excoriation went on, and I started
to wonder what they intended, ultimately, to do with me, I
kept in mind my father's advice from the days when I was
afraid at school: Don't push the panic button.

There was every reason to panic. This was not hazing
from Little League teammates. This was not racial taunting

from ElBoy, the black schoolyard bully. Nor was it the loss of a beloved ball. This was the kind of incident that, in those days, landed people in Russian jails. And in response to the threat I faced, I found (at long last) that I had courage. I would not yield. I had, finally and just in time, toughened up.

I diverted my mind by reciting to myself the Pirates' lineup from 1960. Virdon, center field, Groat at short, . . . and so on, until I got to the ninth batter, and Vern's handsome, eternally youthful face composed itself. And when they were done insulting me, they threw me out of the stadium for the rest of the day. So much for the Olympics bringing people together.

I spent three years in the Soviet Union, then got the job that I had thought I wanted all my life: the Paris bureau. I drove my Russian-made car, known as a Zhuguli, from Moscow to Paris—yes, it took a while—and when I arrived on the hilly outskirts of The City of Light, I pulled over (you could do that then) and looked down on the place I would call home.

There is a quality to Paris that makes it attractive to people from anywhere in the world. You need not speak French—though it helps—to sense the respect for history, the wealth of pleasure, the knowledge of how to live life enjoyably, sensuously, and sensibly, that Parisians possess. If absolute opposites exist, Paris in the 1980s was probably the antithesis of Meridian in the 1930s. That said, the simple realities of life—finding a place to live, figuring out how to get from one place to another, affording the necessities, and squirreling away enough for some non-necessities—are as concrete in Paris as anywhere else.

I found an apartment, learned the Metro route, compromised enough on how often I ate at restaurants and learned which ones were cheap and filling, and for those days when I could not eat out, learned to cook. Like probably every American who has hankered to see his name above his own published words, I began a Paris novel that never got to chapter 2. It was not so much that I had too many diversions as that I had so few original thoughts, a curbing limitation on becoming a novelist. I sauntered through Paris, alone, and tried to drink in its greatness. Too often, I ended up drinking its wine.

The boy who sat in his front yard in suburban Pittsburgh waiting for something to happen became a man who did the same thing in The City of Light. Was it not the fault of the locality but of the person that time seemed to drag and events occurred without my knowledge or appreciation of them? Was anything *ever* going to happen to me?

Vernon Law knew when he reencountered VaNita McGuire in the butter room of the Ada County Dairy that he was a goner. His life would never again be his own. Put another way, he had found the person with whom he wanted to share it. For me, that moment occurred in Bonn, in what was then known as West Germany. I had been sent there to help cover a NATO summit that would be Ronald Reagan's first as president of the United States. When I got to the UPI bureau in Bonn—after failing to be able to pronounce its address in German and being forced, in desperation, to show passersby my pathetic piece of paper on which it was written—the first thing I saw was a beautiful, blonde British girl in a filmy blue dress walking toward me. I knew then how Vern felt in the butter room.

Eighteen months later I was a newly married man with a new job at *Time* magazine, a new home, in, of all places, Bonn, and a partner for life. We roamed Europe together, moved to Latin America, and wondered how things could get any better. The answer came with the birth of our first child, a girl (to whom this book is dedicated), a couple of years later, and then a son, who bears my, and his grand-father's, name.

I tried to teach both of them to appreciate the beauty of baseball, its perfect geometry, its elegant pacing, its electrifying moments of magic. It is hard to explain baseball in a country where soccer is the only sport to be discussed, reported on, televised. Baseball requires a sense of history, a method for comparing and admiring the statistics upon which the game is based, and, more practically, teammates, to allow it to spread the seed of contagion that so completely infected me and my generation of Pittsburghers. When I told my children about baseball, I spoke about the Pirates.

And my Pirates remained the Pirates of 1960. Smoky

Burgess and Hal Smith catching, Dick Stuart and Rocky Nelson at first, Maz at second, paired with Dick Groat at shortstop, and The Tiger, Don Hoak, at third. In left field was the aptly named Bob Skinner, whose slim frame belied his vicious slashes with a bat. In center was the professorial, wire-rimmed-glasses-wearing Bill Virdon, who would go on to manage both the Pirates and, in a later life, their 1960 nemeses, the New York Yankees. Clemente, The Great One, in right. That is the starting lineup, always. No matter what city I put my head down in, and dream in, it is of that lineup. Always.

And always, in my mind, on my mind's mound, is Vern Law.

◆ ◆ ◆

By 1994, my days of living abroad were finished. My children had been reared in four cities on three continents. Enough was enough. It was time to live in a place where the movies were in a language they understood and where ice cream came in as many flavors as they could imagine and many more they could neither imagine nor pronounce.

We planted roots in a suburban village in New Jersey, enrolled the children in public school (we never had the Catholic school debate that had shaped my young life), and turned me from a globe-trotter into a daily commuter, by bus no less. The atmosphere of suburbia was a confusing combination of false-friendly smiles from neighbors who might be accidentally spied getting into or out of their cars (if their electric garage door openers weren't working) and yards full of swings, sandboxes, and tires hanging by ropes from the branches of trees—but completely devoid of the children for whom these things had been bought and built.

As the native-born American in the family, I felt it incumbent upon me to explain this place to my wife, to my children, to myself, to our bewildered dog. My memories of childhood were of the door being pounded by friends who wanted me to come play ball, of the various summoning signals of parents at dinnertime, calling their children in from the lots where we competed ceaselessly, giving each other the names, nicknames, and attributes of the 1960 Pirates whose positions we played.

What had happened to that world, that existence built on batting orders and dreams of greatness that, until 1960 anyway, I believed could only be achieved outside of Pittsburgh?

The answers, of course, are as varied as the number of heinous crimes against children and families that seeped into our culture between the '60s and the '90s: child abduction and abuse, the drug *demimonde* that consumed some of my friends as it did most everyone's, the sense that the United States was no longer a place of innocence, honor, and wholesome values. I was now the parent of children approximately the age I had been when the Pirates won the World Series in 1960. And I would no more let them spend the day out of our yard without my or my wife's eyes on them than I would lead them to a rattlesnake and instruct them to capture it.

My wife tried not to roll her eyes at neighborhood gossip and the incredible lengths to which some parents would go to secure their children's "best interests"—mothers arguing with principals about which teachers were assigned which students, fathers shouting full-throated at coaches who did not recognize their children's brilliance in biddy-league, anonymous tongue-wagging about who hadn't been seen in church for two months running, and you know what that usually means . . .

Then God sent us baseball, though in distinctly odd packaging that I thought provided a glimpse of the Divine's sense of humor. In 1996, a 22-year-old, biracial, bubble-gum-blowing shortstop broke into the New York Yankees' starting lineup. That the Yankees believed Derek Jeter was a special player was evident: He was given the Number 2, the only single-digit Yankee uniform number not yet retired permanently and enshrined beyond the left-field fence of Yankee Stadium in Monument Park. Jeter's flashy play, his dazzling smile, his squiring around of a rock singer, and the youthful zing he added to the hidebound Yankees made him a sensation, if not overnight, then by midseason.

My brilliant British wife suggested that the family sit down together—something we hadn't done much since arriving in America—and watch a baseball game. We focused, of course, on Derek Jeter.

"He's good," I said, displaying my vast knowledge of the game.

"He's fast," said my son, for whom speed was, and remains, the ultimate virtue.

"He's cute," said my daughter, a sentiment shared that year by approximately 98 percent of the girls in her school and the New York metropolitan area.

And so we became baseball fans. All of us, together. Of the Yankees! The Yankees, whom my Pirates had ambushed and humiliated some 40 years earlier. The Yankees bonded us as nothing else. My work, my wife's commitments, our daughter's ballet, our son's friends and sports—all these faded for a few hours most nights, while we watched the Yankees. We hugged each other when they won and assured one another that they would win tomorrow when they fell short.

Jeter led the Yankees to the World Series and the world championship that year, beating the Atlanta Braves, the reigning dynasty, in six games. When the final out landed in third baseman Charlie Hayes's mitt, we screamed and hugged and held each other like—well, like a family. We had found ourselves in America.

It felt odd, traitorous nearly, to root for the Yankees, the ancient and proud foe that my hero had defeated all those years before. The Yankees were still in pinstripes, still arrogant, still expecting to win. But I forgave them their character flaws because they were the tonic of togetherness I needed for my family and could not conjure on my own in this, my strange native land, so different from the one I remembered.

I began to think about writing this book around Christmas of 2003. The tragedy of 9/11 had taken 12 men from the village where we lived. The awful haunting emptiness at the bottom of Manhattan Island, where the World Trade Center had once pierced the sky, still resonated with me eerily. It was as if the terrorists had not just killed 3,000 innocents and punctured our sense of invulnerability. It was as if they had also bruised the hearts of every one of us who survived. I wanted to go back to the first week of September of that awful year and replay the events that had changed us forever. Failing that, I wanted to return to a time when I had been happy.

Try looking up Derek Jeter's phone number in the White Pages. It's not there. Major League Baseball players nowadays are as insulated from unwanted contact with normal humans as presidents of nations, possibly more so. Their salaries allow them to purchase protection from the public. They inhabit a world of private workouts, eat food prepared with their specific body fat and metabolism in mind, walk among bodyguards paid to space them away from the crowds that gather whenever they appear. Were a fan ever to rush into right field, as they had during the 1960 World Series, before the players were safely in their clubhouse, he or she would be manhandled, maybe tasered, possibly shot.

Vern Law's number *is* in the phone book. I knew he lived

in Utah and that he had ever since he had accepted a job coaching the Brigham Young University baseball team. I called directory assistance and got his number, and address, on my first try. He answered the phone himself (no body-guards protect him, except perhaps VaNita) and agreed to meet with me the next time he was in New York.

When I finally got my chance to meet my hero, it was not as a middle-aged man with children of his own. I became again that six-year-old boy who had spent hours with his ear against the radio. True, he was a boy with graying hair, clothed in a grown man's sober blue suit, wearing a red rep tie that all of us wear but none of us wants to. And when I saw him finally, coming through the door of his New York hotel room, he carried not a baseball, nor his venerable leather glove, nor even a bat. He was carrying a corn muffin. Vern Law liked the corn muffins at the hotel where he was staying. Because, for one thing, they were free. We talked for two hours and Vernon Law, the hero of the 1960 World Series (notwithstanding Mazeroski's home run), agreed to tell me his story.

This has been the tale of a hero and of what he believes, of how he helped me realize who my real hero is, and what he taught me to teach my children. Vernon Law is still in-volved in baseball, still a model Mormon, still unblemished by scandal or steroids or the other stupidities that seem to cloud the reputations of every contemporary sports legend. Each of his surviving 1960 teammates also agreed to be interviewed for this book. Their comments appear next. Some would only talk with me after I told them Vern Law had suggested I call. Inevitably, the 1960 Pirates have drifted apart, though they still recall each other warmly. When Law encountered Mazeroski at the Pirates' spring training camp one recent year, he couldn't resist joshing with him. "Heck, Maz, if I hadn't screwed up Game 7, you wouldn't be in the Hall."

Not surprisingly, Law believes, among other things, that sports are being ruined by inflated salaries, egotistical self-centered athletes, and the flood of performance-enhancing drugs. In this he is joined by a vast majority of fans, who know nothing of the hardships of being a professional athlete, but know they hunger for heroes.

Such sentiments are not new; however, in Law's case, they come from a Cy Young Award winner who has a World Series ring, whose son Vance followed him into Major League Baseball, and who even today works quietly, without publicity, to help professional athletes who cannot handle the pressures they encounter.

Vernon Law and his teammates are products of another generation, octogenarians who pass judgment on the superstars of today because they once held that exalted status themselves. It has been 50 years since they won their World Series. Law's skill and decency made him my hero forever. My hope is that more boys and girls can find such heroes of their own. They are worth finding, worth following, worth honoring and, above all, never kissing good-bye.

Courtesy Pittsburgh Pirates

On my mind's mound is The Deacon, always.

What the Others Say

"There is no I in team."

(From Vernon Law's *Words to Live By)*

Dick Groat

1960 Season Statistics

G	AB	R	H	2B	3B	HR	RBI	BB	SO	AVG
138	573	85	186	26	4	2	50	39	35	.325

1960 World Series Statistics

G	AB	R	H	2B	3B	HR	RBI	BB	SO	AVG
7	28	3	6	2	0	0	2	0	1	.214

The 1960 team did not think we were ever supposed to lose. The more comeback wins we made, the more we felt invincible.

Members of that team were very close. We all palled around together and still do to this day.

Every player on that team had a piece of winning that

Series. Everyone sacrificed for the good of the team and that becomes contagious as it did on the 1964 Cardinals—Team First!

Free agency, agent system, multi-year contracts—they're great for players, bad for fans and owners.

Bill Virdon

1960 Season Statistics

G	AB	R	H	2B	3B	HR	RBI	BB	SO	AVG
120	409	60	108	16	9	8	40	40	44	.264

1960 World Series Statistics

G	AB	R	H	2B	3B	HR	RBI	BB	SO	AVG
7	29	2	7	3	0	0	5	1	3	.241

The 1960 Pirates never gave up. We won at least 30 games coming from behind in the eighth and ninth innings.

Every player played a big part in our winning. Joe Christopher was an extra outfielder but didn't play much. He was mainly a pinch runner late in the game. I know we won eight or ten games just because of his baserunning.

We were blessed with a lot of winning players, but we had the best second baseman that ever lived and one of the best outfielders that ever lived. I also believe Dick Groat got more out of his natural ability than anyone who ever played. He was probably the smartest one who ever lived.

Joe Gibbon
1960 Season Statistics

G	ERA	W-L	GS	CG	BB	SO
27	4.03	4–2	9	0	31	60

1960 World Series Statistics

G	ERA	W-L	GS	CG	BB	SO
2	9.00	0–0	0	0	1	2

It was my largest thrill in baseball. I was never on another team like the '60 Pirates. Like one big family. Good teammates. Friendly and good people with a mission to do the impossible. What a raucous year to win the Series.

Dick (Ducky) Schofield
1960 Season Statistics

G	AB	R	H	2B	3B	HR	RBI	BB	SO	AVG
65	102	9	34	4	1	0	10	16	20	.333

1960 World Series Statistics

G	AB	R	H	2B	3B	HR	RBI	BB	SO	AVG
3	3	0	1	0	0	0	0	1	0	.333

There were some nice guys on that team. It carried through their whole life. They're still good people. If Law hadn't pitched on that team, we wouldn't have won. But as a position player, there were just so many good players that any one of them could have been the MVP. I'm just glad we were able to do it for the city of Pittsburgh.

Most of the guys don't really resent the guys now making money. I think the guys that got to the Big Leagues when I played were appreciative of being there. I think you had a lot more guys who could have replaced you. You had 16 Major League teams; now you have twice that many. You go up to bat now and as soon as you're done you run into the clubhouse to see it on tape. I just don't think the guys who get to the Big Leagues now know how to play as well as we did.

Another thing: now you walk up to home plate with armor on. It used to be you walked up there, you had a real chance of getting hurt. And the players' pants that drag over the ground, that's a lack of respect for the game.

Bob Friend
1960 Season Statistics

G	ERA	W-L	GS	CG	BB	SO
38	3.00	18–12	37	16	45	183

1960 World Series Statistics

G	ERA	W-L	GS	CG	BB	SO
3	13.50	0–2	2	0	3	7

All of us started dreaming of playing in the World Series when we were kids. In 1952, we had probably the worst team in baseball history, 42 and 112. (Many of us ultimately played for the '60 Pirates.) When we arrived at Spring Training 1953, Havana, Cuba, Mr. Rickey, our general manager, reminded us at our weekly meetings: The little things in baseball win games. Execution, conditioning, and focus— and there is "World Series potential in this camp." He said this after losing 112 games.

Although it took another seven years, our dream came through. Mr. Rickey laid the foundation. Joe Brown arrived in 1956 and kept the Pirate ship moving with good trades. His best hire was Danny Murtaugh, one of the best managers of all time. He never took credit, but gave all the credit to the players. Danny loved to kibitz and double-talk with his players. Danny was a man's manager. All the players respected him and played hard for Danny.

While sitting at the end of the dugout, watching the game, I felt something hit my chest. It was tobacco. "Sorry, Bart, I thought you were sleeping," Murtaugh said. I was 40 feet away from him.

The 1960 Pirates was a total team effort. All 25 players contributed big time. Many had their best years. Groat, Haddix, Law, Face, Friend, Hoak, Mazeroski, Skinner, Virdon, Clemente, and the so-called "role players": Hal Smith, Dick Schofield, Gino Cimoli, and Smoky Burgess.

Wilmer Mizell won 12 games, Dick Schofield took over short when Groat went down with a broken wrist. We were concerned if we could win, but Schofield played the month of September and hit over .300.

Another thing that really kept us loose was that Bob Prince and Jim Woods had nicknames for us. In other words, it was a total "family affair."

One of my favorite teammates was Vern Law. We first met in 1950 at spring training in San Bernardino, California, shagging balls in the outfield. We roomed together on a few road trips. Vern liked his favorite drink, a "Mormon Martini"—ice water with lots of ice. Vern acquired a good slow curve and slider and became a great pitcher for us, winning the Cy Young in '60. He is a great family man and gentleman and I'm a better person for having known Vern.

Our team knew how to win. Thirty times we came back in the seventh inning to pull games out. We were strong up the middle, [had] strong pitching and a great outfield, and we knew how to play ball!

ElRoy Face
1960 Season Statistics

G	ERA	W-L	GS	CG	BB	SO
68	2.90	10–8	0	0	29	72

1960 World Series Statistics

G	ERA	W-L	GS	CG	BB	SO
4	5.23	0–0	0	0	2	4

To me, winning the World Series meant that I was one of the few men in the world to have a ring to show for it. It was a once-in-a-lifetime experience, along with a great bunch of guys to be associated with. We were the underdogs.

Since then, the game has really changed with [respect to] the players and owners. Because of free agency and expansion, there are lots of players in the Big Leagues who couldn't have made a club in the '50s and '60s. I believe in some cases now, there are minor league players playing in the majors. It's a business now.

Bob Skinner

1960 Season Statistics

G	AB	R	H	2B	3B	HR	RBI	BB	SO	AVG
145	571	83	156	33	6	15	86	59	86	.273

1960 World Series Statistics

G	AB	R	H	2B	3B	HR	RBI	BB	SO	AVG
2	5	2	1	0	0	0	1	1	0	.200

Our comeback victories in the late innings were the team's trademark. During the days I was in left field, around the seventh inning, they used to raise the gates behind left field and let people in. Marty Schottenheimer, the football coach, was at Pitt in 1960. He recently told me that he was always waiting out there to be let in, and as it turned out he got to see the best part of a lot of games for free.

In those days, we were the Cinderella team. We were a
bunch of guys, some of whom had come up through the organization, some who arrived there just in time, and we had
an attitude that made us feel we could beat anybody.

When the Yankees came into Pittsburgh with all those
superstars, we kept reading how we were going to get killed.
I was quite nervous getting ready to run out onto the field
the first game. As I was standing there in the dugout, a guy
jumped out of a plane over Forbes Field and parachuted to
the ground. It turned out he'd lost a bet and that was how he
had to pay it off. But it made me think, heck, he's in more
trouble than I'm going to be. And when I ran out on the
field, I was calm.

For us, money wasn't a factor. I knew I'd be working each
winter. I worked at a factory, welding plane parts. I worked
forty hours a week just like all the other guys. Some of them
knew what I did in the summer, but they weren't particularly
impressed.

It was never tough living in Pittsburgh. The people there
always treated us so nicely. If I didn't live in San Diego,
Pittsburgh might be my next choice, except for the weather.
Even now when I go back, they want to talk and reminisce.
It's a great place. During the World Series, Elston Howard
got hit (by Bob Friend) with an inside pitch. The visiting
team had to go down through the Pirate dugout to get to the
clubhouse in Forbes Field. So Elston comes through our
dugout, past Law, and said something about "Preacher." And

Vern went down the tunnel after him. Man, he was mad! Nothing happened, between them, but I was proud of Vern for standing up for himself like that.

Joe Christopher
1960 Season Statistics

G	AB	R	H	2B	3B	HR	RBI	BB	SO	AVG
50	56	21	13	2	0	1	3	5	8	.232

1960 World Series Statistics

G	AB	R	H	2B	3B	HR	RBI	BB	SO	AVG
3	0	2	0	0	0	0	0	0	0	.000

When I'd go to meetings with Branch Rickey, a lot of the kids would go to sleep in the meeting because they weren't interested in what he was talking about. But I was taught to respect my elders, so I would listen to him. And he would tell us, if you can't help your fellow man, what is the sense of being? That's what he taught me.

I can look at a player and ask his date of birth and from that alone, I can tell him how good he'll be in baseball. You must understand your spirituality. But today's players don't care about that. They only care about bling-bling and money.

The 1960 team was a team that wouldn't give up. Danny Murtaugh was the right man for the job at that time because he knew how to keep everyone happy and in order. Everyone called Clemente names because he didn't act the way they thought he should. But he turned out to be the greatest of them all.

Bill Virdon always said, "When you put that Christopher kid in, things happen." And he was right. Who was playing right field the night Haddix pitched his 12 innings of perfect baseball and still lost? Joe Christopher. That was the first game I played for the Pirates.

Hal Smith

1960 Season Statistics

G	AB	R	H	2B	3B	HR	RBI	BB	SO	AVG
77	258	37	76	18	2	11	45	22	48	.285

1960 World Series Statistics

G	AB	R	H	2B	3B	HR	RBI	BB	SO	AVG
3	8	1	3	0	0	1	3	0	0	.375

We had a group of guys who had played ball [for] a while. All of them were trained to play the game properly. Most of them were seasoned veterans. We had a few young guys like Clemente, and even Maz wasn't that old, but he was so good at second base he could have been a rookie and he'd have been great. The rest—Stuart and Nelson, Groat, Hoak, Virdon, Skinner and Cimoli—they'd been around a long time and knew how to play. They knew how to get a hit, how to run the bases, and how to move a man over, knew when to hit to the opposite field. I would say that that year, every player on our team helped to win a game or two or three or four, each. And our pitching staff, well, what can you say? ElRoy Face would have had so many saves, if they'd have been counting them back then, that no one could ever have touched him.

We all knew what we could do. We didn't choke up. We came together and became close friends.

There are a lot of people coming into this country playing ball now who I think don't realize how lucky they are to be able to play in a country like this, in the Major Leagues. We were in San Francisco once, and Willie Mays was getting ready to hit. And I said to him, "Willie, this is some game, isn't it?" And Willie said to me, in this real high-pitched voice of his, "Smitty, if it wasn't for baseball, I would be picking cotton." And me, I grew up on a farm. And I knew I didn't want to be a farmer if I could be a ballplayer. I worked. I don't think some of these guys want to work very hard. If they're home run hitters, that's all they want to concentrate on.

I get more fan letters today, in the mail, than I did all the years I was playing. Why? The computer. People get our addresses and send us letters. I've signed baseball bats coming through the mail, bubble-gum cards, baseballs that they send to me. We didn't have that then.

I got through the minor leagues by working in the wintertime as a house painter. I made more money in the winter than I did in the summer. The only year I didn't have to work was the year we won the Series, and I got a $6,200 bonus.

Gino Cimoli
1960 Season Statistics

G	AB	R	H	2B	3B	HR	RBI	BB	SO	AVG
101	307	36	82	14	4	0	28	32	43	.267

1960 World Series Statistics

G	AB	R	H	2B	3B	HR	RBI	BB	SO	AVG
7	20	4	5	0	0	0	1	2	4	.250

We didn't have a guy who hit 30 home runs. We only had one guy who won 20 games that year, Law. When Stuart couldn't play, Rocky Nelson came in and did a hell of a job. When Groat got hurt, Schofield came in and did a hell of a job. When you keep winning games in the seventh, eighth, and ninth innings, it gets infectious. Every time we went out onto the field, someone picked someone else up. We got to the point where Murtaugh wouldn't even stay in the dugout in the eighth and ninth innings. He had an ulcer, and he had to go back to the clubhouse at the end of the game. It was just destined that the Pittsburgh Pirates were going to win.

That inning in the seventh game, I got a hit, and Virdon hit a sure double play to Kubek. I was looking right at him when it hit him in the throat.

What kind of pitch did Maz hit? I know it was a high fastball. I don't care what Terry says. It was a fastball.

My dad? His name was Abramo, but people called him Abe. The first game I played at Seals Stadium for the Giants' minor league team I got beaned in the head. And before anyone could do anything, this little old man jumped the fence and ran up to the plate and was standing over me. And the umpire asked him, "Are you a doctor," and this little old man was shouting, "Atsa my son!"

Pittsburgh isn't a flashy city. It was a working city, and the people weren't fancy, they were working folk. I loved it there. I couldn't pay for a drink. But I loved it, and they loved the Pirates.

George Witt
1960 Season Statistics

G	ERA	W-L	GS	CG	BB	SO
10	4.20	1–2	6	0	12	15

1960 World Series Statistics

G	ERA	W-L	GS	CG	BB	SO
3	0.00	0–0	0	0	2	1

By the time I got to Pittsburgh, I already had arthritis in my clavicle. I did have a good curveball. I lost the World Series ring [while] surfing, which may have been my unconscious mind doing what it needed to do. I still have nightmares about my time in baseball. In fact I just had a nightmare last night. I was pitching, but I couldn't find my glove.

I was a loner. I think I was kind of ignored as a newcomer. There were people I admired, Vernon for one. He was open to all personalities and always kind. I would have liked to know Harvey Haddix better. He was the only player I ever called after I got out of baseball, and it happened to be the day before he died. He was a mender of problems.

I had a fight once with Don Hoak in front of the Sheraton Palace in San Francisco. He told me I had to throw more between starts. I knew that wasn't the reason I was sore all the time, so I told him to shut up. He said, "Are you challenging me?" So we went out and did our thing. Tom Cheney said some derogatory things about me in the bullpen so we went to the tunnel beneath Forbes Field and did our thing there.

All I ever wanted to be as a kid was a Major League ballplayer. By the time I got to the Majors I was having trouble with my arm, and it never worked out the way I hoped it would. When we won the pennant, we were on the bus and everyone was drinking. The guys started to get boisterous. I got Hal Smith and threw him on the floor. I pretended I was kidding, but I wasn't, because he had pissed me off. All in all, it was an interesting cast of characters. I was just miscast. I was happy to get out of baseball.

Bob Oldis

1960 Season Statistics

G	AB	R	H	2B	3B	HR	RBI	BB	SO	AVG
22	20	1	4	1	0	0	1	1	2	.200

1960 World Series Statistics

G	AB	R	H	2B	3B	HR	RBI	BB	SO	AVG
2	0	0	0	0	0	0	0	0	0	.000

We had all kinds of guys: religious guys like Law, arm wrestlers like Dick Stuart, nondrinkers like Burgess and The Deacon and Vinegar Bend Mizell, and a guy who could smoke cigars, chew tobacco, and carry on a conversation all at the same time like Rocky Nelson. I had a lot of fun. Before every game at home or on the road, Murtaugh would play Hearts with some of the players. We'd play Hearts like we were going to murder each other, and then go out and play ball together. When we'd go out for dinner, nobody recognized us. We could go out and have fun together.

We got off to a great start that year, and that gave us all confidence. Baseball's like anything else: You get off to a great start and you'll get to believe in yourself. When I came home from the 1960 World Series that October, I had a football game I was supposed to officiate that night. I went and I was just another guy as soon as I got home. It didn't have any effect on my life.

Bill Mazeroski

1960 Season Statistics

G	AB	R	H	2B	3B	HR	RBI	BB	SO	AVG
151	538	58	147	21	5	11	64	40	50	.273

1960 World Series Statistics

G	AB	R	H	2B	3B	HR	RBI	BB	SO	AVG
7	25	4	8	2	0	2	5	0	3	.320

I thought everybody liked each other. It was a close-knit team. Winning makes it easier not to get mad at each other. It was a fun clubhouse to be in. Someone was always messing with someone else, not in a bad sense but as a joke. Murtaugh knew what he was doing. He had a lot of hunches and he didn't go by the book, but some of his hunches worked better than the book. Bobby Bragan used to pinch-hit for me all the time. And it made me feel bad. When Murtaugh came in he called me and said, "I'll never pinch-hit for you." Walking by the office where Milene worked with Danny, he saw me looking at her, and he said, "Why don't you take that girl out?" And I did, and we've been married 51 years.

Pittsburgh isn't like New York where people just walk by you and never get to know you. People in Pittsburgh appreciate quiet workers. If you do your job and don't act like a jerk, people in Pittsburgh will respect you.

The players now, they don't seem to get out and meet the fans. We used to go to Little League banquets and charity causes and meet regular people. I still go to spring training, and if you meet the guys, one on one, they're good guys.

I don't know how it happened that I was chosen to do what I did. The home run was probably the most exciting thing that happened to me, along with just playing in the Major Leagues. There's something special about the guys on the 1960 club. Winning brings you together like nothing else.

Vernon Law was a special person. If you couldn't look up to Vernon Law, you can't look up to anyone. I have as much respect for him as I do for anyone.

Sources

BOOKS

Hart, Arthur A. *Boise Baseball: The First 125 Years.* Boise, ID: Historic Idaho, Inc., 1994.

Lorant, Stefan. *Pittsburgh: The Story of an American City.* Lenox, MA: Kingsport Press, 1980.

O'Brien, Jim. *Maz and the '60 Bucs: When Pittsburgh and Its Pirates Went All the Way.* Pittsburgh: James P. O'Brien Publishing, 1993.

Ostling, Richard N., and Joan K. Ostling. *Mormon America: The Power and the Promise.* New York: Harper One, 2007.

Reisler, Jim. *The Best Game Ever, Pirates vs. Yankees: Oct. 13, 1960.* Cambridge, MA: Carroll & Graf, 2007.

Tarr, Joel A., editor. *Devastation and Renewal: An Environmental History of Pittsburgh and Its Region.* Pittsburgh, PA: University of Pittsburgh Press, 2003.

The Book of Mormon: Another Testament of Jesus Christ. Salt Lake City: The Church of Jesus Christ of Latter-day Saints, 1981.

PERIODICALS

Baseball Almanac
Baseball Digest
Pittsburgh *Post-Gazette*

SOURCES

Pittsburgh Press
Pittsburgh Quarterly
Sports Illustrated
The *New York Times*
The *New York Post*
Time Magazine
Wikipedia

Index

Page numbers in italics indicate images.

Aaron, Henry, 168
Abrams, Al, 204
Adams, Spencer, 24
Adcock, Joe, 170
Agents, 75–78
All-Church Award for Excellence in Athletics, 179–80
Allen, Mel, 221, 263
All-Star games, 182–84
Ambrose, Frank, 233
Angels in the Outfield, 3
Ankle injury, 13–14, 213–16, 225–27
Arm injury, 313
Ashton, Marvin, 179–80
As I Remember, 17–18

Balog, Drew, 298, 300–301
Baltimore, Maryland, 207, 210–11
Baltimore Orioles, 207, 210–11
Bardot, Brigitte, 236
Barr, Mayor, *305*
Baseball, author loses, 57–63
Beehive House, 179–80
Beery, Wallace, 47, 66
Benny Benack and his Iron City Six, 196–97
Benson, Ezra Taft, 260–61, 306–7
Berra, Yogi: on Yankees roster, 2, 237; Game One and, 240, 241–42; Game Four and, 249; Game Seven and, 264–65, 278–79, 281–82, 296, 301
Bierbauer, Louie, 3–4
Black, Joe, 164
Blanchard, Johnny, 251, 270, 281–82, 299
Bloom, Sy, 196
Boggs, Lilburn, 33
Boise, Idaho, 16–17

Bonn, West Germany, 333–35
Book of Mormon, 29–32
Bowling alleys, 42–43
Boyer, Cletis, 266, 270, 282
Boyer, Ken, 191, 282
Bragan, Bobby, 147, *148*, 358
Broglio, Ernie, 191
Brotherhood (baseball league),
    3–4
Brown, Joe E., *150*
Brown, Joe L., 8–9, *150*, 151,
    347
Brown, Kevin, 7
Buhl, Bob, 203
Burdette, Lou: Law pitches
    against, 142; Harvey Haddix
    and, 170; Braves and, 191;
    Dick Groat and, 194; career
    statistics for, 226
Burgess, Forrest "Smoky," *167,
    256;* pennant celebration and,
    10, 216; on Pirates roster,
    151; lifestyle and career of,
    166–69; makes National
    League team, 183; Game
    Four and, 250; Game Seven
    and, 265, 280; Bob Oldis on,
    357
Burwell, Bill, 104–6, *105*

Cancer patients, 184–86
Career statistics: of Vern Law,
    225–26; of Pittsburgh Pirates,
    343–59
Carnegie, Andrew, 136
Carnegie Library of Pittsburgh,
    132
Castleton, Roy, 23–24

Castro, Fidel, 199–200
Catholic nuns, 153–55, *154,*
    181–82, 308–9
Cerv, Bob, 249, 252
Charity, 184–88, 221
Cheney, Tom, 260, 356
Chesnes, Bob, 116
Children's Hospital of
    Pittsburgh, 184–86, 221
Christiansen, ElRay L., 111
Christopher, Joe, 172, 280, 344,
    351–52
Church, Frank, 66–67
Church of Jesus Christ of Latter-
    day Saints: doctrine of,
    23–27; history of, 27–37;
    Law as ambassador for,
    118–19
Chylak, Nestor, 278
Cigars, 75–78, 174
Cimoli, Abramo, 161–62, 284,
    355
Cimoli, Gino: on pennant
    celebration, 7–8; on Pirates
    roster, 161–62; Game Four
    and, 250; Game Seven and,
    284–85; on playing for
    Pirates, 354–55
Clark, D. Worth, 66
Clemente, Roberto: nickname
    of, 86; reputation of, 151–53;
    image of, *152;* Bob Skinner
    and, *162;* career with Pirates,
    163–66; as outfielder, *165;* on
    Pirates roster, 183; Game One
    and, 241; Game Two and,
    244; Game Four and, 251,
    253; Game Seven and,

269–70, 288–90; with teammates, *318;* Joe Christopher on, 351–52
Coates, Jim, 241–42, 287, 289–90
Conn, Billy, 219
Corey, Jill, 273
Coryell, Joyce, 104, 110–11
Cowdery, Oliver, 30–32
Crosby, Bing: career of, 47–48; Herman Welker and, 66; recruits Law, 76–78, 174; letter of, *78;* Prince and Murtaugh with, *178*
Crosetti, Frank, 279
Cy Young Award, 313

Davenport Pirates, 76–78, 104–7
Death, acceptance of, 22
DeMaestri, Joe, 286
Dietrich, Marlene, 129
Ditmar, Art, 239, 246–47
Douglas, Paul, 3
Down, Fred, 203

Eisenhower, Dwight, 198
Ejection of Law over swearing, 147–50
Employment of Vern Law, 42–45
Endorsements, 258
Euripides, 15

Face, ElRoy: nickname of, 86; career of, 170–72; Vern Law and, *171;* objects to team policies, 177; on Pirates

roster, 183; Game One and, 242–43; Game Four and, 251–53; Game Seven and, 275–83; with teammates, *318;* on playing for Pirates, 348–49
Fairless, Benjamin, 138
Faith, 145–47
Finegold, Joseph, 285
First Vision, 28–29
Flood, Curt, 191
Follett, King, 34
Forbes Field, *118*
Ford, Whitey, 2, 246, 247, 260
Forgiveness, 211–12, 216–19
Fort Eustis, Virginia, 124–27
Fort Myers, Florida, 174–78
Frick, Ford, 182–83, 237
Friend, Bob: pitches against Braves, 144–45; career of, 169–70; as starter, 178; makes National League team, 183; Game Two and, 243; Game Six and, 257–58, 259–60; Game Seven and, 283–94; on World Series, 346–48

Galbreath, John Wilmer, 4, *9*
Game Seven of World Series: events preceding, 260–62; Law pitches in, 262–77; ElRoy Face pitches in, 275–83; Bob Friend pitches in, 283–94; Harvey Haddix pitches in, 294–97; final moments of, 297–301
Garagiola, Joe, 5
Garments, 11–13

Gibbon, Joe, 245, 345
Gibson, Bob, 191
Golden Triangle, 139–40
Gold plates, 29–31
Green, Fred, 243
Groat, Dick: pennant celebration and, 10, 229; career of, 155–57; Bill Mazeroski and, *156;* on 1960 season, 175; makes National League team, 183; wrist injury of, 194; Game One and, 240; Game Seven and, 287; with Law and Haddix, *295;* on playing for Pirates, 343–44
Gromyko, Andrey, 199
Groupies, 106–7

Haddix, Harvey: nickname of, 85; on Pirates roster, 151; loses in thirteenth inning, 170, 268; Game Five and, 253–54; Game Seven and, 293, 294–97; with Law and Groat, *295*
Hall of Fame, 226–27
Haney, Fred, 142–43
Harris, Martin, 30
Hayden, Mike, 139–40, 299, 318–19
Heinz, H.J., 138
Henry, O., 133
Herman, Babe, 76–78, 174
Hinckley, Gordon B., 26
Hoak, Don: nickname of, 85; on Pirates roster, 151; career of, 158–61, 192–93; images of, *159, 160, 197;* Game One

and, 239; Game Four and, 249, 253; Game Seven and, 264–65, 267, 273–74, 276; George Witt and, 356
Houk, Ralph, 249
Howard, Elston, 237, 242–43, 350

Immigration, 16–17
Integrity, 145–47
Ironing, 309–10

J&L Steel Plant, *89*
Jack (Law family dog), 38–40, *39*
Jackowski, Bill, 299
Jackson, Larry, 191
James, Bill, 225
Jenkins Arcade, *56*
Jesus Christ, 28–29, 35
Jeter, Derek, 337–38
John the Baptist, 31–32
Joubert, Joseph, 304
Journalism: author's beginnings in, 321–25; in Moscow, 325–32; in Paris, 332–33; in Bonn, 333–35

Kaufmann, Edgar, 129, 138
Kelley, Leo, *234*
Kennedy, John F., 200–201
Khrushchev, Nikita, 199, 236
Killebrew, Harmon, 46
Kimball, Spencer W., 119
Kiner, Ralph, 4–5, 122
King, Ed and Wendy, 84–85
King Follett Discourse, 34
King, Nellie, 147, 221
Klein, Edwin, 235

Index

Kline, Ron, 145, 161
Kubek, Tony: Game One and, 237, 239, 243; Game Four and, 249, 259; Game Seven and, 263, 274, 285–86
Kuhn, Bowie, 191

Labine, Clem, 244–45
Labor movement, 323–25
Landess, Stanley, 147–50
Law, Audrey Packer Perkins, 19
Law, Charles, 23
Law, Dennis, *44*
Law, Evan: birth of, 19; Vern Law and, *20;* with family, *44;* Law plays without, 70; recruited by Pirates, 77; marriage of, 104, 110–11; practices with Law, 176–77; death of, 192
Law, Isaac, 23
Law, Jesse, 19, 37–38, *44,* 192
Law, Joyce, 104, 110–11
Law, Melva Christina Sanders, 19, 41, 76–77, *234*
Law, VaLynda, *188, 189*
Law, Vance, 188, *189*
Law, VaNita McGuire: courtship and engagement of, 71–75; Vernon Law and, *74, 108, 113, 146;* marriage of, 107–12; moves to Pittsburgh, 116–22; gives birth to Veldon Law, 126–27; supports Law, 143–44; home life of, 188; injures wrist, 188–90; with family, *189;* at pennant parade, *230*

Law, Varlin, 188, *189*
Law, Vaughn, 188, *189*
Law, Veldon, 126–27, 188, *189*
Law, Vernon: pennant celebration and, 10–14; Wally Westlake and, *12;* memoirs of, 17–18; personality of, 18–19; family and childhood of, 19–23, 37–42; Evan Law and, *20;* employment of, 42–45; with family, *44, 193;* plays high school sports, 45–48, 69–70; author compares himself to, 63–64; Herman Welker and, *67;* VaNita Law and, *74, 108, 113, 146;* Davenport Pirates and, 99–107; marriage of, 107–12; New Orleans Pelicans and, 112–16; moves to Pittsburgh, 116–22; signs autographs, *120;* plays major league baseball, 122–24; images of, *123, 180, 187, 342;* at Fort Eustis, *124, 125;* military service of, 124–27; pitches for Pirates, 141–45; at bat, *143;* faith and integrity of, 145–47; gets ejected over swearing, 147–50; ElRoy Face and, *171;* speaking engagements of, *185;* home life of, 188; Danny Murtaugh and, *205;* ankle injury of, 213–16, 225–27, *238;* on forgiveness, 216–19; at pennant parade, *230;* Game One and, 239–42; after Game

One, *244;* Game Four and, 248–52; prepares for Game Seven, 260–62; Game Seven and, 262–77; with Haddix and Groat, *295;* celebrates World Series win, 306–7; retirement of, 310–15; after retirement, *316;* with teammates, *318;* interview with, 339–41; on teamwork, 343; Bob Friend on, 348; Bill Mazeroski on, 359

Law, Veryl, 188, *189*

Law, William and Wilson, 23, 34–35

Lawrence, David, 136, 137–38, 231, *232*

Leigh, Janet, 3

Levey, Charles, 231

Logan, Johnny, 159

Long, Dale, 253, 294, 296–97

Lopat, Eddie, 298–99

Lopez, Hector, 239, 242

Lorant, Stefan, 129–31

Macmillan, Harold, 199

Major League baseball: Law plays, 122–24; Law retires from, 310–15

Mantle, Mickey: on Yankees roster, 2; Game One and, 237, 242, 243; Game Two and, 245; Game Three and, 247, 249, 250–51, 252; Game Six and, 259; Game Seven and, 264, 277–78, 295–97

Marichal, Juan, 227

Maris, Roger: Dick Groat and, 156; Game One and, 237, 240; Game Four and, 249; Game Seven and, 263, 267, 277, 281, 294–95

Mary Edna, Sister, 181–82

Mary Raphael, Sister, 308–9

Masloff, Sophie, 131–32, 133–34, 137

Mathews, Eddie, 2, 204

Mayfield, Molly, 201

Mays, Willie, 168, 353

Mazeroski, Bill: on pennant celebration, 7; Dick Groat and, 155–57, *156;* Bob Oldis on, 195–96; Game One and, 239, 242; Game Seven and, 266, 267, 281–82, 298–301; after World Series win, *301;* with teammates, *318;* on playing for Pirates, 358–59

McCarthy, Joseph, 66

McDougald, Gil, 251

McGuire, VaNita. *See* Law, VaNita McGuire

McHugh, Roy, 205–6

Mellon, Richard King, 137–38

Meridian, Idaho, 15–17

Military service, 124–27

Minor league baseball: recruitment into, 75–78; first season in, 99–104

Mission(s), 25, 100–101

Mizell, Wilmer "Vinegar Bend," 247, 293, 347, 357

Moody, John: starts school, 49–53; as Pirates fan, *51;* childhood of, 53–57, 81–85,

Index

88–98; image of, *54;* loses baseball, 57–63; with parents, *63;* at Forbes Field, *213;* adolescence of, 319–21; beginnings in journalism, 321–25; works in Moscow, 325–32; works in Paris, 332–33; works in Bonn, 333–35; moves to New Jersey, 335–37; interviews Pirates, 339–41

Moody, John Sr.: lessons learned from, 206–13; with wife, *208;* as journalist, *210;* at Forbes Field, *213;* encourages son in journalism, 321, 323–25

Mormons. *See* Church of Jesus Christ of Latter-day Saints

Moroni, 29–30

Moscow, USSR, 325–32

Murtaugh, Danny: influence of, 5–7; image of, *6;* on pennant celebration, 9–10; with Joe E. and Joe L. Brown, *150;* nuns and, *154;* at spring training, *175, 176;* Bob Prince and, *176;* during 1960 season, 177; with Prince and Crosby, *178;* Vern Law and, *205;* pennant celebration and, 229; Game Four and, 248; Game Seven and, 274–77, 284, 285, 294; Hal Smith and, *292;* suggests retirement for Law, 314; Bob Friend on, 347; Joe Christopher on, 351; Bob

Oldis on, 357; Bill Mazeroski on, 358

Murtaugh, Kate, 229

Mussolini, Benito, 265

National League pennant, 2–14, 184, 203, 204–16

Negri, Joe, 196, 320

Nelson, Glenn Richard "Rocky": Dick Stuart and, 157; career of, 161; Game Seven and, 263–64, 269, 287–88; Bob Oldis on, 357

New Orleans Pelicans, 112–16

New York Yankees: World Series roster of, 237; Game One and, 237–43; Game Two and, 243–47; Game Three and, 247; Game Four and, 247–53; Game Five and, 253–57; Game Six and, 257–60; Game Seven and, 262–301; author cheers for, 337–39

Nixon, Richard, 200–201

Nuns, 153–55, *154,* 181–82, 308–9

O'Toole, Joe, 115–17

Oceak, Mary, 155

Oldis, Bob: on Danny Murtaugh, 5–6; on Pirates roster, 172; on Bill Mazeroski, 195–96; injures Law's ankle, 206; Game One and, 239; on playing for Pirates, 357

Olympic Games (1980), 327–32

Otero, Reggie, 161

Parade for Pirates, 228–33
Paris, France, 332–33
Parton, James, 81
"Party Line," 84–85
Payette High School, 46–48
Pee-wee baseball, 92–98
Perkins, Audrey Packer, 19
Piche, Ron, 204
Pioneers, 16–17, 36–37
Pittsburgh baseball club, *4*
Pittsburgh, Pennsylvania:
author's childhood in, 54–57,
81–85, 88–98; Jenkins
Arcade, *56;* history of, 79–82,
128–40; downtown, *82;* in
winter, *83;* Law moves to,
116–22; pollution of, *130,
132;* 1936 flood in, *135;*
Pirates return to, 228–33;
prepares for World Series,
233–37
Pittsburgh Pirates: celebration of,
2–14, 203–6, 213–16; radio
broadcasts and, 85–88; Law
recruited by, 116–22; Law
plays for, 122–24, 141–45;
1959 changes to, 151–53;
fans of, 153–55; 1959
infielders for, 155–61; 1959
outfielders for, 161–66; 1959
catchers for, 166–69; 1959
pitchers for, 169–72; team
photo of, *172;* 1960 spring
training, 174–78; 1960
season, 178–98; pennant
celebration for, 228–33;
Game One and, 237–43;
Game Two and, 243–47;

Game Three and, 247; Game
Four and, 247–53; Game Five
and, 253–57; Game Six and,
257–60; Game Seven and,
262–301; Law retires from,
310–15; impact of, 315–19;
recollections of, 343–59
Point, The, *80*
Polygamy, 27–28, 33–34, 37
Post, Wally, 158
Prayer, 181–82
Priesthood, 31–32, 118–19
Prince, Bob: as sports announcer,
85–88, *87;* at spring training,
176; Danny Murtaugh and,
176; with Crosby and
Murtaugh, *178;* Law's ankle
injury and, 214, 216;
celebrates pennant, 215; life
and career of, 219–24; image
of, *220;* relationship with
Law, 224–25; Bob Friend on,
348
Prince, Frederick Seaton, 135
Purkey, Bob, 151
Purkey, Bob Jr., 151
Pyle, Ernie, 133

Queen, Mel, 142

Racism, 114–15
Radio, 84–88
Reagan, Danny, 101–2
Reisler, Jim, 262
Retirement of Vern Law, 310–15
Richardson, Bobby: Game One
and, 237, 240, 241–42;
Game Two and, 244; Game

Four and, 251; Game Six and, 260; Game Seven and, 262–63, 272, 293
Rickey, Branch, 4–5, 351
Rigdon, Sidney, 32
Riggs, Ada, 17
Riggs, H.C., 17
Rivera, Mariano, 170
Roberts, Curt, 157
Roberts, Robin, 122–23, 226
Robinson, Jackie, 158
Rojek, Stan, 122
Roosevelt, Theodore, 133, 228
Rosewell, Rosey, 87
Rules of Vern Law, 103–4
Russell, Mrs., 96–98
Ruth, George Herman "Babe," 68–70

Salt Lake City, Utah, 36–37, 179–80
Santa Rosa Pirates, 99–104
Schofield, John Richard "Ducky," 172, 194–95, 345–46, 347–48
Schottenheimer, Marty, 349
Scouts, 75–78
Sebak, Richard, 319
Segregation, 114–15
Shantz, Bobby: Game Two and, 245; Game Seven and, 270–71, 279–80, 282, 284–85, 287
Simmons, Curt, 191
Skinner, Bob: nickname of, 85–86; career of, 161; Roberto Clemente and, 162; makes National League team,

183; Game One and, 241; Game Seven and, 263, 287; on playing for Pirates, 349–51
Skowron, Bill "Moose": Game One and, 237, 242; Game Four and, 250, 251, 253; Game Seven and, 265, 268–70, 279, 281, 289–90, 297
Smith, Emma Hale, 30
Smith, Hal: Game Seven and, 281, 290–91; Danny Murtaugh and, 292; on playing for Pirates, 352–54; George Witt and, 356
Smith, Hyrum, 23, 35
Smith, Joseph Jr., 23, 27–35
Smith, Joseph Sr., 28
Snider, Duke, 243
Snow, 82–84
Spahn, Warren, 191, 204
Speaking engagements, 118–19, 184–86
Spring training, 174–78
St. Louis Cardinals, 1, 7, 203–4
St. Valentine's Roman Catholic School, 49–53
Stafford, Bill, 265–66
Statistics: of Vern Law, 225–26; of Pittsburgh Pirates, 343–59
Stengel, Casey: on Yankees roster, 2; Game One and, 239, 240–41, 246–47; Game Seven and, 282–83, 285–86, 287
Stover, Harry, 3
Stringer, Robert, 186

Stuart, Dick: career of, 157–58; Game One and, 239; Game Four and, 249, 253; Bob Oldis on, 357
Stuart, Lois, 157–58
Sunday, playing baseball on, 100
Swearing, 147–50

Tarr, Joel A., 89–90
Temper of Vern Law, 150–51
Temples, 11–12
Terminal, Wabash, 139
Terry, Ralph, 250, 286, 291–92, 298–99
Test Oath, 27
Thomas, Frank, 151
Thomas, Nancy, 223
Thulin, Ron, 315–18
Tickets for World Series, 233–34, 260–61
Tilley, Darrell, 71
Tithing, 24–25, 146–47
Tobacco, 258
"To Each His Own," 73
Turley, Bob, 263, 265

Uecker, Bob, 222
United Mine Workers, 323–25
United Press International, 323–25

Virdon, Bill: nickname of, 85; career of, 162–63; Dick Groat and, 193–94; Game One and, 240; Game Two and, 243–44; Game Four and, 250–51, 252; endorsements and, 258;

Game Seven and, 267, 285; on playing for Pirates, 344; on Joe Christopher, 352

Welker, Herman, 47–48, 65–68, 67
Westlake, Wally, 11, 12
Williams, Ted, 202–3, 247
Wills, Maury, 315
Witt, George, 203, 245, 355–56
Wolf, Warner, 222–23
Woodruff, Wilford, 37
Woods, Jim, 85, 215, 216, 348
Words to Live By, 103–4
Work ethic, 317
World Series: pennant celebration and, 2–14, 203–6; current events and, 198–203; Pittsburgh celebrates, 228–33; Pittsburgh prepares for, 233–37; Game One, 237–43; Game Two, 243–47, 246; Game Three, 247; Game Four, 247–53; Game Five, 253–57; Game Six, 257–60; celebrations following, 302–3, 304–7, 311–12; author's recollections on, 307–10; impact of, 315–19. See also Game Seven of World Series

Yankee Stadium, 183, 246, 248, 254
Young, Brigham, 36

Zorilla, Pedrín, 163